Aaron Noonan is an Australian motorsport media veteran with a career spanning more than two decades. A former *Motorsport News* magazine reporter, he spent time working in motorsport public relations and has served as a TV commentator, host and reporter for *Supercars* and associated motorsport telecasts on Channel 7, Channel 10 and FOX Sports. Co-host of the popular *Shannons Legends of Motorsport* TV series, Aaron also worked as part of Channel 7's 2016 Rio Olympic Games broadcast team. Publisher of the award-winning V8 Sleuth website and host of its weekly podcast, Aaron runs his own motorsport media agency and has written a range of books on the sport, including working with legendary motorsport commentator and racer Neil Crompton on his autobiography, *Best Seat In The House*, which was published in 2021. Aaron lives in Melbourne with his wife Jaylee and their chocolate labrador Rosie, and, when not writing about motorsport, is a tragic Hawthorn AFL supporter.

Also by Aaron Noonan

*Best Seat in the House*
with Neil Crompton

# THE
# GREAT
# RACE

## 60 YEARS OF THE BATHURST 1000

## AARON NOONAN

HarperCollins*Publishers*

*This book is dedicated to my dad, Les.*

**This book is not authorised or endorsed by the organisers and/or promoters of the official Bathurst 1000 race.**

**HarperCollins***Publishers*
Australia • Brazil • Canada • France • Germany • Holland • India
Italy • Japan • Mexico • New Zealand • Poland • Spain • Sweden
Switzerland • United Kingdom • United States of America

HarperCollins acknowledges the Traditional Custodians
of the land upon which we live and work, and pays respect
to Elders past and present.

First published in Australia in 2023
by HarperCollins*Publishers* Australia Pty Limited
Gadigal Country
Level 19, 201 Elizabeth Street, Sydney NSW 2000
ABN 36 009 913 517
harpercollins.com.au

A catalogue record for this book is available from the National Library of Australia

Printed and bound by CPI Group (UK) Ltd, Croydon, CR0 4YY

ISBN 978 1 4607 6356 8 (paperback)
ISBN 978 1 4607 1594 9 (ebook)

Front cover images: Cars by AN1 Images/Graeme Neander; Mount Panorama by istockphoto
Back cover images (from left to right): Dick Johnson and John Bowe celebrate their first Bathurst win together in 1989 by AN1 Images/Graeme Neander; Jason Bargwanna and Garth Tander didn't hold back their excitement at Bathurst in 2000 by AN1 Images/Graeme Neander; Larry Perkins and Russell Ingall raise aloft their trophies at Bathurst in 1997 by AN1 Images/Graeme Neander; Smiles all round as Steve Richards and Craig Lowndes celebrate their 2018 Bathurst win by AN1 Images/Dirk Klynsmith
Author photograph by Supercars Media
Typeset in Adobe Garamond Pro by Kelli Lonergan

# Contents

# FOREWORD
## by Garth Tander

**W**henever I think of Bathurst, I usually think about the track and the challenge of the race, but then my thoughts always go back to before I started racing and my memories of growing up and watching the Bathurst 1000 all day with my dad.

It was an annual ritual in the Tander house and it made for a particularly early get-up on Sunday morning, given we lived in Western Australia and the race started around 7.30am our time.

It wasn't realistic for us to travel to Bathurst when I was young, considering we were on the opposite side of the country, but I have vivid memories of watching the Top 10 Shootout on television on Saturday and then the race all day on Sunday.

It took me until 1998, the year I made my Bathurst debut driving one of Garry Rogers Motorsport's Commodores, to see the track with my own eyes for the first time.

It didn't disappoint.

I've been lucky enough to win the Bathurst 1000 on multiple occasions. The best way to describe how special it is and its importance to the nation is not so much how I feel about it, but how other people I meet in life feel about it.

When someone asks me what I do for a job and I tell them I race cars, often you can see that they don't quite get it.

'Do you know Bathurst?' I say, and they'll nod and engage further.

When they realise you've won the Bathurst 1000, it instantly changes the way they look at you.

There's an understanding of what the race is, where it sits in the Australian sporting landscape and the currency it has – not just in motorsport, but in Australian sport.

There's no better feeling professionally than winning the Bathurst 1000.

On four of the five occasions I've won it driving with a first-time winner – I first experienced it in 2000 – I've told each of them, 'Your life will change the moment you walk out onto that podium as a Bathurst 1000 winner.'

From up on that podium, looking down across the crowd, with your race team just below you alongside your race-winning car, is extremely special. The crowd under the podium just swells and spreads down Pit Straight. There's no other podium like that in Australian motorsport.

It's often been said that the Bathurst 1000 sits in the Australian sporting landscape alongside the Melbourne Cup, the AFL and NRL grand finals and the Boxing Day Test, and it's totally true.

The race has withstood, in motorsport terms, so many evolutions. It's gone from a 500-mile race for series production road cars into more modified Group C cars, international Group A cars and then what we know today as Supercars.

The race has never shrunk; it's never faded or lost its importance in Australian sport. The myth continues to grow. It's bigger and bolder every year and captures people's imagination like no other car race in Australia.

Not everyone watches every horse race during the year,

but millions of people tune in for the Melbourne Cup. The same is true for the Bathurst 1000. You don't have to follow every race in the Supercars Championship to casually observe what unfolds each year in the Bathurst 1000.

Most of the population know it's on and will either watch every lap, take a passing view, follow it on social media or catch the latest on the evening news.

That doesn't happen in any other race in the championship.

I'll have a lifelong connection with the race, but when I think of lifelong connections it's the generations of fans and supporters that have been going to the race as spectators and camped on top of the Mountain that sit most prominently in my mind.

There are campsites that have been in families for decades across generations. The measure of Bathurst's importance is the huge number of people who take a fortnight of their four-week annual holidays to go to Mount Panorama and soak up the event – and they've been doing it for generations.

No other sporting event of its size and stature has that sort of attraction. Nothing compares to the Bathurst 1000 pilgrimage of passionate supporters.

Once Bathurst has got you, it's got you for life. The whole story of Bathurst and its famous race is captivating.

The 60th anniversary of the Great Race at Mount Panorama is a special milestone and one to celebrate.

Enjoy this gripping look back at its history and stories from six decades of racing.

Garth Tander

# INTRODUCTION

In 2023 the 'Great Race' at Bathurst's famous Mount Panorama marks its 60th anniversary.

This special milestone provides the perfect opportunity to look in the rear-view mirror and celebrate what's happened over the past six decades, but it's also a chance to ponder how the road ahead looks for Australia's most popular motor race.

The Bathurst 1000 is Australian motorsport's version of its four-legged cousin, the Melbourne Cup.

Each is 'must-watch' sporting theatre and both are their respective sport's day in the sun in front of a national and international audience.

Bathurst's banner-head race evolved from simple, humble beginnings – when signage on race cars was banned, television broadcasts were in black and white, and motorsport was largely an amateur enthusiast pursuit.

Since 1963 the Great Race (as it's been lovingly dubbed for years) at Bathurst has made and broken the biggest stars of the sport and provided the stage for drivers and teams to show their wares and become household names.

Mount Panorama's legendary 6.213-kilometre ribbon of bitumen has made household names of Peter Brock, Allan Moffat, Dick Johnson, Larry Perkins, Jim Richards, Craig Lowndes, Mark Skaife and so many other drivers.

The cars they've driven to victory are fan favourites, evolving from humble road-going racers of the 1960s and

1970s – largely conceived for regular road driving – right through to today's high-tech, purpose-built, millimetre-perfect V8-powered Supercars missiles.

Drivers, teams and cars have all played their part in the story of the Great Race, but it's been the parochial fans that have elevated the Bathurst 1000 to its position as an icon of Australian sport – and culture.

Perhaps the ever-present theme of 'us' versus 'them' best explains why the race's fans have played such a large part in shaping its history. Fans have committed and been prompted to pick a side. Whether trackside, leaning on the fence watching the cars hurtle at speed across the top of the Mountain, or kicking back on the couch watching on television at home, everyone watching has someone or something to cheer for.

Driver versus Mountain, Holden versus Ford, Brock versus Moffat or Australia versus the world: the race has always supplied a side to take. Indeed, there are no shades of grey when it comes to this Australian institution.

This book shouldn't be viewed as an attempt to tell the complete history of the Bathurst 1000; rather it is a celebration of an event so many Australians hold close to their hearts. It's a series of stories, images, historical reflections and fun facts all based around our Great Race.

Let's hope this book helps readers of all ages to reminisce about their favourite eras, cars and stars. Perhaps it will also capture the imagination of the next generation of pilgrims to the Mountain.

1

# Start Your Engines

The history of the Great Race at Bathurst began when a field of 56 cars set off on a 500-mile journey on Sunday October 6 in 1963. Even then, racing at Mount Panorama, and indeed Bathurst overall, was far from a new thing.

Bathurst is located in the central tablelands of New South Wales and was originally occupied by the Muurrai clan of the Wiradjuri people. It is the oldest British colonial settlement in Australia and was founded in the early 1800s. The area boomed in the gold rush of the 1850s.

In terms of motor racing – for which Bathurst now has worldwide acclaim – an area outside the city was chosen as the site of Bathurst's first motor racing track. It was set up in 1911 – before World War I broke out. A 26.5-kilometre route using highway roads east of the city, its popularity died out rather quickly and racing moved to the 11.5-kilometre 'Vale' circuit south of Bathurst. This consisted of gravel public roads and was used for motorcycle racing from Easter 1931 onwards.

The venue hosted the Australian Tourist Trophy, however by 1937 the sheer speeds the motorcycles were reaching had risen to uncomfortable levels and the surface was deteriorated badly and causing blinding dust clouds that made visibility tricky for riders. Additional to all of this was the fact that the roads couldn't be completely closed to the public while racing was taking place. Now the permit for racing at the Vale circuit was in doubt.

Because the annual Easter motorcycle races were a financial windfall for Bathurst's shopkeepers, hotels and guest houses (in the same way the Bathurst 1000 is today), something decisive had to happen if racing at the Vale circuit was to continue.

The Mayor of Bathurst since 1931 (the year of that first Easter event at the Vale circuit), Martin Griffin had been a motorcyclist in his younger days and he was interested in bringing car racing to the area in addition to motorcycle racing. He also recognised the financial benefits of keeping motorsport in the locality and the injection of funds that came with it visiting town every year.

Economic conditions were tough the world over in the 1930s; Australia was no exception. Aware that seeking public funds post-Depression for the stated purpose of the construction of a new motor racing circuit could perhaps be harpooned politically or by public lobbyists, Griffin came at things from a different angle.

Griffin's approach was simple. So as not to raise too much attention, he would make it seem like one of the employment schemes that were common in New South Wales coming out of the Great Depression: dole recipients were sometimes put to work digging drains and building roads and pathways.

He proposed the construction of a scenic tourist drive that would attract visitors to the city to see the sights, to picnic on the mountain and take in the breathtaking views. Travellers from far and wide would visit and spend money in Bathurst, he asserted.

The angle worked and, with the support and engagement of Eric Spooner, the NSW Minister of Works and Local Government – it's likely he also knew of the real intent of the project, it must be said – the Federal Government tipped in additional funding to turn the formerly rugged area known as Bald Hill and Wahluu (meaning 'to watch over' in the language of the local Wiradjuri people) into the new Mount Panorama circuit.

Construction began in mid-1936 and Spooner officially opened the 'Mount Panorama Scenic Drive' on St Patrick's Day, 17 March 1938. Within weeks the first race weekend kicked off. On Easter Saturday, 16 April, it was reported that over 20,000 spectators watched motorcycles compete in the Australian Tourist Trophy; the cars took part in the Australian Grand Prix on Easter Monday, April 18. Englishman Peter Whitehead won at the wheel of an ERA, taking just under three hours to complete the 40-lap distance on the all-dirt surface (tarmac was laid in time for the Easter 1939 race meeting).

No doubt there's been a little bit of sugar sprinkled onto the story over the years, but at its core it's a wonderful tale. In 1937, when the business community of Bathurst felt something decisive had to happen to ensure the continuation of racing, what ultimately resulted was the creation of one of the best known racing circuits in the world.

Without Griffin, Spooner and many others who were involved in making the Mount Panorama Scenic Drive, the history of the Great Race may not have been as great as it's turned out to be.

Racing continued at Mount Panorama during Easter 1939 and 1940 before the Mountain fell silent to racing as World War II raged around the globe and, for a time, on Australia's doorstep. Racing resumed in 1946, after the war ended, and carried on into the 1950s.

The circuit hosted the Australian Grand Prix three more times: in 1947 (won by Bill Murray, after whom Murray's Corner on the circuit is named), 1952 (won by Doug Whiteford's Talbot-Lago) and 1957 (won by Lex Davison, grandfather of future Bathurst 1000 winner Will Davison, aboard a Ferrari).

A second annual race meeting, in October, was established at Mount Panorama in 1950, which included production sedan cars for the first time. Another important part of the Great Race story followed: the Sydney-based Australian Racing Drivers' Club took over the circuit in the mid-1950s.

These were two of the key elements that later combined to form Bathurst's Great Race. But further south was where the Great Race was born.

The road to the creation of the Great Race at Bathurst came in 1960 when Ron Thonemann, the owner/operator of a small automotive public relations consultancy, had the idea that a long-distance race for showroom-stock family road cars would be beneficial for one of this clients, Jim Thompson, the managing director of Armstrong York Engineering.

The business made shock absorbers; Thonemann saw a race as the perfect platform to help generate publicity for the company – and generate business with major car manufacturers, including Ford and GH-Holden.

Armstrong were in on the idea and when it was taken to the Light Car Club in Victoria, they were too. Originally they wanted to run the race at Albert Park, on the circuit around a man-made lake in Melbourne, now the modern home of the Formula 1 Australian Grand Prix. Although Albert Park had hosted major motorsport events in the 1950s, the Melbourne City Council closed it down after the 1958 Melbourne Grand Prix.

The only other circuit near Melbourne was the one on Phillip Island, operated by the Phillip Island Auto Racing Club (PIARC). When approached with the concept, they embraced it, and so the 'Armstrong 500' – inaugurated on the weekend of November 19–20 in 1960 – came to be.

Run for touring cars of the period under the Appendix J rules for Australian touring car racing set out by governing body CAMS (the Confederation of Australian Motor Sport), cars had to be assembled or manufactured in Australia to be eligible for the race and 100 examples had to have been registered for road use.

All cars had to complete the first 100 miles (160 kilometres) without stopping for fuel, oil or driver change, and any mechanical trouble that occurred within this opening stage of the race had to be fixed by the driver alone, without any assistance from pit crew.

Cars had to be in showroom specification. As far as safety items went, seat belts and laminated or shielded windscreens were the only permitted additional items.

No outright winner of the Armstrong 500 was to be officially recognised: only the five class winners were to receive prizemoney and no one driver could drive more than 300 of the 500 miles.

That very first 500-mile race began at 7am and was telecast on GTV-9 in Melbourne. Five classes of car, ranging from Renault 750s to Simca Arondes, Morris Majors and Ford Falcons, competed in this first classic, and the Vauxhall Cresta of Frank Coad and John Roxburgh completed the 167-lap distance first. A total of 34 of the 45 starters were finishers.

The second Armstrong 500 – in 1961 – couldn't capitalise on the excitement generated by the debut race and the field size shrank to just 26 starters.

The Mercedes-Benz 220SE of Bob Jane and Harry Firth was the first to complete the 500 miles and the duo would continue to write themselves into Great Race history in several of the years that followed.

They returned to Phillip Island in 1962 and once again were first to complete the distance: remember, there was no 'official outright winner' at this stage. This time Jane and Firth raced in a Ford Falcon XL, which was the Ford Motor Company's first official works entry in the Great Race.

A field of 40 cars competed in that year's race, a marked improvement over the previous running. But these cars lapping the cold-mix track, coupled with weeks of heavy rain in the lead-up to the event, caused big holes to open up in the track surface that made the race more of a rally than a road race.

Flying stones cracked plenty of windscreens and radiators were holed by plenty more and, as the cars were taken away at the end of racing, the toll on the circuit was revealed. The track was heavily damaged and the PIARC was left with a massive bill.

The ruined track couldn't be re-surfaced with hot mix for a simple reason: the bridge that connected San Remo on the mainland to Phillip Island couldn't carry the weight of the road-making equipment required to repair the track.

And just like that, after three years, Phillip Island was no longer a viable venue for the Armstrong 500.

So, where to take the Great Race for 1963?

Sandown in Melbourne, opened in 1962, was offered as a potential substitute, but in the end Mount Panorama at Bathurst – run by the ARDC – became the new location of the Armstrong 500.

While the venue and organisers had changed, the premise of the Armstrong 500 at its new home held true to its roots. The cars were divided into separate classes, only Australian-built or manufacturer cars were permitted, and cars were arranged on the grid by class and drawn from a hat.

The race attracted a field of 56 cars but, truth be told, it was just another race. No one at the time was making predictions it would become a national sporting institution and the banner-head race on the Australian motorsport calendar.

That 1963 Armstrong 500 field comprised four classes. Class A was for cars costing less than 900 pounds and was made up of small machines, including a Fiat 770, Morris 850s, a Triumph Herald and Volkswagen Beetles.

From there the classes were divided by increasing showroom price brackets – all the way up to Class D for cars between 1201 and 2000 pounds, including a Ford Zephyr, Chrysler Valiants, Peugeot 404s, Studebaker Larks and a Vauxhall Velox.

But the cars that were 'hot to trot' were in Class C, a battle between Ford's Cortina Mk I GT and Holden's EH S4.

Unlike today's four-day Bathurst 1000 race meeting – packed with multiple practice sessions, qualifying and then the Saturday Top 10 Shootout – the 1963 Armstrong 500 was a far simpler two-day affair. Saturday saw just three one-hour practice sessions before Sunday's 500-mile race kicked off at 9am.

That little Cortina that won the race, as Jane said in 2008, was good for 93 horsepower and a top speed down Conrod Straight of 129mph (207.6km/h). It reportedly ran like clockwork and there was nothing the big, heavy cars could do to stop it.

Little cars dominated the Armstrong 500 for the next few years, but the race itself was about to become a really, really big deal …

## What's in a Name?

The Bathurst Great Race has been known by a range of titles over the years.

It began as the Armstrong 500 in 1963 and stayed that way until Gallaher cigarettes took over as the naming rights sponsor for 1966.

The race became known as the Hardie-Ferodo 500 in 1968 and was renamed the Hardie-Ferodo 1000 when the race moved from 500 miles to 1000 kilometres for 1973.

Parent company James Hardie took over as presenting partner in 1981 before race organisers signed up Sydney-based brewing giant Tooheys as naming rights backer from 1988 through to the end of 1995.

Banking and finance company AMP then came on board so the race became the AMP Bathurst 1000, a moniker that continued through the two Super Touring races – in 1997 and 1998.

The establishment of the V8 Supercars Bathurst 1000-kilometre race in 1997 had backing from Primus Telecommunications and the race was known as the Primus 1000 Classic.

Insurance giant FAI sponsored the race from 1998 to 2000, however the 'Classic' word was dropped from the race's title for 1999 and 2000.

The 2001 race stands out in Bathurst Great Race history as the only one to be void of a naming rights sponsor. It was simply known as the V8 Supercar 1000.

Bathurst and racing legend Bob Jane picked up the sponsorship from 2002 to 2004 via Bob Jane T-Marts before Supercheap Auto signed up to back it over a 16-year period – from 2005 through to 2020.

The race became the Repco Bathurst 1000 in 2021 in a deal set to run through until at least 2028.

Despite so many name changes, Bathurst's fans have remained incredibly loyal.

2

# Small Cars On A Big Mountain

The early years of the annual Bathurst endurance race were dominated by small cars. They may have had less power under the bonnet than some of their rivals, but their light weight meant they were kinder on their brakes and tyres and spent less time in the pits.

Bob Jane and George Reynolds won the race overall in 1964 in a Cortina GT, though the race organisers, the Australian Racing Drivers' Club, still didn't officially acknowledge an outright winner in those days, instead focusing on recognising each of the different classes in the race.

That stance only changed later in the decade. Being 'first across the line' mattered to drivers, teams, manufacturers and the viewing public.

Jane and Reynolds had inherited the lead in the 1964 race from another Cortina – driven by brothers Ian and Leo Geoghegan – when a generator bracket broke. Six Cortinas finished among the first seven finishers and the winning car completed the 130 laps in 7 hours, 35 minutes and 32.1

seconds, which was 13 minutes faster than the race-winning time of the 1963 winning Cortina.

The creation of the Cortina GT500 model in 1965 gave Ford another Bathurst-winning car. It was one of the first 'Bathurst special' cars produced. The imminent threat of the Mini Coopers had prompted Harry Firth, then-Ford competition chief and three-time winner of the Great Race – two with Bob Jane at Phillip Island and the inaugural race in 1963 at Bathurst – to come up with the GT500 Cortina. A limited-build model, it featured a host of performance modifications tailored to the Mount Panorama circuit.

Among the modifications were an uprated drivetrain, competition suspension, long-range fuel tanks and various changes with its engine – all designed to make it a better weapon to win at Bathurst.

Cortina GT500s were the first three cars across the line in 1965 as Barry 'Bo' Seton and Midge Bosworth teamed up in a Fairfield Motors entry to beat home the Grawill Motors GT500 of Bruce McPhee and Barry Mulholland.

The new Cortina had managed to fight off the rising threat of the diminutive Morris Cooper S 'Minis' on the Mountain, but there was more to come from the little 'flying bricks'.

The overlords of the Great Race prioritised support for local car manufacturing, which was why the rules stipulated that for a car to be permitted to race, 100 cars of its exact model had to be registered for the open road in Australia. When they revisited the requirements in 1965, they lifted that number to

250 and the consequences were surprisingly dramatic. Ford didn't want to make the investment in another 250 special cars, and besides, the new Falcon was soon to come into the marketplace, so it took a gap year for 1966.

Such was the Mini domination of that year's race, they filled the first nine outright positions, led home by Bob Holden and Finnish ace Rauno Aaltonen, who became the first international driver to win the Great Race.

Holden, who suffered from polio as a child – and was stuck in plaster for three and a half years – said that having Aaltonen alongside him was one of the greatest incentives to do well in that race.

'When you get put in with [a driver of] that sort of heritage, it would have been very hard to put up with the fact if I did something wrong,' he told me for an episode of the Shannons Legends of Motorsport video series during a sit-down chat at Phillip Island in 2018.

'The track was good, the cars were a bit funny, but the tyres were sort of alright and this little car felt pretty special. Rauno reckoned it was the best Mini he'd ever driven.

'When you used to go down that straight at those speeds, the trees used to rush past you at a thousand miles an hour [and] it used to be scary, especially in a little car. The road was humpy, with a crest on it, and the big cars would go past, and the bloody car would jump sideways with the wind. It was all part of the experience!'

That 1966 Bathurst victory remained the banner-head achievement of Holden's motorsport career.

He made a total of 28 Bathurst Great Race starts – right through to when he was 65 years old, in 1998 – more often than not in smaller capacity class cars that he prepared and ran himself, including Ford Escorts and Toyota Corollas.

Holden, who turned 90 in December 2022, hasn't slowed down since his last Bathurst 1000 start either. He's continued to compete into his 80s in historic events – at the wheel of the same Corolla he and Aaltonen drove at Bathurst in 1991, when they reunited to tackle Mount Panorama 25 years on from their Great Race victory in the Mini.

The second-placed Mini behind Holden and Aaltonen on the day in 1966 they won the Gallaher 500 (as it was known then) was driven by rising star Fred Gibson, paired with Bill Stanley.

Gibson only had to wait another 12 months to know the feeling of being a winner of what was fast becoming Australia's most famous race. In 1967, he played a major role in the return of Ford in its quest for Mountain glory.

## An Older Holden Model

1966 Bathurst winner Bob Holden was on the grid for the first Great Race at Mount Panorama in 1963 at the wheel of a Peugeot 404.

He remains the oldest known Bathurst Great Race driver in history, given he was 65 years and 307 days old when he lined up for the 1998 AMP Bathurst 1000 – his last start in the race – at the wheel of a BMW 320i.

Paired with Justin Matthews and Paul Nelson, Holden finished ninth overall in the race.

Holden made 28 Bathurst starts, however it could have been more. He missed the race in 1969 as his Datsun 1000 was crashed in practice, and after his Toyota Celica's engine failed on the warm-up lap in 1983, he was not credited with starting the race.

He was set to race his Toyota Corolla in 1993 but didn't make it to the Mountain; he was injured in a road accident just before the event. A broken nose and several rib fractures left Holden on the sidelines for race week.

Lou Stoopman (61 years old in 1977), Allan Grice (59 in 2002), Murray Carter (59 in 1990), Peter Brock (59 in 2004) and Jim Richards (59 in 2006) are the other oldest known Bathurst 1000 starters.

## Not Quite Always in October

The Bathurst 1000 is often referred to as the October classic, but over the course of history, it hasn't always been held in October.

Race organisers had traditionally run the event over the New South Wales October long weekend. This is organised around the Labour Day public holiday, which is on the first Monday in October, and every now and again, the calendar fell in such a way that the long weekend was in September. That's why the race was run on the last day of September in 1973, 1979, 1984 and 1990.

The V8 Supercar/Super Touring Bathurst split of the 1990s saw the V8 Supercars race on the Mountain in November in 1998, 1999 and 2000.

It was the ongoing COVID-19 pandemic that forced the most extreme date change: organisers pushed back the 2021 race to the first weekend of December.

3

# The King

No one is bigger than Mount Panorama – but Peter Brock sure comes close.

The nine-time Bathurst winner transcended the sport through the 1970s, '80s and '90s like no one before or since, his deeds at Bathurst making him a mainstream, household name. Generations of fans literally worshipped him and followed his every gearchange.

The Brock and Bathurst story is a well-told one, but it's compulsory to re-tell it when delving into the history of the Great Race.

In the late 1960s Brock was a bearded, wild young racer from Melbourne who had made a name for himself in a rudimentary Austin A30 Sports Sedan powered by a Holden engine.

Racing legend Harry Firth spotted his talent and gave him a drive in the 1969 Bathurst Great Race – alongside veteran Des West – aboard one of his three Holden Dealer Team Monaros. The duo finished third and Brock became part of the Bathurst furniture for the next 35 years.

His breakthrough came in 1972 driving solo in the

nimble six-cylinder Torana XU-1 up against the mighty V8 Falcons led by Allan Moffat.

The #28 Torana qualified fifth and race day dawned wet, exactly the conditions that Brock and the lightweight Holden could exploit to their advantage.

When the 500-mile, 130-lap race started, the conditions were terrible and immediately Brock and the Torana pack latched onto the back of the big Falcons in the slippery conditions.

Applying that pressure paid off: Moffat spun on lap 28 near Reid Park, allowing Brock to sail through to the lead. He swapped the lead with John French and Moffat as the conditions improved, but then he picked up a one-minute penalty on lap 90 for restarting the car too early after refuelling.

It wasn't enough to hold him back. Before long others had their dramas: French had a puncture and Moffat picked up two one-minute penalties, also for refuelling miscues.

The then 27-year-old Brock couldn't be caught, and he charged home to win, one lap clear of French's Falcon and two laps up on Doug Chivas' Charger.

It was the day that David beat Goliath at Bathurst and the day the Brock legend was born.

From there the floodgates were open and the wins kept flowing. The rise of Bathurst through the 1970s and '80s via its ground-breaking television coverage coincided with the emergence of poster-boy Brock and each fed the growth of the other.

Keen to spread his wings, the prodigiously talented Brock left the Firth-run Holden Dealer Team at the end of 1974 and won Bathurst again in 1975 in a privately prepared and run V8 Torana alongside co-driver Brian Sampson.

Brought back into the HDT fold for 1978 in a bid to bolster Holden's ranks in the wake of the crushing Ford 1-2 form finish at Bathurst in 1977, Brock proceeded to launch the most successful blitz on the Great Race in its history.

By the time he crossed the line at the front of his own 1-2 form finish in 1984, Brock had won the Great Race a staggering six times in the space of seven years. He and his team simply crushed the field, pure and simple.

Brock's period of domination started in 1978 when he and Kiwi Jim Richards won the race in their first attempt as a combination and went even better the following year – they won by a whopping six laps, just over 37 kilometres in front of their nearest opposition.

They swapped their A9X Toranas for a new Commodore in 1980 and the result stayed the same, though their pathway to victory was a little shaky in the early stages when Brock pitted after hitting a slower Gemini across the top of the Mountain. But they recovered to eventually reclaim the lead, aided by Dick Johnson famously smashing into an errant rock that had rolled out onto the track just after the Queensland Ford hero had swept past Brock to put him a lap down.

Johnson got his revenge on the Mountain in 1981 and stopped the Brock/Richards bid for four straight wins when he and John French won a race stopped early due to a multi-car crash at McPhillamy Park.

But Brock and his Holden Dealer Team were back on top in 1982, this time with new co-driver, ex-F1 driver Larry Perkins.

They went on to win three in a row, including the 1983 race that required them to swap to the team's second

Commodore after their own #05 car blew its engine in the very early stages of the race.

Brock and Perkins led home the sister Commodore of John Harvey and David Parsons in 1984 with a 1-2 form finish to end the era of Group C racing at Bathurst, a series of uniquely Australian regulations and rules.

International Group A regulations were introduced for 1985 and largely removed a lot of the advantages Brock and his HDT outfit had long enjoyed, exposing them to a worldwide pool of manufacturers, teams and drivers all keen to dominate touring car racing, rather than the locally developed rules and 'king of the local sandpit' situation Brock had previously been in.

But his split with Holden in February 1987 in the wake of a range of issues, including his insistence at fitting a box of magnets and crystals dubbed a 'Energy Polarizer' to his HDT Special Vehicles road cars and race cars, had far more of an impact on his ability to fight for Bathurst 1000 glory.

Losing Holden factory backing meant the supply of parts and technology dried up, however Brock still found a way to win the 1987 Great Race – a round of the inaugural World Touring Car Championship – in one of the all-time fairytale wins.

In a repeat of the 1983 race, Brock's #05 Commodore blew its engine early and he and co-driver David Parsons jumped into the team's back-up #10 Mobil Commodore in order to continue in the race; fully legal under the 'cross entering' rules of the time.

They pressed on through wet weather and driving rain, eventually surviving the tricky conditions to cross the line in third place, a few laps behind the two Swiss-run Texaco-backed Ford Sierras that dominated the race.

But the two turbocharged Fords were flung from the results post-race for illegal bodywork, promoting Brock, Parsons and Peter McLeod (who had driven the opening stint in the #10 car) to victory!

In perhaps the most turbulent year of his professional life, Brock had proved the knockers wrong in a script not even the most optimistic of Hollywood blockbuster writers could have conjured up.

That result left Brock with his ninth win from his first 19 starts in the race, a win rate of just under one win for every two times he lined up on the grid.

Peter Brock made another 13 Bathurst 1000 starts after his 1987 win but couldn't manage to finish on the podium in the back end of his career, let alone claim an elusive 10th Bathurst Great Race win.

It's proof that there's only so long a magical stretch of even the greatest sportspeople's careers can run for. All the same, Brock's golden run was so long that it will stand the test of time in Bathurst's history books.

Brock was still a massive crowd favourite and a skilled driver, but the competition levels, sponsorship budget levels and constant technological evolution of the cars he raced against made for a much tougher pathway to victory than in his heyday of the late '70s and early '80s.

In fact, Brock's only Bathurst 1000 podium appearances after his ninth win came in the pair of races held in 1997 – the year of his retirement from full-time racing. He was invited up there with the winners to acknowledge the adoring fans and spray some farewell champagne – as is customary for drivers appearing on the podium – despite not finishing in the top three positions.

In the wake of his bust-up with Holden a decade earlier, Brock had moved to race BMWs in 1988 but the small four-cylinder cars were out-gunned on the long straights up and down Mount Panorama and he didn't stand a chance of victory.

By that time the turbocharged Ford Sierra was 'the car to have' in international Group A touring car racing, so Brock and his Mobil team made the previously unthinkable move in order to be competitive in 1989. However, his cars never carried the Ford blue oval badge in this period.

He drove one of the whistling Fords to pole position at Bathurst that year, but a jammed wheel nut put paid to his winning chances. Blistered tyres on the resurfaced circuit in 1990 forced his car to make multiple unscheduled pit stops to change tyres, however he and Englishman Andy Rouse still managed to finish fourth.

The result remained his best Bathurst 1000 finish in his post-1987 Great Race career.

A move in 1991 back to racing a V8 Commodore was a winner with the fans, especially given his car was prepared and run by his former Bathurst winning co-driver Larry Perkins, but the locally produced Holdens were simply no match for the all-conquering Nissan GT-Rs.

It took until 1994 for Brock to become a genuine contender at Bathurst again: that year he was brought back into the Holden factory fold and signed to drive for the Holden Racing Team as teammate to Tomas Mezera. It gave him the car and backing capable of winning the Great Race in a way he hadn't had for a decade.

'There was no one more recognised in the country – and still now – as Peter Brock,' Mezera recounted to me on the V8 Sleuth Podcast in 2020.

'There will be no one else like him. People say Lowndesy [Craig Lowndes] is like him, but he's not anywhere near it. There will never be another one [like Brock].

'I got more known and recognised because I drove with Brock! Even these days, I go to check my golf clubs in at the airport and guys behind me spot me and ask about how I had driven with Brock – it was nearly 30 years ago!'

Ultimately, Brock's opportunities to win his 10th Bathurst once joining the HRT slipped through his fingers and on more than one occasion it was of his own doing.

Ask Mezera which Bathurst win was the 'one that got away' and he quickly nominates 1994 as the one that should have been his second win and Brock's record 10th.

That race was controversial for many reasons. The race promoters offered Brock a $100,000 bonus payday should he at last win his 10th Bathurst Great Race. The HRT's #05 Commodore (a brand-new car built for the Sandown and Bathurst long distance races) that he shared with Mezera was in hot water during race week over the location of its suspension towers.

Rival teams were spitting chips at what they deemed a cheating car, but a fix was made that satisfied officialdom and the Commodore was permitted to continue into the Sunday race, which was lashed by rainstorms.

'About lap 120, I'm in the lead by about 20 seconds,' recalls Mezera.

'We knew we had to make one more pit stop before the end of the race. Dick [Johnson] behind us and our other [HRT] car with Bradley [Jones] and Lowndesy [Craig Lowndes] both had to make two stops to be able to make it home from there.

'Because of the rain earlier in the race and the way it jumbled things up, they didn't have enough fuel to go to lap 130 or so. We did. I stayed on slick tyres through the wet part of the track, and I drove to a lap-time number to get the right number of laps [completed] so we didn't need an extra stop.'

Mezera wheeled into the pits to hand over to Brock on lap 131 then walked back inside the pit garage confident they were in the box seat to win the race with 30 laps remaining.

'Brock jumped in, and we knew we could make it to the end with the fuel we had,' he says.

'He was about 20 seconds behind them [John Bowe in the Johnson Falcon and Lowndes] on the track and both have to make a stop. They could only make it to about lap 155 [of 161], they can't get any further.

'But he decided to chase them! He was trying to catch up and get close to them and unfortunately no one told him to just relax. I went to have a shower and thought, "This is great; we're going to pull this one off and get the win."'

Then it all went wrong, and Brock did something he had never done in 25 years of competing in the Great Race to that point.

He crashed out of the race.

The fan favourite had lost the rear end of the Holden over the top of the Mountain, spun, then slammed the unforgiving concrete wall. The car was smashed.

That brought out the Safety Car to bunch up the field at a slow speed while the recovery crews loaded the crashed car onto the back of a tilt-tray truck. There were six laps of slow speed driving, allowing those marginal on fuel – including the top two cars of Bowe and Lowndes – to save more fuel and thus be able to make it to the finish line in first and second respectively without the need for another visit to pit lane.

'That was Brocky's 10th Bathurst that got away,' muses Mezera.

'Everyone's got a story like that about the Bathurst race. It was a shame for Brocky because he was already running out of time [to win his 10th Bathurst Great Race]. He was getting on; he was in his 50s. He did extremely well to get to that age and still be reasonably competitive. I'm kind of straightforward though. When he screwed up, I told him. Lots of people never told him that, they'd be dancing around him.'

From there the Brock error rate at the Mountain grew. He crashed the duo's Commodore in the Saturday morning Top 10 Shootout the following year. During practice for the Super Touring race in 1997, he even rolled the Triple Eight team's front-wheel-drive Vectra when he lost control and tumbled over and over in the sand trap at the Chase on the high-speed Conrod Straight. It was the first and only time he'd ever rolled a car at Mount Panorama.

However, Brock's performance at his last full-time V8 Supercar race – in 1997 at Bathurst (a fortnight after the Super Touring race) – was more befitting of the man and the moment.

He blasted away from pole position to head the chasing pack, duelled with former co-driver Larry Perkins in the opening laps and handed over at the first pit stop to partner Mark Skaife in the lead of the race.

The car had an under-bonnet backfire during Skaife's stint that caused race-ending damage, but Brock had stepped out of the famous #05 Holden as race leader.

It was proof that on his day and with the right car he could still turn on some magic at the Mountain.

Post-retirement comebacks to the Bathurst 1000 in 2002 (in an, at best, mid-pack Team Brock Commodore) and 2004 (in the second Holden Racing Team Commodore) were largely unsuccessful and underlined that his best days at the Mountain were behind him, however that simply didn't matter to the spectators.

Fans queued for hours for his autograph; merchandise sales went through the roof; and the media turned an even bigger spotlight on the race than it normally would have – thanks to the return of its most winning driver.

Brock couldn't get enough of Bathurst and Bathurst couldn't get enough of him.

It's inevitable that stars fade as the years tick by from when they first made the stage their own. New heroes rise and take their place; it's just how it is.

But Brock's legacy will endure.

He's the one all the modern heroes of Bathurst are compared with. No one can, has, or will replace him. He had sparkle, charisma and X-factor. Blokes wanted to be him, women just wanted him.

Brock wasn't merely 'good for his time' or relevant for a fleeting moment. He was box-office stuff at Bathurst for three decades – and the reason so many attended the Great Race or tuned in on television.

There are reminders everywhere of Peter Brock at the Mountain and at its most celebrated race to ensure his name and deeds will remain prominent and relevant for decades to come.

His record of nine wins has been etched in the history books as the benchmark and is unlikely to ever be toppled. Only someone very special could do it.

A statue of Brock and his 1984 race-winning 'Big Banger' Commodore welcomes guests at the front of Bathurst's National Motor Racing Museum, and Skyline on the Mount Panorama circuit has been re-named 'Brock's Skyline' in his honour.

Every year since his death in 2006, the winners of the Bathurst 1000 have been awarded the Peter Brock Trophy – designed and created by Hardy Brothers jewellers, the same company that manufactured the Melbourne Cup at the time.

Each of these elements keep Brock connected to the Mountain that made him an icon of Australian sport, and keep the Mountain connected to its most successful challenger.

He's a Bathurst 1000 immortal.

*A bearded Peter Brock tackles Mount Panorama for the first time in 1969. He and Des West finished third in the V8-powered Monaro.*

## Most Podium Finishes

With his record-making nine Bathurst 500/1000 wins, Peter Brock cemented his place in Great Race history. But his protégé Craig Lowndes has Brock and all other drivers covered for podium finishes at the Great Race.

Lowndes has racked up 14 podium finishes from 29 starts as of the completion of the 2022 race. He opened his account immediately on debut in 1994 by finishing second.

Since then he's taken seven wins, a further four runner-up finishes and two third-places to give him a podium finish 48% of the time he's started the race.

Brock and his former winning partners – Jim Richards and Larry Perkins – have 12 podium finishes.

Mark Skaife is next best with 10 podiums from Steve Richards (nine) and Greg Murphy (eight).

# 4

# Marvellous Moffat

**A**llan Moffat is a giant of Australian motorsport and his name takes pride of place in the list of figures to have shaped the Great Race over its journey.

He was intense, focused, emotional, determined and, at times, standoffish. His commitment to winning was absolute. Winning at Bathurst became his obsession.

Moffat's pathway to racing at Mount Panorama came in a very different way to that of his contemporaries.

Originally hailing from Canada, Moffat moved to Australia as a teenager in the early 1960s when his father was sent 'Down Under' by his employer, tractor manufacturer Massey Ferguson.

A few years later his parents returned to their homeland without him. Moffat wanted to further his interest in motorsport and he had a firm focus on carving a career behind the wheel. He proceeded to divide his time between Australia and the United States.

After starting his racing career with a Triumph TR3, he then did a stint in the United States as a gopher for the famous Team Lotus squad, helping them at events, including the Indianapolis 500. Moffat convinced them to sell him one of their Lotus Cortinas, a machine he sent back to Australia to race in the mid-1960s.

He spent plenty of time in North America racing in Trans-Am. It was also in the States that he set up his connection with Ford, working as a development driver for the Kar Kraft special vehicles division.

Moffat decided to settle permanently in Australia in 1969 and secured a brand-new Boss 302 Trans-Am Mustang from Kar Kraft to bring back to his adopted homeland. It famously was sponsored by Coca-Cola and became his car of choice in his challenge on the Australian Touring Car Championship.

In those days the ATCC was contested by modified touring cars – known as Improved Production cars – however the annual Bathurst Great Race over 500 miles every October was run for more standard, Series Production-specification cars that could be road registered and driven around the streets.

By coincidence, in 1969, when Moffat made his first start at Mount Panorama, so too did a young bloke from Melbourne named Peter Brock. Both got their first taste of the race that shaped their lives.

Moffat drove a works Falcon GT-HO with Alan Hamilton (who would later be Colin Bond's co-driver in the famous 1-2 Moffat/Bond Ford form finish at Bathurst in 1977) and crossed the line fourth, one spot behind Brock, who finished third in a Holden Dealer Team Monaro GTS 350 with Des West.

Neither of the two young drivers grabbed the headlines that day, but their careers and common goal of conquering Mount Panorama guaranteed that they would appear together in the headlines for the two decades that followed.

'Bathurst made them and they made Bathurst,' says veteran Aussie motorsport journalist David Hassall, who closely followed the careers of the two racing icons during the period.

'You can't separate the two things. It's hard to imagine what Bathurst would be without either of them, let alone Australian motorsport.'

Moffat's first Bathurst Great Race win came in just his second start – in 1970. He was lead driver of a three-car factory Ford assault. He took pole position then saw off an early race challenge from Colin Bond's new, nimble Torana XU-1.

Moffat's early race pace set up a lead he was able to carry all day, claiming his first Bathurst victory by 39 seconds over his teammate, 1968 Bathurst winner Bruce McPhee.

Driving the full 500-mile (805 kilometre) distance solo in those days – as some drivers opted to do – required extra preparations. A driver tackling the Bathurst race had to ensure sufficient hydration to complete the six-hour-plus race. Without a co-driver to provide the main driver some time to rest and recharge, toilet breaks were not really an option. But Moffat wasn't expecting a Channel 7 camera crew to interrupt his in-car, er, self-relieving during his last pit stop.

As his crew leapt into action to service the big V8 muscle car, its pilot figured he had about two and a half minutes to relieve himself. While fluid was going in at one end of the day, it was coming out of the other!

All was going fine until a Channel 7 reporter and his cameraman appeared at the driver's window looking to get a quick word with the race leader before he powered back out onto the track.

The interview took place, live on television around the nation, while Moffat carried on his business below the window line. After all, it's hard to stop some things once they've started ...

The Ford pit crew gave their pilot the signal to take off and Moffat blasted back into the race.

Moffat became the only driver in Bathurst history to win the race solo in successive years, romping home to victory in 1971 at the wheel of one of the classic Aussie muscle cars of all time, the Ford Falcon GT-HO Phase III.

Such was his dominance, he qualified 13 seconds faster than the existing race lap record and three seconds faster than teammate John French.

In 1971, he had a few anxious moments thanks to a pesky beer carton that blocked his radiator for a time after blowing over the fence from the spectator area. The cardboard prevented clean air from flowing into the engine of his Falcon V8, which soon threatened to overheat. Luckily the cardboard dropped off. Once again it seemed that nothing could stop Allan Moffat from winning for the second year in a row.

He finished the 130 laps some 23 minutes faster than he'd taken to complete the same distance in 1970 –

quite the leap of speed from year to year and proof that the manufacturers kept finding more and more pace as they introduced new models and advancements via tyres, brakes and suspension.

The following year, 1972, marked the final time drivers could tackle the Bathurst race solo and Moffat aimed to become the first driver to win the race three times in a row.

Ultimately though it wasn't his day. Instead it became the first win for Peter Brock – at the helm of the Holden Dealer Team's XU-1 Torana.

A couple of things made the 1973 race notable: it was the debut of Group C specification cars as well as the year the race expanded from 500 miles to 1000 kilometres.

The increase in distance meant co-drivers were mandatory, so Moffat shared his new Ford XA GT Falcon with Ian 'Pete' Geoghegan.

They qualified third then set about battling Brock's Torana all day. When the XU-1 ran out of fuel with Brock's co-driver Doug Chivas at the helm, that let the Ford off the hook and opened the path for Moffat to take his third Bathurst win in the space of four years.

Moffat's rivalry with Brock was every publicist's dream in the 1970s, particularly when it came to the annual Bathurst race. They were complete opposites in so many ways and that only helped fuel the fascination for the fans.

Moffat was Canadian, a Ford driver, could be prickly to the media and fully focused.

Brock was the Aussie lad born and bred in Melbourne, a Holden driver, the media darling and usually appeared far more relaxed than his counterpart.

'Moffat and Bob Jane and Moffat and Norm Beechey were genuine rivalries in that they clashed on the track, but Moffat and Brock never clashed,' notes veteran motorsport journalist David Hassall.

'Sure, there were plenty of dark looks across the pits at one another, but it didn't translate to the track. It was clean between Brock and Moffat on the track, and it didn't create the bad blood like other rivalries Moffat had with other drivers. Allan was certainly intense and determined. He was very isolated and had a siege mentality of "us versus the world" in the way he went about his racing.

'It's a popular misconception he wasn't naturally gifted as a driver and I think that aggravated him a little – the guys who worked with him and even some of his rivals had the highest regard for his ability behind the wheel. He was a gun, and he got the most out of the cars.'

Moffat and Brock dominated Bathurst through the 1970s and into the early 1980s. From 1969 – when both made their Great Race debut – through to the end of the local Group C touring car racing era in 1984, they won 12 of the 16 Bathurst 500/1000s held in that time, with eight to Brock and four to Moffat.

Indeed, they drove for the best teams and therefore had the best cars with the best preparation and access to the best technology available at the time, but such a level of domination for such a sustained period by two drivers of Australia's most famous race has not happened before or since, and nor is it likely to ever occur again.

That level of domination at the peak of the Ford versus Holden battle at Bathurst made them household names.

But the withdrawal of Ford from Australian touring car racing at the end of 1973 left Moffat without the crucial financial and technical support of the 'blue oval'.

He forged on as a privateer, racing Falcons with the backing of loyal sponsors, but had to take a far greater load on his shoulders than when he was a Ford factory driver and turned up with his helmet to drive, free of the obligations of running a team. He had to find the sponsorship funding and deal with the day-to-day issues of keeping the doors of his race team open.

His 1974 Bathurst program, his first under his own banner and outside of the Ford factory squad, had all the hallmarks of a Moffat Bathurst assault. He air-freighted the Falcon he intended to race at Bathurst to the United States in the months prior for testing and tinkering in a project he dubbed 'Project B-52', conducted away from the prying eyes of rival teams and drivers.

Unlike his rivals of the era, he looked beyond Australia's border for his co-driver that year, signing German Dieter Glemser, one of the best Ford touring car drivers in the world of the period. It was just one occasion of many that he secured top-line international co-drivers for his Bathurst assaults. Moffat was a visionary, he dreamt big and had a worldly view of racing in a way no one in Australian touring car racing did at the time.

A student of military history and strategy, he ran his race team and campaigns much like the general of an army. He pondered deeply over strategy and formed strong alliances with people and organisations both locally and overseas. Letting any form of intelligence out the door to rivals was indeed a no-no.

Another of Moffat's 'project' examples was his 1976 Bathurst campaign. In June of that year his Falcon race car burned to the ground in its transporter after catching fire en route to the Adelaide International Raceway round of the Australian Touring Car Championship.

So, appropriately, the Falcon XB GT that was built as a replacement for the destroyed car was built under the banner of 'Project Phoenix', literally rising from the ashes.

That car appeared in a striking white paint scheme under the Moffat Ford Dealers banner with renewed backing from Ford via head office and its dealer network.

Aussie international Vern Schuppan signed up to drive with Moffat at Bathurst and the new car claimed pole position, but engine dramas sidelined them when the crankshaft pulley broke, thus giving the water pump no drive and cooking the motor.

It was later revealed that the failed pulley was one of the items salvaged from the Adelaide fire that somehow ended up fitted to the Bathurst race engine.

However, the very same car had a much better ending to the race 12 months later – in 1977.

Moffat was at the peak of his powers in 1977, a season that was simply the best of his career.

He wooed Colin Bond away from the Holden Dealer Team to make the jump across the manufacturer fence and become his teammate in a pair of Moffat Ford Dealer hardtop Falcons for the season.

The addition of American Carroll Smith as team manager added another piece to the puzzle and the team went on a tear, dominating the Australian Touring Car Championship as Moffat claimed his third championship and second in succession.

But the thing that motor racing fans – both hardcore and casual – remember from that year above all else is the 1-2 form finish at Bathurst, forever one of the most famous moments in the history of the Great Race.

The two Moffat team Falcons were the only cars on the lead lap at the end of the 163-lap race. Ahead was the #1 car that the team boss shared with Belgian ace Jacky Ickx – coming home victorious after starting third on the grid.

Moffat and Bond each drove double stints (the former copping a rather nasty blistered hand) before handing over to their respective co-drivers, who each ran a stint.

But Belgian Ickx, a Le Mans 24 Hour winner and more used to precise F1 and sportscar machinery, had given the brakes in the lead car a fair caning in his first taste of a touring car at Bathurst, forcing Moffat to limp home in the latter stages as they cried 'enough'.

'The front brakes went metal to metal and the pistons started to melt and popped something out,' Moffat told me in 2015 of the closing stages of his 1977 victory.

'The pistons had gone out so far that the hydraulic seal jumped out of the brake caliper and as such all the brake fluid poured out – and the smoke I saw was all the brake fluid on the hot rotor. It only took three or four brake applications, and the brake fluid reservoir was empty.'

But no one other than Bond was a threat and the #2 pilot played the last part of the race with a straight bat, crossing the line alongside team owner Moffat for a memorable finish.

The simple mention of Moffat and Bond driving across the line two abreast to greet the chequered flag at Bathurst in 1977 still infuriates Holden fans to this very day.

Moffat's fourth Bathurst win came on a day when the big Falcons swept aside all comers. They simply crushed the opposition in what proved to be his day of ultimate Bathurst glory.

*Allan Moffat acknowledges the crowd on the podium at Bathurst in 1977. The victory was his fourth Great Race win and one of his undoubted banner-head career achievements.*

Smarting from being dusted up by Ford at Bathurst in 1977, Holden responded for 1978 by doubling down and enticing Brock back to the Holden Dealer Team after his three years racing as a privateer.

On the other hand, Moffat found Ford going the other way. They trimmed his backing and eventually bailed out altogether, leaving him once more as a Falcon-mounted privateer paddling his own boat against the ever-flowing tide of Toranas.

He endured three years of unsuccessful Bathurst campaigns – between 1978 and 1980 – failing to finish the race each time. In fact, he drove two cars in 1980 – his own Falcon, which had been prepared late and expired after just a few laps, as well as the Bob Morris/Bill O'Brien-driven car he had been cross-entered in – and both failed to finish.

Ford's manufacturer support had been a crucial element in Moffat's success in the 1970s but was no longer forthcoming in the new decade of the 1980s, so he linked with Japanese manufacturer Mazda in 1981 to drive a rotary-powered RX-7, backed by Peter Stuyvesant cigarettes.

The small coupe, with its distinctive engine note, was referred to as 'the rice burner' by many of its rivals yet it proved to be a more than competitive car in the Australian Touring Car Championship. In fact, Moffat drove the Mazda to victory in the 1983 championship, his fourth national title in touring car racing.

But there was one place where victory eluded the Mazda – Bathurst.

Moffat simply couldn't overcome the power of the V8-engined cars up and down the long straights of Mount Panorama and, despite finishing on the podium three times in four visits with the Mazdas to Bathurst (third in 1981, second in 1983 and third again in 1984), he was forced to watch on as Dick Johnson (1981) and Brock (1982, 1983 and 1984) collected the silver James Hardie Trophy on offer for the winner.

Then the rules for touring car racing in Australia were revisited once again and there was a move away from the locally developed Group C regulations to internationally developed Group A cars for 1985. That prompted Mazda to pull out of the sport: it didn't have a suitable car for the new era.

Moffat was left without a drive all year, including for Bathurst. Nothing if not adaptable, he donned a red blazer and joined the Channel 7 television commentary team for the weekend.

If Moffat's absence from the grid for a Bathurst 1000 was strange enough, things really took a twist in 1986 when he was signed up to a drive a Holden – and with Brock!

The long-time rivals got together for the 1986 season and shared a Mobil Holden Dealer Team Commodore in a campaign that included select rounds of the European Touring Car Championship and the big endurance races in Australia, including Bathurst.

But Moffat's first, and indeed only, Bathurst assault in a Holden didn't start well. He lost control of the #05 Commodore in Friday morning's practice session at McPhillamy Park.

He just slid a couple of feet wide, dropped the right rear wheel into a small, muddy hole on the outside of the track and the car slewed across the circuit and hit the wall hard, riding up and along the concrete for some 50 metres before coming back down and coasting to a halt on the grass on the outside of Skyline.

The team went to extraordinary lengths in order to fix the damaged car overnight. Front-end mechanicals had to be flown up from Melbourne (an Australian Airlines jet was held at the terminal so the parts could be loaded onto the flight!) and body panels were taken from an HDT show car on display in one of Bathurst's banks. It all came together and the car was back on track on Saturday.

But race day didn't pan out for the dream Moffat/Brock combination. The latter had hauled the car up from 11th on the grid to run second in the early stages, but their hopes of a victory were dashed at their second pit stop.

It turned out that the car's oil cooler had incurred damage. The crew realised this when they removed the front wheels and the pool of oil became visible. Over two laps were lost as they frantically worked to bypass the damaged unit. Brock returned to the race in seventh place and they eventually finished fifth, one lap down.

The Brock/Moffat partnership only lasted one year before Brock's notorious and very public break-up with Holden in early 1987.

Moffat did a deal via a third party to purchase Brock's new and unraced VL model Commodore race car and he and former Brock co-driver John Harvey joined forces to tackle select rounds of the World Touring Car Championship.

They crossed the line seventh in the season-opening race at Monza in Italy, then were elevated to victory when the top six finishers – all BMWs – were all excluded from the results, thus making Moffat and Harvey the inaugural winners of a WTCC race.

But the rise of turbocharged Ford Sierras as the dominant car in worldwide touring car racing couldn't be ignored. Moffat elected to abandon his V8 Commodore in favour of leasing Brit Andy Rouse's Sierra for the 1987 Bathurst race, which was also a round of the world championship.

History shows he should have run his Commodore. The Sierra's driveline failed without Moffat getting to turn a lap in the race and Brock won in his second-string Commodore.

Moffat's 19th and last Bathurst start came in 1988 at the wheel of a Sierra sourced from Swiss Ford guru Ruedi Eggenberger, with backing from ANZ Bank.

Eggenberger's gun German driver, Klaus Niedzwiedz, also came as part of the package to drive with Moffat and Gregg Hansford. They led 101 of the 161 laps before the engine overheated after driving slowly behind the pace car while in a clear lead.

'Ruedi had a computer system where we had instant feedback from the car to the pits – the oil and water temperature being the most important,' Moffat explained to me during an interview in 2013.

'We just assumed it was OK. With a three-lap lead, we could do whatever we want. I didn't want to overrule Ruedi: we had hired him as team manager.

'It's the worst defeat in my whole career. I couldn't believe it could have happened.'

Moffat continued to run a succession of Sierras and later a Falcon at Bathurst as a team owner until the mid-1990s. The racing legend quietly ended his career as a driver with victory in the Fuji 500 in Japan at the wheel of one of his Sierras in 1989.

He continued his association with Bathurst as a Channel 7 commentator in the 1990s and, since 2010, his son James (who finished second in 2014 in a Nissan with Taz Douglas, and again in 2021 in a Mustang with Cam Waters) has been on his own quest to claim victory in the race that made his father a legend.

Allan Moffat and his contribution to the story of the Great Race will never be forgotten.

# Winning From the Front

Sitting on pole position isn't a guarantee that a car will go on and win the Great Race at Bathurst.

The tallying of practice and qualifying times to determine grid positions began in 1967. Since then the pole-sitting car has gone on to win the race only 13 times.

First to pull it off were Bruce McPhee and Barry Mulholland in their Monaro GTS 327 in 1968, and Allan Moffat followed suit for his first two Bathurst wins, in 1970 and 1971.

Peter Brock and Jim Richards achieved it in 1978 and 1979 and Richards was next to do so – in 1991 in a Nissan GT-R alongside Mark Skaife. They won from pole again in 2002.

The most recent pole-to-victory win came in 2021, with Chaz Mostert and Lee Holdsworth for Walkinshaw Andretti United.

Second place on the grid has gone on to win the race 11 times, third place has generated eight wins and fourth grid position has had five winners.

# Same Names

There have been a handful of instances in Bathurst 1000 history where two drivers competing in the race share the same name but are unrelated.

For instance, there were two Peter Williamsons. One competed in a Morris Cooper S in 1973; the other was made famous by being the first driver to carry Channel 7's RaceCam in-car camera in the 1979 race.

However it's highly unlikely there will again be two drivers with the same name – including the same middle name – who share a car in the race, as was the case with the pairing of David John Parsons and David John Parsons in 1999.

It helped that one was nicknamed 'Skippy'. He was four years older than his driving partner and was the Tasmanian David

Parsons who won at Bathurst in 1987 with Peter Brock and Peter McLeod. He'd made his Bathurst 1000 debut five years earlier and finished runner-up in the Holden Dealer Team 1-2 form finish of 1984.

The latter David Parsons, who was dubbed 'Truckie', was a transport business operator from Castlemaine in Victoria. In 1995, he had made the move from racing trucks to racing V8 touring cars after purchasing a customer Commodore race car from Larry Perkins.

The pair linked up in 1999 to drive together at Bathurst at the wheel of a Gibson Motorsport-prepared Commodore VT in the blue colours of sponsor Challenge Recruitment. They missed qualifying on Friday when 'Truckie' crashed the car at Griffins Bend. It was repaired and, after starting 54th on the grid, they finished a solid 11th in the race, two laps down on the sister Gibson-run, Wynn's-backed Commodore that won the race, driven by Steve Richards and Greg Murphy.

While it had no bearing on their performance in the race, the fact that the two men shared the same car, first name, middle name and surname is an amazing coincidence.

It's yet another quirky part of Bathurst's rich Great Race history.

5

# Holden v Ford

An integral part of the story of Mount Panorama and its Great Race is the epic battle between Holden and Ford.

Many other car manufacturers have tackled the race, and there have been plenty of occasions in Bathurst history where it wasn't all about V8-powered cars, so it was never a forgone conclusion that the event would evolve into a two-horse race.

What's surprising is that this never really detracted from the broad general interest that Australians have had in the Great Race.

It worked for a reason.

The public fell in love with the Holden and Ford battle partly because it reflected their driveways at home. A family in the 1960s or 1970s may not have been able to afford the limited-run V8 muscle car Falcon, Monaro or Torana that their racing heroes drove, but they had as their daily drive the six-cylinder base model that looked close enough to the cars that raced around the Mountain.

The two local giants of the Australian car industry of the period dominated the race from its inception.

Holden and Ford won 20 of the first 21 Bathurst 500/1000s from 1963 to 1984. The only time neither of the 'big two' won the race outright in that period was in 1966, when Mini Coopers tasted success.

The first V8-powered car to win the Great Race at Bathurst was the XR GT Falcon of Harry Firth and Fred Gibson in 1967. Powered by a 289 cubic inch (4.2 litre) V8 engine, the XR GT Falcon broke the trend of the race being won by small cars.

Holden's new Monaro GTS 327 made its Mountain debut in 1968 and won first time up in the hands of Bruce McPhee and Barry Mulholland. It was the first win for a Holden car in the race, but not the first for a Holden engine, given the Monaros were in fact powered by a 327 cubic inch (5.3 litre) Chevrolet engine sourced from General Motors in America.

The victory is an important one in the history books though, because it was the first of a record 36 times that a Holden would win the Bathurst Great Race.

It does, however, remain one of the quirky wins in the history of the race. The regulations of the period dictated that each car required two drivers, however it did not specify a minimum or maximum number of laps each driver was required to complete.

Not a fan of being forced to have a co-driver, McPhee had co-driver Mulholland drive one single lap in the 130-lap race. Nobody could say he failed to meet the requirements of the regulations and McPhee drove the other 129!

It was a strategy he'd employed in previous years too. The duo finished sixth – in a Cortina – in 1964, second in another Cortina in 1965, third in a Mini in 1966 prior to the victory in the Monaro in 1968, and then second again in a Falcon, in 1969. That meant Mulholland drove a mere five Great Race laps across six years (he and McPhee didn't compete in the 1967 race), making him the most successful on a lap-to-result ratio in the race's history!

In the 1960s General Motors had a worldwide policy of no circuit racing. But Holden in Australia found a way around that in 1969 when it clandestinely formed the Holden Dealer Team run by former Ford ace driver and car preparer Harry Firth.

Holden was absolutely involved behind the scenes. It was presented, however, that its dealers and some subsidiary sponsors, including Castrol, were the ones supporting the racing program, thus getting around the global edict from head office back in Detroit.

The creation of the HDT introduced the wider Australian sporting fanbase to not only Peter Brock, but also a Sydney rally and race driver, Colin Bond, who was a pivotal figure in the Holden and Ford rivalry at Bathurst of the late '60s and '70s.

'Harry Firth had always been with Ford and prepared and raced them in the early days,' Bond told me during a sit-down chat on the V8 Sleuth Podcast in 2019.

'Then suddenly Ford decided they'd bring Al Turner out to Australia from the United States to run the motor racing side of things, so Harry was out of a job. The next minute, GM picked him up.

'I used to rally against Harry in my Mitsubishi days, and he had a Cortina. We used to give him a hard time. I think [influential motoring journalist] Mike Kable had talked to Harry and told him I'd been doing a bit of circuit racing. And that's why I think he rang me to offer me a drive at Sandown alongside Spencer Martin and then picked me in the team to go to Bathurst.'

The 1969 Monaro that was due to tackle Bathurst was a HT model GTS 350. It was a step up from the previous model, with a bigger 350 cubic inch (5.7 litre) V8 engine, wider track, a four-speed Muncie gearbox and thicker front brake discs.

But before the team made its debut at Bathurst as the HDT, it entered a single car for the Sandown Three Hour race in Melbourne to gauge its competitiveness against the new GT-HO Falcons.

The outcome was a disaster: open-wheeler ace Martin crashed the Monaro at the end of the main straight when it lost its brakes. There was an ominous crunch and within seconds it caught fire, hardly an inspiring first showing for HDT, which appears in the history books as one of the legendary acronyms in Australian motorsport.

Bond had missed the Sandown race due to an existing commitment that weekend – a rally in New Guinea – but he was absolutely on board for Bathurst.

'With Spencer out of the equation for Bathurst, he [Firth] got Peter Macrow and Henk Woelders, who were both Formula 2 [open-wheeler] drivers to drive what we used to call the number one car,' he recalls.

'Tony Roberts and I were in the number two car – we were both rally people and Tony worked for GM as an engineer and had been around for quite some time. He won the Sandown race in 1968 with Bob Watson and came third at Bathurst.

'And then you had Peter Brock and Des West. Des had been to Bathurst lots of times and he was a Holden dealer in the past and even used to race humpy Holdens going back further than that. That was the team; it was virtually only a couple of months old.

'In those days we used to drive the cars to and from the track. So often you'd put the standard (brake) pads in and you'd run the discs in driving around on the road before you'd get there and put the race pads in there for going on track. Tatey [HDT crew member Ian Tate], Brocky and one of the other boys drove the cars up for 1969 from Melbourne to Bathurst.'

Bond describes the race itself as relatively easy. He started seventh on the grid and the factory Fords, though fast, proved fragile as their untried Goodyear racing tyres continually let them down. His Monaro, shod with Michelin radial road tyres, took the lead and never looked back.

'It was the first time I'd been to Bathurst with a competitive motor car,' says Bond.

'I'd not driven the race car until the Saturday practice at Bathurst! You had to stroke the cars along. You had to look after the brakes as much as possible. But it just ran perfectly. I did notice we had a slight dint in the door; it must have been Tony with that one!'

The 1969 Bathurst win launched Bond's career and the Monaro win further elevated the Holden and Ford rivalry as the race grew in importance as the decade ended.

'Des West said to me after the race, "Oh my God, this race is becoming so professional." I said, "What do you mean?" And he said, "Well, I'm really having trouble having a cigarette now on the way around!" He'd light it going up the Mountain and just hold it down (below the window line) when he drove past the pits!'

Holden made a big move in 1970 when it took the decision to downsize in its bid for Bathurst glory. Rather than fight Ford with a V8-powered challenger, it opted for the smaller, six-cylinder powered Torana XU-1.

The little Holden was lighter than the big Falcons, kinder on its tyres and more fuel efficient. It was a solid-sounding theory but Ford immediately proceeded to steamroll its way to Bathurst wins, with Allan Moffat driving in 1970 and 1971.

'We went to the XU-1s but, in hindsight, we should have run the Monaro for one more year,' says Bond.

'The first year we just had stupid problems with them, like carburettor jets falling out. With the XU-1 it was still difficult at Bathurst. We could win everywhere else, but at Bathurst you still needed a V8 to get up the Mountain.

'We were going to put a V8 in the XU-1 but it all got knocked on the head when it got bad publicity in the press.'

What he was referring to was the 1972 'Supercar Scare'. Winning Bathurst had become a big deal for Holden, Ford and Chrysler and each planned to build enough new, faster and more powerful cars for the road to be permitted to race them at Mount Panorama.

Ford planned a Phase IV version of its Falcon GT-HO (based on the new XA Falcon coupe), Holden planned to beef up its XU-1 Torana and replace its six-cylinder engine with a V8 and Chrysler had planned to fit a V8 engine to its six-cylinder Charger.

But a series of newspaper articles trumpeting that these '160mph Supercars' would be sold to the public, let loose on roads and cause bloody carnage around the country had garnered a lot of attention. Journalists, politicians and other segments of the community had immediately jumped on the bandwagon. The whole uproar caused the cars to be canned.

Holden abandoned its V8 plans and stuck with its six-cylinder Torana XU-1 for that year's Bathurst race, which worked just fine for Brock, who went on to win his first Great Race.

But it worked out far from fine for teammate Bond, who crashed and rolled his Torana in the opening laps of the race in wet, slippery conditions at the top of the Mountain.

'We only had one set of wet (fully grooved) tyres and one set of (slightly grooved) intermediates,' he recalls.

'I said I'd have the wet weather tyres, but I got in the car on the grid, and it's got the intermediate tyres on it. Harry said, "Don't worry, cock, this rain will pass." He was right – the rain did pass – but I didn't get that far!

'I walked back to the pits and the boys asked how bad the car was. I said it wasn't bad, it had just hit the wheel and hit the Armco and slipped onto its roof. It wasn't all that bad, though after the race, the tow truck driver came along and put a chain through the roof to pick it up and destroyed it!'

Ford and Holden continued to slug it out at Mount Panorama for the remainder of the 1970s. The former made the decision to withdraw its factory support at the end of 1973 and that handed Holden a free pass to dominate for the rest of the decade.

Its move to an LH Torana in 1974 paved the way for the first V8 Torana Bathurst race car, the L34-option of the SLR/5000. The new car proved fast but fragile and Falcon privateers John Goss and Kevin Bartlett came out on top in that year's rain-affected race.

Privateer Torana L34s won the next two Bathurst races – in 1975 with Peter Brock and Brian Sampson and 1976 with Bob Morris and John Fitzpatrick.

The latter proved one of the most dramatic finishes in the race's history. Brit Fitzpatrick limped his way around the final laps with a broken axle and a smoke plume caused by a blown gearbox seal blowing oil onto the clutch.

A nervous Morris could only pace around the pits with fingers crossed and wait and watch as his co-driver gradually limped through the last few laps and greeted the chequered flag in front.

Holden debuted its ultimate Bathurst Torana in 1977: the A9X, which featured more power, four-wheel disc brakes and a hatchback version that was adopted by most teams. It was defeated by Allan Moffat's Falcons that year but finished off the decade in style with two Bathurst wins in a row – in 1978 and 1979 – with Peter Brock and Jim Richards at the helm.

The 1970s at Bathurst were all about Torana and Falcon, so it was perhaps appropriate that the start of the 1980s coincided with new cars for both sides of the fence.

Holden's new Commodore made its Bathurst debut in 1980 at the same time Ford teams were starting to run the four-door XD model Falcon.

Commodore and Falcon shared the track with the emerging challengers from Nissan, Mazda and BMW in the early 1980s until the adoption of Group A international touring car rules changed things from 1985.

The Falcon was not eligible under the rules and those wanting to run a Ford product, including Dick Johnson, had to opt for the non-Australian Mustang sourced from overseas for the 1985 and 1986 seasons.

Group A evened the playing field for Bathurst and, given it was an internationally developed formula, took away much of the local advantage that Holden and Ford had enjoyed in the years of the domestically created Group C rules.

With the influx of overseas teams and cars to Bathurst, the local heroes had to measure themselves against Volvos, BMWs, Jaguars and the like. The shakeup also put something of a pause to the direct Holden and Ford rivalry for a period.

Holden's Commodore remained its Bathurst challenger in the face of all of this competition and still racked up wins on the Mountain in 1986 and 1987, however Ford's move of developing the Sierra for racing overseas turned its turbocharged touring car into the car of choice in Australia in the later years of the 1980s.

The imported Fords won at Bathurst in 1988 and 1989, though both the 'blue oval' and Holden were forced to take a back seat to Nissan when the Japanese manufacturer's four-wheel-drive GT-R was introduced in 1990.

While it won Bathurst two years in a row – in 1991 and 1992 – the international formula of touring car racing didn't seem to be able to capture the hearts and minds of fans in the way that the Holden and Ford battles of the 1970s and early 1980s had done.

So Australia changed course and opted to 'return to the future' to a Commodore and Falcon V8 formula, pitting the two traditional rivals in a largely two-horse race from 1993 onwards.

A handful of the new-era cars, complete with rear wings and moulded front spoilers, appeared in the 1992 Bathurst 1000 (two Holden Racing Team Commodores, one Peter Brock Mobil Commodore and one Falcon from Glenn Seton's team) before becoming the 'main show' the following year, with the turbo Sierras and Nissans consigned to the history books.

Larry Perkins and Gregg Hansford won the 1993 race, the first of the new five-litre era, in their Castrol Commodore. It proved to be the last time a Holden V8 engine won the Bathurst 1000 as the new era permitted Commodore teams to use a Chevrolet-based engine in their cars. This stayed in place right through until 2022, when the Commodore nameplate bid its farewell to the Bathurst 1000.

BMW M3s and older model Commodores left over from the Group A category and smaller two-litre cars filled up the field for the '93 and '94 races before Bathurst became a purely Holden and Ford V8 race in 1995.

Holden and Ford battled one another exclusively in the Bathurst 1000 each year until 2013, when the new 'Car of the Future' regulations saw Nissan and Erebus Motorsport's privately developed Mercedes-Benz AMG E63 join the grid for that year's V8 Supercars Championship and the Bathurst classic.

Volvo joined in the fun in 2014 but, one by one, each of the new brands left the sport and the exclusive Ford versus Holden battle picked back up again in 2020, the same year that General Motors announced it would kill the Holden brand in Australia.

Bathurst Great Race cars had been very much production cars modified for the race track in the early era. But the modern era of the Holden and Ford battle saw the cars become purpose-built racing machines from the ground up. They had very little in common with their road-going versions.

The passion for the Holden and Ford rivalry carried on through the bulk of the V8 Supercars and Supercars era (the category changed its name in 2016). It remained strong enough to continue as a major selling point for the annual race. Year after year, fans kept coming back to the Mountain and television viewers kept tuning in to see which of the two would conquer the 161-lap, 1000-kilometre classic.

The Holden and Ford battle at Bathurst is now consigned to history. The Falcons, Monaros, Toranas, Mustangs and Commodores that used to tackle the Mountain over the years are as much a part of the folklore of the race as the drivers that steered them.

Over more than five decades, in their efforts to win the Great Race, each manufacturer and their representatives poured piles of everything into Bathurst: money, people power, marketing clout, technical know-how, political manoeuvring and so much more.

Beyond the Bathurst 1000 there are other classic races around the world – the Monaco Grand Prix, Indianapolis 500, Daytona 24 Hour and Le Mans 24 Hour – but none of them have, or ever will, see such a sustained, tribal, passionate rivalry between brands quite like the Ford and Holden battles at Mount Panorama.

## 1-2 Double Punches

Only four times in the history of the Bathurst race has a team finished 1-2. It's happened twice with Ford teams and twice with Holden teams.

The factory Ford Falcon GT-HO Phase IIs of Allan Moffat and Bruce McPhee came home 1-2 in 1970 and Moffat led home a more famous 1-2 formation finish with teammate Colin Bond in 1977 in their pair of Falcon XC hardtops.

Peter Brock led home his second Holden Dealer Team Commodore VK in 1984, driven in the final stint by David Parsons to take a 1-2 form finish.

Triple Eight matched that by finishing 1-2 in their first year at Bathurst racing Holdens in 2010, with Craig Lowndes and Jamie Whincup crossing the line in formation.

There's also an outlier in the history books for 1-2 finishes.

In 1967 the top two finishing Falcons were both entered by the Ford Motor Company but were prepared and run completely independently of one another – by Victoria-based Harry Firth and the New South Wales-based Geoghegan brothers, Ian and Leo. That result hasn't been counted in this list of 1-2 finishes.

# 6

# Lights, Camera, Action

**T**he television coverage of the Great Race turned the Bathurst 1000 into a phenomenon on the Australian, and indeed world, sporting stage.

Technology that enhanced the coverage became world-leading, cutting-edge stuff and advances were made that took viewers right into the heart of the action at every turn in a way no other sport was able to.

But it wasn't always so big.

Channel 9 (GTV-9 in Melbourne) broadcast the Armstrong 500 at Phillip Island 1960 to 1962. Then, in 1963, when the race moved to Bathurst, Channel 7 (ATN-7 in Sydney to be exact) took over the broadcasting.

Channel 7 had just four cameras to cover the six-plus kilometre circuit for that first telecast of the 1963 event. The minimal camera coverage meant that only Pit Straight, the bottom of Conrod Straight and partway up Mountain Straight, as well as the exit of the Cutting, were captured and beamed onto black and white TV screens around the country.

There were no in-car cameras, no helicopter shots and not a speck of colour was to be found!

With no video links between Bathurst and Sydney, crews were forced to camp out in the Blue Mountains to set up microwave links to help carry the TV images back to Epping in Sydney. It was the only way viewers at home could see this new race for road-going cars.

Unlike the modern Bathurst telecast tallying multiple days and including an entire Sunday smorgasbord of speed, the inaugural race in 1963 on ATN-7 in Sydney was a case of blink and you could have missed it.

The coverage ran from 8.30am to 10.30am in Sydney before breaking for a 90-minute movie, returning at midday for an hour before the 'Blacklock 10,000 pounds-to-win' tenpin bowling final took priority for the next half an hour.

A five-minute update at 1.30pm led into a Sunday matinee movie (a 1935 American thriller, *Car 99*, of all things!), with a couple more five-minute updates in between a game show, *Party Time*, and a religious program, *Stop, Look and Listen*. Then at last rev heads got the chance to be returned to Mount Panorama at 4pm for the final hour of the race in order to see the Cortina of Harry Firth and Bob Jane eventually cross the line as winners, nearly eight hours after the field had been sent on its way.

Coverage of the race expanded in the years that followed, though a one-hour lunch break – which allowed the stations in Sydney and Melbourne to screen the regular lunchtime sports panel shows in each respective market – still stayed in place until 1977, the first year the race was shown in full into the Sydney market.

Two of the advancements in the television broadcasting of the Bathurst Great Race stand out above all others: the move to colour television in 1975 and the introduction of RaceCam, an in-car camera system, in 1979.

Both thrust the race even deeper into lounge rooms – of rev heads and casual viewers alike – across the country and turbocharged its growth.

'The race was born at Phillip Island but, in reality, didn't achieve any notoriety or real general public profile outside of the motor racing fraternity until it went to Bathurst,' says Garry Wilkinson, host and commentator of Channel 7's Bathurst telecast from 1978 to 1998.

'Even then it was a narrow-focused sporting event. But even when Channel 7 televised it from 1963, they toiled away and showed it in black and white. But it had a fairly narrow audience.

'Colour television just transformed the whole spectacle of not just motor racing, but Bathurst in particular. It showed off the complexity, the drama and the colour of the event by 1000-fold. It reached a much broader public audience as a result.'

As much as colour added a new dimension for viewers, the decision to fit a TV camera inside the Toyota Celica of Sydney Toyota dealer Peter Williamson in the 1979 race took the viewing experience to a whole other level – and made 'Willo' a part of Bathurst history.

Broadcasters putting cameras into race cars for TV wasn't a completely new idea, however Channel 7 was first to get it to really work. It developed an in-car camera that could feed pictures and sound up via a microwave link from the car to a helicopter that, in turn, beamed it on to an outside broadcast truck and into the main feed.

Viewers responded enthusiastically to the fast-talking, fast-driving Williamson. At various times during that 1979 race, if he wasn't bemoaning how slow the only Volvo in the race was, he was buzzing with energy as he willed the big, lumbering Chevrolet Camaro to move out of his nimble Celica's way across the top of the Mountain.

It was mesmerising stuff and proved to be a huge hit.

The technology ended up going worldwide and became the norm for motorsport telecasts in countries everywhere.

'RaceCam was a massive transformational event, not just for Bathurst but racing and sporting coverage around the world,' says Wilkinson.

'That wouldn't have happened had it not been for the foresight of Geoff Healey, the Head of Engineering at Channel 7. He had the concept in his head.

'He was able to juggle the finances between some of his budgets and have a bit left over for projects like this one. And he hired the right people to do the job: chief engineer John Porter, a genius, along with men like Rob Brear and John Symanovicz.

'The first cameras were huge. When Healey first put the proposition to the ARDC and to some drivers, they shied away in horror. The weight of the camera and its brace added quite a few kilograms to the car, and no one wanted to carry the extra weight!

'Williamson was never averse to a commercial opportunity though, and he could see the advantages for flogging Toyotas at his Peter Williamson Toyota dealership, so he took it on.

'That first camera had no provision originally for audio. It was just for pictures. But there was audio there so the camera engineers could talk to Willo and he could respond to them. Healey was standing there in the shed with them at Bathurst in '79 and the engineer was pointing out some of the dials and bits to Williamson.

'"Hang on," he said. "If he can talk to us and we can talk to him, why can't we patch it to air?"

'And that's exactly what happened.'

Very soon the high-profile drivers wised up to the impact that carrying a RaceCam in the Bathurst 1000 could have – it provided brilliant nationwide exposure for their sponsors – so they jumped in to become mobile cameramen for Australia's biggest motor race.

'Williamson was very good; he was terrified out of his wits, but he was the trailblazer. And gradually a few other drivers thought, "Holy hell, our sponsors need to be in on this!"' says Wilkinson.

'They all followed in succession: Dick Johnson, Allan Moffat, Peter Brock. The weight of sponsorship and television exposure overcame whatever the few seconds a lap here or there the drivers may have lost by using some of their powers of concentration on what they were saying in addition to their driving.'

Along the way the Bathurst 1000 television coverage hasn't always gone smoothly, particularly with the in-car cameras in race-winning cars.

Three years after RaceCam was introduced, Peter Brock and Larry Perkins became the first combination to win the Bathurst 1000 in a car carrying an on-board camera – in 1982 in their Holden Dealer Team Commodore. Unfortunately viewers were robbed of clear car-to-commentator conversations in that day's broadcast by an audio issue aboard the #05 Holden.

Ten years later the race-winning car – the Nissan GT-R of Jim Richards and Mark Skaife in 1992 – also had a problem that curbed its effectiveness for the broadcast. Its on-board fire extinguisher somehow triggered mid-race and coated extinguisher foam all over the lens of the camera, rendering it useless to the TV director!

Two years on, in 1994, the in-car camera in the eventual winning Ford Falcon of Dick Johnson and John Bowe also proved useless to Channel 7 in the tense closing stages of the Great Race.

The RaceCam in the car's front passenger seat area failed to capture his fight with young gun Craig Lowndes – it had gone haywire and sent itself into a constant 360-degree spin that couldn't be stopped remotely by technicians in the TV compound!

It didn't distract Bowe enough to stop the Tasmanian from taking his second Bathurst 1000 win.

Over time, cameras popped up in more and more places every year at Bathurst.

They were implanted in the track, on the door and within the headlights of cars, atop concrete walls and even on pit crew members.

Each year during the 1980s and '90s, Channel 7 found a way to come up with an innovation that would take viewers somewhere they'd never been before in a Bathurst 1000 telecast.

Things went another step in 1983 when a hole was cut in the roof of Jim Richards and Frank Gardner's JPS BMW to allow a periscope camera to poke through, which spun a full 360 degrees above the roof line!

As much as Channel 7 had a range of brilliant technicians, management and engineering minds that constantly raised the bar, no one brought the annual Bathurst race to life quite like Mike Raymond.

A former speedway promotor and commentator, Raymond started commentating on Seven's Bathurst broadcast in 1977 and voiced some of the biggest moments and wins in Great Race history, right through to his last Bathurst broadcast in 1995.

Publicly visible as a commentator, he was so much more than that, acting later as executive producer and helping to guide the telecast from on-air in the commentary box.

'Mike was larger than life in so many respects it's not funny,' says Wilkinson.

'He was a big man with a big voice and big ideas, with an insatiable appetite for motorsport, beginning with speedway. He grew up with oval track racing and had an inbred interest and devotion to stock car racing in America. He adopted that kind of Americanisation, terminology, slang and a tinge to his voice.

'He quickly grasped that motor racing for the public was not so much about the cars. Mike saw you had to create personalities. The people behind the wheel came first and selling the cars came second. Otherwise, they were anonymous drivers at 260km/h.'

It was Raymond who came up with a bunch of nicknames to bring the Bathurst stars of the 1980s and 1990s to life to viewers and they are nicknames that have stuck ever since. Peter Brock became 'Peter Perfect', Talmalmo-based Nissan racer George Fury became 'Farmer George', the youthful-looking Glenn Seton became the 'Baby Faced Assassin', the quiet Jim Richards became 'Gentleman Jim' and forceful young gun Tony Longhurst became 'No Baloney Tony', among many others.

'He was the conductor and leader of the chorus,' says Wilkinson of Raymond, who died in November 2019.

'We'd lob at the track, and he'd produce a telecast out of his briefcase. He had it all in his head of how he wanted it to go. He had contacts and knew everyone. Motor racing on Channel 7 would have died a natural death long before it did if it wasn't for Mike. He was a genius, essential to the survival of motorsport over that period as a product on TV.'

These days the telecast of the annual Bathurst classic is bigger than ever before. The 2022 Repco Bathurst 1000 saw just over 40 hours of coverage in race week created with 199 cameras, a production crew of over 250 people, 52 kilometres of broadcast cable and the use of four high-definition outside broadcast trucks.

Produced by Supercars for its broadcast partners, Fox Sports and Channel 7, the modern Bathurst 1000 telecast has a deep bag of tricks. From former drivers in commentary and pit lane to technical tools and even an in-commentary box former Supercars race engineer providing key strategic and technical analysis, pretty much every angle is covered.

A veteran of 16 Bathurst Great Race starts behind the wheel between 1988 and 2002, Neil Crompton has been the voice of the Bathurst 1000 since his retirement from full-time racing.

He's sure the step-up in the Bathurst race's broadcast year on year has helped educate viewers in a way the 'glory years' of the '70s and '80s couldn't.

'I reckon it's the same premise as education,' he says.

'If you explain and expand on topics, you bring your class of students along with you. I think if you graphed the engagement within our motor racing audience, it is a wedge shape – from casual to the deeply engaged. For the group from the middle and up, there's now so much information available.

'In the old days the commentary was, "The red car is in front of the blue car" and all very simple, whereas now we have so much data to support things; we have history files on hand of previous years' strategies, a deep level of statistics and the insight that a range of drivers provide in the on-air team. Unmistakably the viewing audience has also come along with the advancements over time, no doubt.

'As a kid watching the race on TV in Ballarat, I knew nothing of the fuel range of a two-door hardtop Falcon versus the XU-1 Torana. It was simpler back then: you were barracking for Ford or Holden or Moffat or Brock. It was all very top line.

'These days social media is a megaphone and it's shortened up time frames and broadened the contact base. When I was a kid the only way to know what was going on in the race at Bathurst was to turn on the television. Now the information is at your fingertips flowing by the second and you can tap into so much more information than ever before if you choose to.'

The race and its broadcast have evolved significantly over the years, but one thing has stayed the same.

The Bathurst 1000 remains the must-watch motor race on the national sporting calendar.

## Pacing the Field

The Safety Car (or pace car as it was then known) was first introduced to the Bathurst 1000 in 1987. Its purpose is to pace the field at a slow, controlled speed to allow track officials to remove crashed cars, debris or any other situation that needs to be addressed.

Since its introduction there have only been two years that the Safety Car hasn't been called upon – in 1989 and 1991.

All manner of brands have been used as the Bathurst Safety Car: Nissan (the first – in 1987 – was a Nissan Skyline), Mazda, Holden, Volvo, HSV, Ford, Audi, Chrysler, Lexus and Porsche have all paced the Bathurst 1000 field in the past.

Over the years there have been some interesting Safety Cars for the Bathurst 1000.

In 1992 a black Nissan GT-R filled the role and just months later the very same car was back at the Mountain competing in the Bathurst 12 Hour production car race in Falken Tyres colours!

In 1993 that year's Bathurst 12 Hour-winning BP Mazda RX-7 served in the Safety Car role for the Bathurst 1000 in October, seven months later.

The inaugural Holden Safety Car for the Bathurst 1000 was a Jackaroo – in 1995 – and the first Ford was an AU XR8 Falcon in 2001.

# 7

# **Lucky Escapes**

I t's been said there are two types of racing driver. Those who have crashed and those who are yet to crash.

At Bathurst there have been some horrifying accidents over the years and fortunately, more often than not, the drivers behind the wheel have emerged to tell the tale.

Most have been captured by television cameras for the broadcast and beamed worldwide, but some of the biggest crashes in Great Race history weren't caught on film.

Take for example John Keran's accident at McPhillamy Park in a Torana XU-1 in 1970.

An amazingly fast rally driver, he had a tyre blow that caused a catastrophic accident. The little Holden smashed into a barrier head-on instead of turning into the fast left-hand sweeper that connects the cars to the next corner at Skyline.

Its rear wheels launched into the air from the collision as the car cannoned into the fence and came to a stop in an instant. The front of the Torana was demolished, its right front collapsing violently in the sickening shunt. Keran suffered a badly broken leg, an injury that effectively ended his career.

While Keran's accident was certainly a huge one, it's rarely referred to when Bathurst tales of big crashes and great escapes are being told.

That can largely be put down to the fact that there was another spectacular accident in the same location in the next year's race – in 1971 – that had one major difference: it was caught by television cameras.

*The field races by the leftovers of John Keran's destroyed Torana in 1970. This was 17 years before the Safety Car was introduced to Bathurst to slow down the field and allow for the safe retrieval of crashed cars.*

Mention Bill Brown to Bathurst fans and they won't instantly recall his debut in the race in 1964 in a Vauxhall Viva or the fact he made 10 starts in the race in the 1960s and 1970s.

But they absolutely do remember his almighty crash in the 1971 race when he rolled his Falcon GT-HO along the wooden fence at McPhillamy Park, not far down the road from where Keran's Torana came to grief.

Brown's spectacular crash remains one of the most talked about crashes in the history of the Great Race.

Like Keran, Brown's car blew a tyre, but it didn't plough into the McPhillamy Park gate Armco fence. Instead it rode up a small earth bank, which acted as a vault and flung him into a wild series of rolls along the wooden trackside fence, the only barrier stopping the big V8 muscle car from launching itself into the crowd of spectators. The Falcon had a tyre rubbing on the guard and Brown had intended to come to the pits to have it dealt with in a couple of laps' time. But the tyre didn't make it that far and blew as he came over the top of McPhillamy Park at an estimated 170km/h.

Footage of the almighty accident also showed a pair of trackside marshals running for their lives as the fast-approaching (and already rolling) Falcon bore down on them. Somehow, they got out of the vehicle's path in the nick of time to escape with their lives, and the Great Race avoided what could have been its first fatalities.

The accident was caught by Channel 7 cameras. Amazingly, Brown emerged with not much more than a black eye, even though the Falcon had come to rest upside down on the fence, bowed and nearly broken in half.

Multi-car crashes at Bathurst have stopped the race on two occasions: in 1981 and 1984. The first brought the race to an end whereas the latter came at the start of the race.

In 1981 a massive accident at McPhillamy Park – the same area where Keran and Brown crashed – stopped the race in its tracks at three-quarter race distance.

Falcon pilot Bob Morris – the 1976 Bathurst winner, who was running second and trying to beat Dick Johnson's similar Ford – had attempted to make a pass on the inside of Christine Gibson (wife of 1967 winner Fred Gibson) turning into the fast left-hander at McPhillamy.

The two cars collided and were carted wide into the outside fence. In later years that fence was removed, and a sand trap installed to allow for greater run-off, however in 1981 the two crashed Fords were sitting ducks stuck on the racetrack. Before anyone had time to react, they were quickly ploughed into by the next cars on the scene: they were out of sight because of the blind turn-in point of the corner.

David Seldon's Gemini, Tony Edmondson's Commodore, Kevin Bartlett's Camaro and Garry Rogers' Commodore all quickly became part of the accident zone and the track was blocked by shattered cars.

Rogers, later to win the race as a team owner in 2000, smashed into Gibson's Falcon at high velocity. He emerged with his life, however the savage accident damaged his middle ear and permanently affected his balance. Conscious but dazed through the entire ordeal, Rogers' feet were stuck in the footwell of the smashed Commodore between the buckled pedals. Winded and struggling to get out, he was helped from the car by a couple of drunken fans who had leapt the fence to render assistance. As the clean up began, Rogers was carted away to hospital in an ambulance.

The race was not restarted; Johnson and French were declared the winners. Morris' Falcon was classified second in the final results as they were declared from the last completed lap of the race. His brand-new car was completely destroyed.

Rogers and his Commodore's owner, Clive Benson Brown, were classified fourth despite their car also being smashed to pieces. The result remained the former's best Bathurst 1000 finish in his driving career.

In among the numerous cars involved in the 1981 crash was Kevin Bartlett's Channel 9 Sport-backed Camaro. The big American V8 coupe remains a cult car in Bathurst history. It had started from pole position for that year's race thanks to its pilot's inspired driving in a wet Hardies Heroes Top 10 Shootout session on Saturday morning.

The very same car featured in the next multi-car crash, which stopped the 1984 race within moments of it starting. By that time the Camaro was in different colours to the black and yellow Channel 9 livery that had made it famous, and was being driven by privateer racer John Tesoriero. He collected the back of the stalled Jaguar of Tom Walkinshaw shortly after the flag had dropped.

The Jaguar's clutch had fried so the Scotsman – who took over Holden's factory racing team a few years later – was stranded sitting on his 10th grid position and the majority of the 63-car field were left to pick their way through.

Walkinshaw very nearly survived without panel damage until the Camaro – which had started 46th on the grid – clipped the Jaguar and spun it into the path of Peter Williamson's Toyota Supra. The track was blocked in the blink of an eye, forcing officials to stop the race. They were able to restart it just over half an hour later.

One of the most publicised driver line-ups in Bathurst 1000 history also descended into a start-line shunt at the Mountain – and it happened in the same 10th-place grid position that had also proven the downfall of Walkinshaw.

The combination of three-time Formula 1 World Champion Jack Brabham (not yet knighted at that stage) and Stirling Moss – widely viewed as the greatest Grand Prix driver to never be crowned World Champion – in a Torana L34 in 1976 provided a big splash of publicity for the Great Race.

Brabham had retired from Formula 1 racing and Moss's career had ended 14 years earlier – cut short following a massive accident at Goodwood.

But their Bathurst 1000 debut was largely over before it began when Brabham's gearbox selected two gears at once and his blue Torana V8 went nowhere from its 10th grid position.

On this occasion Brabham was also collected by a following car: in his case it was the Triumph Dolomite driven by Ballarat (Victoria) racer John Dellaca. The little Dolomite biffed straight into the boot of the Torana, severely crunching both cars. The Torana was patched up and sent back into the race despite being many laps behind, though its engine later blew to end the famous duo's day with a mere 37 laps completed.

The Dolomite fared slightly better. It was able to return to the race after repairs and completed 67 laps – not enough however to be classified as a finisher.

Despite the introduction of the Chase at Bathurst in 1987 – a right/left/right chicane on Conrod Straight designed to slow cars down in a safe manner – it has been the site of two of the biggest crashes in Bathurst's V8 Supercar history.

The modification to the track had been in place for a decade when Tomas Mezera found himself barrel-rolling through the sand trap there in the early stages of the 1997 Primus 1000 Classic. He was at the wheel of a Commodore owned by privateer racer John Trimbole.

A delaminated tyre ripped away his brakes and sent the 1988 Bathurst winner on a wild ride into retirement from that year's race. The crash occurred during a commercial break for broadcaster Channel 10, but the spectacular vision was quickly rolled into the broadcast when the coverage resumed.

'I nearly got killed!' exclaims Mezera. 'It just comes to tyres. The most important thing on a car to go fast is the tyres. In those days, there were tyres for the top runners and there were tyres for the also-rans and privateers. You never got the same tyre that Dick Johnson got from Dunlop or Allan Grice, or Fred Gibson got from Yokohama or Brock got from Bridgestone. You always get the leftovers.

'Dunlop did some testing with the new tyre and Dick did the testing and they found the tyres kept delaminating. Obviously, they didn't choose that tyre, but it was kept in stock and sold to us. The tyre delaminated and ripped the brake line off and I nearly killed myself.

'I had a bit of a bloody headache, but I was alright – I walked away. I was very lucky. Mind you, when I saw I was in trouble, I tried to spin the car and roll it in the sand, trying to absorb the energy, because I couldn't arrow it straight into the sand trap: it would have hit the earth bank and concrete wall there head on. I did what I had to do. I'm very happy I managed to do that. It was the biggest crash of my career.'

Mezera's black and red Commodore was eventually repaired and returned to Bathurst three years later to compete in the Great Race, and finished 19th in the hands of Queensland privateers Tim Sipp and Shane Beikoff.

Another red and black Commodore rolled spectacularly in the Chase – Fabian Coulthard's Bundaberg Red-backed, Walkinshaw Racing-run Commodore from 2010. Unlike Mezera's car, it wasn't able to make a racing comeback.

The Kiwi also suffered a tyre blow-out that sent him spiralling, however it was a rear tyre that pitched his car into an out-of-control series of rolls just as he turned into the full-throttle, flat-out right-hander that begins the Chase section nearing the end of the opening lap of the race.

Stripping itself of its doors and other panels as it erratically flew around like a t-shirt in a tumble dryer, the exposed chassis eventually came to rest in the sand trap with its pilot OK inside. Dazed but uninjured, Coulthard was able to step from the car, or what was left of it, without assistance.

The left-rear tyre blow-out was traced back to a minor bump at the start line as the lights went out to commence the race. Coulthard had scrambled to go around the sluggish-starting Michael Caruso. The touch and resultant damage to the Kiwi's tyre made it a ticking timebomb that exploded at the fastest corner on the track, where cars are travelling at near enough to 300km/h.

'It happens pretty quick,' said the British-born Kiwi. 'You're just waiting for it to end. I knew I was on my head, and that I was barrel-rolling multiple times, but you just wait for it to finally run its course and stop. I was flat out, so it was 290-kay plus.

'I had full communication with the team. Rob Starr, my engineer, was on the radio to me straight away saying, "Can you hear me? Are you okay?" I responded straightaway. I was conscious throughout the whole thing. It was better than any ride at Dreamworld. It was the fastest and biggest [crash I've ever had].

'I knew a fair bit had come off the car, because I didn't have to open the door to get out.'

The crash remains one of the instant topics of talk when Coulthard and Bathurst are mentioned in the same sentence together.

Winless in the Great Race in 19 starts, dating back to his debut in a Tasman Motorsport Commodore alongside countryman Jason Richards in 2004, it took Coulthard until his 14th start – in 2017, sharing a Shell-backed DJR Team Penske Falcon with Tony D'Alberto – to score his first Bathurst 1000 podium finish, with a third-place result.

He finished in the top 10 in five straight Bathurst 1000s between 2014 and 2018 and shared second place in a Walkinshaw Andretti United Commodore with Chaz Mostert in the 2022 race.

Just as winning at Bathurst defines a driver's career, so too does crashing at Bathurst.

Whereas a tiny percentage of starters get to finish, let alone win the race, plenty of drivers – Bill Brown is the perfect example – are far more widely known for their crashes at Bathurst than any other wins they had at other tracks.

Winning Bathurst is the only real way to truly shake free of being associated only with a spectacular accident at the Mountain.

But even then, it will still be one of the next things discussed; such is the power and importance of the Great Race at Bathurst in the hearts and minds of fans around the nation.

## The Fastest of the Fast

Peter Brock's mark of nine Great Race Bathurst wins looks unlikely to ever be bettered and his record of most pole positions in race history looks every bit as unbreakable.

Brock took pole for the race six times – in 1974, 1977, 1978, 1979, 1983 and 1989. Mark Skaife's five Bathurst 1000 poles, the last of which came in 2006 just weeks after Brock's sudden death, is the only body of work that comes close.

Of the current Bathurst 1000 crop of Supercars drivers, Mark Winterbottom, David Reynolds, Chaz Mostert and Cam Waters each sit on two poles apiece, so Brock's record looks safe for the foreseeable future.

# 8

# Wheeling and Dealing

**M**otorsport runs on money and the Bathurst 1000 is no different. It's an Australian motorsport commercial beast.

Advertising logos pop up literally everywhere. From every available square centimetre of the cars competing in the race, to trackside signage, driver and team uniforms and television coverage branding. Each year hundreds of deals are done for brands, products and organisations to connect themselves to the biggest day on the domestic motorsport calendar.

But it wasn't always so.

Advertising on cars was not permitted in Australian motorsport by the governing body, CAMS (the Confederation of Australian Motor Sport) when the Great Race moved to Bathurst in 1963.

Except for the drivers' names, the name of the entrant of the car and the racing number and letter denoting which class it was competing in, early Bathurst race cars – and indeed all racing cars of the period – were otherwise blank, with advertising signage forbidden on their flanks.

Brands were permitted to advertise their wares on trackside signage, but it took until 1968 for cars to be allowed to be turned into mobile billboards when the ban on sponsorship signage was lifted.

That wasn't to say that previous years hadn't featured some subliminal advertising.

The Geoghegan brothers, Ian and Leo, had a novel approach to get some exposure for Grace Brothers, a Sydney clothing store, when they raced a Cortina GT500 in the 1965 race.

Rather than driving the 500-mile, 130-lap race wearing racing overalls, they instead donned business suits available from Grace Brothers and wore them all day behind the wheel!

The brothers finished the race third but were instantly booted from the results. They had started their engine while refuelling during a pit stop, a breach of the rules. Black-flagged and called into pit lane, they were allowed to re-join the race under protest, which was dismissed post-race.

The BMC-run Mini Coopers that dominated the 1966 race were painted in Castrol oil green rather than their traditional British racing green, another subliminal piece of branding, given they couldn't run Castrol signage.

In 1967 the innovative Geoghegan brothers faced the same challenge. They were backed by Castrol in their other racing endeavours and their polar white Falcon XR GT at Bathurst that year ran with green racing stripes – across the bonnet and roof and down the side. It was a way of legally signalling Castrol backing when Castrol branding and signage was not permitted!

The floodgates opened in 1968 when advertising was allowed on cars in Australian motorsport and all sorts of brands, businesses and products started appearing on Bathurst Great Race cars.

Automotive businesses, logically, dominated the list of those that got involved as car manufacturers, car dealerships and oil, fuel and tyre brands all quickly jumped on board.

But it was cigarette companies that really took over in the 1970s. They carried through with spending big bucks into the 1980s and 1990s until tobacco advertising in sport was banned by the Federal Government at the end of 1995.

Philip Morris brand Marlboro inked a deal to sponsor the prolific Holden Dealer Team in 1974, and Camel signed up with Allan Moffat's Falcon team. The former was carried to victory at Bathurst by Peter Brock and the Holden Dealer Team six times, the latter once by Moffat – in his famous 1977 victory.

W.D. & H.O. Wills tried to 'win' Bathurst through the 1970s. It started with its Craven Mild brand – supporting Allan Grice's Holdens – before swapping to JPS branding on BMWs in the 1980s and later Benson & Hedges, which ultimately won for them in 1988 via the Sierra of Tony Longhurst and Tomas Mezera.

The list of cigarette brands that aligned themselves with top-line cars at Bathurst was seemingly never-ending. Peter Jackson sponsored the works Nissan team and later Glenn Seton's Ford Sierra and Falcon team, and Peter Stuyvesant backed Allan Moffat's Mazda program of the 1980s.

The former also sponsored a 'Search for a Champion' competition in 1990 run by Grice (who won that year's Bathurst 1000), offering the prize of a Holden Commodore race car and an entry into the Great Race for the two winners. South Australian Peter Gazzard and Canberra's Rick Bates got the nod from the judges. Thanks to winning the competition, they made their Bathurst 1000 debuts.

The last cigarette backer to win the race was Winfield, the Rothmans brand that backed the 1992 race-winning Nissan GT-R in a deal that helped offset the millions of dollars Nissan had tipped into its motor-racing program.

Tyre companies have also played a considerable part in the growth of the Bathurst Great Race.

They invested millions of dollars in sponsorship arrangements and product development in order to champion their brand via Australia's most famous race.

From the narrow, grooved tyres of the 1960s right through to the fat 'slick' racing tyres of modern motorsport, the rubber that has connected Bathurst race cars to the bitumen of Mount Panorama has been an ever-present element of the race.

Dunlop, Michelin, Olympic, Goodyear, Bridgestone, Yokohama and Pirelli have all won the race over the years supplying various teams and cars but, surprisingly, Bridgestone and Goodyear can both lay claim to winning the race in 1974.

John Goss and Kevin Bartlett's Falcon, backed by Sydney Ford dealer Max McLeod, had a sponsorship deal to use Bridgestone tyres, but when heavy rain lashed the circuit, the team found itself without appropriate wet-weather rubber to change to from its regular Bridgestone slick tyres. Allan Moffat (whose Falcon was already out of the race) stepped up to offer a set of his Goodyear wet tyres. They were fitted to Goss's car and he and Bartlett splashed their way through the remainder of the race to triumph.

It remains the only known time a Bathurst Great Race winner has started the race on one brand of tyre and finished on another!

These days all Supercars teams and drivers competing in the Bathurst 1000 use the same Dunlop 'control' tyre. The concept of a single tyre provider – a system designed to provide equality for teams and a cheaper unit price – came into V8 Supercars in 1999 with Bridgestone. They held the contract for three years before it was awarded to Dunlop in 2002.

They've retained it ever since, meaning every Bathurst 1000-winning car from 2002 onwards has won on Dunlop tyres. This will be the case until at least 2024 as the brand has a multi-year contract in place with Supercars.

## The Oldest Bathurst 1000 Winners

Seven-time winner Jim Richards has accrued a brace of Bathurst 1000 records over his storied career. He is set to retain the mantle of the oldest driver to ever win the race for many years to come.

The Kiwi was 55 years and 41 days old in 2002 when he paired with Mark Skaife to win the race for the Holden Racing Team. That victory came 10 years after Richards had called the crowd a 'pack of arseholes' during a hostile reception from the fans gathered around the podium after the unpopular Nissan win.

Next on the list is John French, who was 50 years and 310 days when he won with Dick Johnson in 1981. Then comes Harry Firth, who at 49 years and 166 days won the Great Race in 1967.

The most recent of the mature winners are Paul Morris (46 in 2014) and Jim Richards' son Steve (46 in 2018).

## Starting From Way Back

Chaz Mostert and Paul Morris triumphed in one of the most dramatic finishes of a Bathurst 1000 when they crossed the finish line first in the 2014 Bathurst 1000.

They led one lap in the whole 161-lap race, but it was the one lap that mattered most – the final lap!

In winning the race, they also broke the record for the lowest grid position for a Bathurst Great Race-winning car. The duo started at the tail of the field – 25th on the grid – because Mostert had been excluded from the Friday qualifying session for passing a car under red flags.

The previous record was for starting 19th and was achieved in 1987 by the winning #10 Mobil HDT Racing Commodore driven by Peter McLeod, Peter Brock and David Parsons. Brock drove the car across the line third, but it was elevated to victory when the top two finishing Ford Sierras were excluded from the results post-race.

The only other Bathurst Great Race winners to start outside the top 10 were Jason Bright/Steve Richards in 1998 (starting from 15th), Greg Murphy/Steve Richards in 1999 (starting from 12th), Craig Lowndes/Steve Richards in 2015 (starting from 15th) and Will Davison/Jonathon Webb in 2016 (starting from 17th).

# 9

# Queensland's Favourite Son

**H**e smashed through trackside trees, crashed into an errant rock and won the race on three occasions. Dick Johnson's Bathurst 1000 career has had it all.

A veteran of 26 starts in the Great Race, Johnson is a true icon of Australian motorsport. In his younger years he would prepare his race cars at night at his service station business but he went on to become the head of one of the most loved race teams in the country, Dick Johnson Racing.

Even today, more than two decades on from the end of his own racing career behind the wheel, Johnson's large fan base continue to follow his every move, as they have since his very first days. He's relatable, always quick with a quote and has been a household name since his infamous collision with a rock at Mount Panorama over 40 years ago.

The Queensland racing hero started racing Holdens at his local Lakeside circuit in the 1960s, and many casual race fans would be shocked to know he made his Bathurst 1000 debut in 1973 at the wheel of a Holden Torana XU-1, rather than aboard a Ford Falcon.

He and Sydney privateer Bob Forbes finished fifth outright in a car that Johnson had prepared for the big race.

'We got there on Saturday morning,' Johnson recounted to me on the V8 Sleuth Podcast in 2021.

'I was still at Shell Orange garage welding the exhaust up on Saturday morning!'

The laconic Queenslander wasn't a total newcomer to the Mountain though. Johnson had been a mountain devotee since the early 1960s. He would make the annual trek down from Brisbane after work on a Friday afternoon, sleep in the car across the weekend then drive home on Sunday night in time for work the next day.

In 1969, Johnson had a front row seat to one of the most dramatic moments in Great Race history. Because one of the drivers involved was his good mate, and future Bathurst co-winner, John French, it was personal.

'(My wife) Jillie and I were with his wife Marie, standing just up from the Dipper, after they come over Skyline,' recounts Johnson.

'We saw this car come over Skyline upside down. I said, "Gee, this is gonna be interesting!" And sure enough there were cars going everywhere …'

The upside-down car was that of Bill Brown, who had ranged down the inside of Mike Savva at Skyline, only for the latter to reclaim the line and force Brown up the grass embankment to the inside, sending his Ford Falcon GT-HO into a gentle roll onto its roof.

It was the opening lap and the pair had been battling for 11th place, meaning that some 50-plus cars were about to crest Skyline at race speed to find the track almost blocked.

French, near the head of the next group of cars, all but stopped in time, but a hard hit from behind tipped his Alfa Romeo 1750 GTV into a violent roll.

The white Alfa copped yet more hits as the smaller class cars arrived; by the time the dust settled, four cars were out on the spot, including the inverted Brown and French, and almost a quarter of the 63-car field had sustained damage of some sort.

What worried Johnson was the growing pool of red fluid coming from his mate's Alfa.

'All I could see was this red stuff running out of his car – I thought he's got to be hurt or something,' Johnson recalled.

'So I leapt over the fence to drag him out of the car, then realised it was only coolant from the radiator of the Alfa that was running out of the car.

'Fortunately, Frenchy was fine, but you can imagine what his wife was feeling like while she was standing there watching all of this transpire!'

Incredibly, none of the drivers involved was injured, and the trackside marshals managed the situation brilliantly.

A dozen years later, Johnson and French teamed up to win the Bathurst 1000. Ironically, the 1981 race they won was stopped by a multi-car crash that blocked the circuit at McPhillamy Park, just a short distance back from where Johnson had helped French clamber from his upturned Alfa in 1969.

But the pathway to getting to the winner's podium at Bathurst had been far from simple.

Johnson traded in racing Holden Toranas in the 1970s and swapped to driving Ford Falcons, which had the backing of Queensland Ford dealership, Bryan Byrt Ford.

He finished fifth at Bathurst in 1978 in a Byrt Falcon hardtop. Johnson was proving himself to be more than capable of being competitive in the top tier of touring car racing, even if he lacked the firepower of the likes of Allan Moffat's Ford team and the factory-backed Holden Dealer Team, which ran out front more often than not.

The Queenslander wasn't a household name like Brock or Moffat. That was about to come via the most unlikely of means.

When the Byrt dealership pulled out of racing at the end of 1979, Johnson was able to use the running gear from one of its superseded Falcon race cars to bolt into an XD Falcon body shell (an ex-police car purchased from an auction!). Between that, $35,000 and a mortgage on the family home, Johnson had himself the basics with which to build his Bathurst challenger for the 1980 race.

And the blue #17 Falcon was undisputedly fast. After a few races in the lead-up, Johnson and his new Ford were quick at Bathurst. He qualified second on the grid and jumped into the lead to head the field in the biggest race of the year.

After 17 laps he was in control of the race he desperately wanted to win. He had just lapped Peter Brock (who had made an unscheduled pit stop to inspect damage after a collision with a slower car) when out of the blue everything went horribly wrong.

Unbeknown to Johnson, an errant rock had rolled down an embankment and landed in the middle of the track on the exit of the Cutting. As fate would have it, moving along the track nearby was a tow-truck carrying an already expired car back to the pits. He had no choice but to smash into the rock.

The consequent collision with the concrete destroyed the left-hand side of the blue Falcon, flinging the car topsy-turvy along the concrete retaining wall. Johnson's dream of winning Bathurst was crushed in an instant.

Johnson's tearful follow-up appearance on Channel 7's national television coverage connected with those who saw it. Affection for the Queensland battler kicked into gear.

While the crash could have been a brutal 'end of the road' moment for Johnson's racing career, it proved to be the complete opposite.

Touched by his misfortune, Channel 7 viewers started calling and offering to donate money so Johnson could get his racing program back on track. Edsel Ford II, Deputy Managing Director of the Ford Motor Company, pledged to match the donations dollar for dollar.

Far from breaking him, the rock exposed Johnson to a national audience and did more good for his career than bad!

Amazingly, the sheer volume of donations funded the build of a new XD Falcon race car for Johnson, and he used it to win his first Australian Touring Car Championship, in 1981.

And, to repay the faith of the fans who'd put up thousands of dollars in donations, he and French went on to win a crash-shortened Bathurst 1000.

'I don't think there was any other year in motorsport that I felt as much pressure after what had happened in 1980 – with a lot of people donating money to keep the thing going and get up and running again for the following year,' says Johnson.

'1981 for me was one hell of a year as far as pressure goes.

It really was heart-warming to see. Kids emptied their piggy banks to donate to us and I still have all of the letters to this day. It's pretty special.

'At Daisy Hill (in Brisbane) I had a letterbox at our house but I used to have the mail van back up to my front door and give me these big canvas bags full of letters, which was just amazing.'

The car that the fans helped fund, the #17 Tru-Blu Falcon XD, remains one of the most special cars in Johnson's career. Unlike the modern-day Bathurst 1000 Supercars that are built and finely tuned in purpose-built race workshops, the 1981 Bathurst-winning Ford was put together in Johnson's home garage.

'It was in the garage at home at Daisy Hill where we'd prep the car. And we'd work until 11 or 12 o'clock at night and be back there at 6 o'clock in the morning and Jillie (Johnson's wife) would come and cook for the guys,' says Johnson.

'I had one full-time guy, Roy McDonald: he was the one and only paid team member. And a mate of mine, Leon (Hortsmann), and my brother Dave. We had a few (extra) guys we'd take down to Bathurst to be able to do the pit stops and things like that. It was very much a family-oriented thing, which it still is today, just on a different level.

'I used to build all the engines and gearboxes and Roy and I used to build and prepare the car. I understood exactly what was going on with my car, which some of the drivers today lack a little bit. Those cars back in the Tru-Blu days were hotted up road cars whereas the cars today are purpose-built.'

Johnson and John French made for a solid combination at Bathurst, where they raced together five times in the 1980s. Every now and again in the aftermath of a Mount Panorama campaign, Dick would find a 'souvenir' from his co-driver's time behind the wheel.

'The XD and XE Falcons had a real deep centre console, and Frenchy was always good on the tooth; he loved eating,' says Johnson.

'He'd make these little Vegemite sandwiches and some quarters of oranges, and he'd put them in the console. And while he was coming down Conrod Straight, he'd grab one out and have a bit of a chew.

'After each Bathurst we'd pack the car up, put it into the truck and take it home. And it would sit in the garage until we'd start looking at what we were going to do for the next race. And there'd be this horrible stink.

'It was Frenchy's (leftover) food he'd had in the console of the car!'

Johnson's encounter with the errant rock in 1980 indeed launched him into a concrete wall, but it proved not to be his biggest crash at Mount Panorama.

That came in 1983 during the Hardies Heroes Top 10 Shootout at the wheel of his mighty green XE Falcon, when Johnson flew off the track at the exit of Forrest's Elbow and crashed through trackside trees. This was a few years before concrete walls fully surrounded the racing surface at Bathurst.

The Queensland hero had been pushing hard to knock Peter Brock off pole position and claim the $7000 prizemoney on offer for being the fastest car against the clock.

The green machine's tail had slid out and touched the fence on the exit of the corner that led onto Conrod Straight, dragging the front-right wheel into the concrete-filled tyre stack at the end of the wall, breaking the steering and sending the car on a hair-raising ride into the trees.

Incredibly, Johnson clambered out the destroyed car's passenger side door, uninjured.

'At the end of the wall coming out of Forrest's Elbow there was a bunch of tyres, which were there for people coming up the other way (on the road) every other day of the year,' recalls Johnson.

'But the trouble was, they were full of concrete! I touched the wall, using every bit of the road, and when I got to the end of the wall it (the stack of tyres) grabbed a hold of the front wheel and broke the tie-rod off. And then it landed on that wheel and headed into the bush. And I thought, "I could be in trouble here."

'Fortunately, the car was second-hand, but I was fine. I was extremely lucky.'

The car was completely destroyed, and Johnson and co-driver Kevin Bartlett appeared set to sit on the sidelines for Sunday.

Then came another of the amazing Bathurst stories that make Johnson's career the stuff of legends.

Keen to see Johnson on the grid for the Great Race, several other teams offered up their cars for him to take over and race.

One offer came from Falcon privateer Andrew Harris, whose XE Falcon was re-built overnight by a crew of volunteers and team members and had the engine and gearbox from Johnson's destroyed car installed. It was repainted in Johnson's familiar green #17 livery just in time to line it up for the start of the big race. In fact, the paint was still wet as it rolled out onto the grid!

Sadly, the most notable car swap in the history of the Bathurst 1000 didn't lead to a fairy-tale result: electrical issues sidelined the car after completing 61 of the 163 laps.

After the race came the task of transporting both cars home and there were complications with the wreck that had been destroyed among the trees on the Saturday at Bathurst.

'We borrowed a trailer off Andrew Harris to tow the wreck home,' Johnson says.

'One of the guys was towing it home and he didn't even get to Orange. He got into a big tank-slapper, fired off the road and through a fence, and rolled the trailer. That was insult to injury, that one ...'

The wreck of Johnson's 1983 Bathurst Falcon met its final end the following year at Sims Metal.

'We helped them launch their new piece of equipment by putting the body shell of the Greens Tuf Falcon through it!' Johnson says.

Hundreds of the fragments were made into paperweights. These small pieces of Bathurst history occasionally pop up for sale on eBay.

Something that never existed though is RaceCam vision of the crash from inside the Johnson Falcon, despite the fact that the car was carrying one of Channel 7's world-leading in-car camera systems. A simple error robbed us all of what would have been some of the most amazing footage ever captured at Bathurst.

'The camera operator in the OB (outside broadcast) van that stood there with the joystick controlling the camera unfortunately forgot to push the record button!' laughs Johnson.

Johnson went on to win Bathurst two more times – in 1989 and 1994 – with loyal lieutenant John Bowe as co-driver.

The Tasmanian open-wheeler ace joined Johnson's team in 1988 and spent 11 years with the Queensland-based Ford squad, playing pivotal roles in each of these Bathurst wins with 'DJ'.

They were the red-hot favourites in 1989 at the wheel of the team's turbocharged Ford Sierra. Johnson and Bowe had finished first and second in that year's Australian Touring Car Championship and led every lap to seal victory at Mount Panorama.

It marked the first time Johnson had won a full-length Bathurst race. After all, his 1981 win had come when a multi-car crash stopped the race with slightly over 40 laps to run.

'1989 would have been the most perfect Bathurst we had because we had so many different elements to that event,' says Johnson.

'We led every single lap of the race, even during pit stops, and it was just very gratifying. I don't think we've ever run such a perfect Bathurst with the team. It's all about the people you've got with you. We made the right decisions at the right time, and it paid off in the end.'

Five years later things weren't quite as clear cut. The 1994 race was marred by a rainstorm. That meant the start of the event was held in slippery, treacherous conditions. And that meant Bowe went missing, deliberately, not keen to be forced to drive in the rain.

'The start of that race was wet, and JB was nowhere to be found. He disappeared!' says Johnson.

'Ross Stone (then DJR team manager) said, "I gotta find JB because Dick wants him to start the race." I said, "Of course

I do; that's his forte doing this." We finally found him: he'd locked himself in one of those port-a-loos out the back of the pits somewhere! But we sorted that out and he got in the car and did a fantastic job.'

Bowe was at the wheel of the car for the end of the race, and he was able to shake off a pesky rookie in the form of Craig Lowndes to bring home the #17 Shell-FAI Falcon to victory five years after he'd driven the #17 Sierra to Bathurst glory.

'I'll never forget getting onto the radio to JB towards the end of that race when Lowndes was hunting him down and passed him into turn two at the top of Mountain Straight,' says Johnson.

'I got on the radio and said, "JB, this is a kid you're playing with here. You're not going to let the famous John Bowe get beaten by a kid. Pull your finger out!"'

Johnson and Bowe visited the Bathurst 1000 podium as runners-up on three occasions: in 1988 and 1992 at the wheel of Sierras and once more in a V8 Falcon in 1996. Their last start together came in 1997.

For his final two Bathurst starts – in 1998 and 1999 – Johnson teamed with son Steven.

The pair finished fourth in Johnson's Mountain farewell, the Ford veteran able to bring the car home safely despite running out of brakes in the last stint of the race. It was one step short of a podium finish but a nice way to end his career behind the wheel at Bathurst.

One of the quirks of Great Race history is that Johnson won the Bathurst 1000 three times but never had the pleasure of driving across the line himself to see the chequered flag.

John French was behind the wheel in 1981, when the race was stopped, and John Bowe drove their winning car across the line in 1989 and 1994.

But it's nothing more than a tiny detail of Bathurst history – Dick Johnson is forever a legend of the Mountain, a 'rock' star in every sense of the word.

*The Dick Johnson/John Bowe #17 Shell Ford Sierra approaches the Dipper at Bathurst in 1989, the year the duo took a dominant win at the Mountain.*

## The Young and the Restless of Pole-Sitters

Craig Lowndes remains the youngest ever pole-sitter for the Bathurst 1000 – he was just 21 years and 102 days old when he drove his Holden Racing Team Commodore VR to pole position for the 1995 race.

Scott McLaughlin's spellbinding 2017 pole lap puts him second on the list at 24 years and 120 days and Mark Skaife's first pole in 1991 puts him next at 24 years, 186 days.

Marcos Ambrose (in 2001) and Shane van Gisbergen (in 2014) both took pole for the Bathurst 1000 aged 25 and Mark Winterbottom (in 2007) and Cam Waters (in 2020) achieved the feat aged 26.

On the flip side, Dick Johnson's pole position in a Sierra in 1992 makes him the oldest Bathurst 1000 pole-sitter. He was 47 years and 161 days when he topped the Top 10 Shootout that year.

Only five other drivers have taken pole position for the Bathurst Great Race aged in their 40s: Peter Brock (44 in 1989), Larry Perkins (43 in 1993), Bruce McPhee (41 in 1968), Kevin Bartlett (40 in 1980 and 41 in 1981) and Wayne Gardner (41 in 2000).

# 10

# A Famous Stage

The drivers and teams who put on the show that is the Bathurst 1000 have, in the Mount Panorama Motor Racing Circuit, quite the stage upon which to perform.

The 6.213-kilometre circuit that hosts the Great Race has evolved significantly over the years from when it was first carved out into what had been known as Bald Hill.

Unlike the racetrack designs of today, the Mountain layout was designed in an age long before complex computer modelling and simulation software produced unimaginative, cookie-cutter track layouts.

The traditional names of the different corners (of which there are officially 23), straights and sections of the Mount Panorama circuit have become part of the Australian and world motor racing lexicon. Other tracks simply refer to 'Turn 1' or 'Turn 23'. Not so at Bathurst, where history and heritage mean so much more.

Sponsorships for different events at Bathurst dictate that these traditional names are tweaked year on year in deference to whoever is paying the bills for trackside signage, but it's the original names that have stood the test of time.

The run along the Pit Straight leads up to the first corner of the circuit, Hell Corner, a 90-degree left-hander that begins the long climb up Mountain Straight.

It's a relatively simple corner but it's hard to negotiate when a car has deposited oil all over the road, as Jim Richards found in 1985 at the wheel of his gorgeous black and gold JPS BMW 635.

He famously speared off into the sand trap on the outside of Hell Corner and was instantly joined by teammate George Fury, who had also lost control on the slippery approach to the corner. Alas, he promptly smacked into the door of Richards' bogged car and smashed the window!

As it was two years before the introduction of the Safety Car, the duo had to dig their own way out. Once his car was free of the sand though, Jim jumped back in and left poor George to it!

Its grim name doesn't make Hell Corner sound like much fun at all, but it's said to date back to the days when a tree stump sat, unprotected by barriers, on the inside of the corner. Clipping it would make for a hell of a day for any driver. This would have been more pronounced for a rider, given the lack of protection for motorcycle racers and high risk of injury or death.

The run through Hell Corner leads onto Mountain Straight, which then leads to a right-hander at Griffins Bend, named in honour of former Bathurst Mayor, Martin Griffin.

It's the first braking area for cars after they've exited the pit lane and blended back onto the track on the inside of the left-hand side of Mountain Straight. This turn has witnessed its fair share of action over the years.

Although the road runs uphill on the approach to the corner, that didn't help David Besnard in 2011 in the Great

Race. He crashed a Dick Johnson Racing Falcon there and it promptly erupted into flames: the fire followed a trail of fuel on the road that had escaped from the smashed Ford.

As Besnard and plenty of others have found, the corner catches out drivers who re-join the track after a brake-pad change then, on the run up the 1.1-kilometre Mountain Straight, forget to tap their brake pedal enough to ensure they have total braking power when required for the upcoming corner.

Once drivers negotiate Griffins Bend they keep climbing and head to the narrow Cutting (the origin of the name is obvious given the track is cut into the rock of the Mountain). It's a steep left-hand corner, with limited room for passing, that connects to a very slight kink to the right dubbed Quarry Corner, not commonly referred to in the modern era. It's this spot where Dick Johnson famously hit a rock in 1980's Great Race.

The run across the top of the Mountain features a range of sweeping corners named after the parks that surround them. It's here where certain campers set up their tents and campsites for the five days of race week (and sometimes before!); they are the true diehards of the Bathurst 1000.

Reid Park is named after Bathurst City Council engineer Hughie Reid, who was tasked with designing the layout of the 'tourist drive' that became the Mount Panorama racing circuit, using existing tracks where possible.

It's followed by the highest point of the track at Sulman Park (it's 862 metres above sea level), named in honour of former racer Tom Sulman, who died in a crash on Conrod Straight in a Lotus sportscar in 1970.

Sulman Park leads to McPhillamy Park, named in honour of Walter J. McPhillamy, who donated a significant parcel of his family's land at the top of the Mountain. He died aged 78 in June 1938, mere months after the circuit hosted its first race event.

The point at which the circuit begins its downhill plunge was originally named 'Skyline' for the view it provides drivers. Peter Brock's name was added as a tribute to the nine-time Great Race winner ahead of the 1997 Primus 1000 Classic.

Brock's Skyline leads to the Esses and Dipper as the bitumen surface snakes its way down the Mountain and through a significant dip, sending cars into Forrest's Elbow, the tight left-hander that opens up onto Conrod Straight.

This corner was originally called 'The Elbow' and sometimes 'Devil's Elbow' before motorcycle racer Jack Forrest crashed there in 1947.

Forrest smashed his elbow on the ground in the accident, but remarkably returned to race the next day. Fellow racer Harry Hinton is credited with dubbing the corner Forrest's Elbow.

Conrod Straight is the circuit's longest straight, but it hasn't always been called that. Prior to the Easter race event in 1939, it was named 'Main Straight'. Then Frank Kleinig's Hudson Special had a conrod failure so spectacular that the straight was later renamed in its honour!

Originally the Straight ran all the way down to Murray's Corner, however this was modified in 1987 with the introduction of a three-corner sequence. Initially named 'Caltex Chase', in reference to sponsorship from the oil giant, The Chase, as it's more commonly referred to now, added 40 metres to the track length. It was a safety upgrade as part of a major amount of track works to satisfy the world governing body of motorsport, FISA (now known as the FIA), in order to secure a round of the World Touring Car Championship for the Mountain in 1987.

There had been concerns that the introduction of the new Chase would negatively alter the character of the Mount Panorama circuit, but that's not proven to be the case. It's become one of the most challenging parts of the circuit, particularly the flat-out right-hander at the beginning of it that is now the fastest corner in Australian motorsport – somewhat ironic given the series of corners was introduced to slow cars down.

The circuit's final turn was called 'Pit Corner' until Bill Murray spectacularly crashed his Hudson Special into the sandbags there in the 1946 New South Wales Grand Prix. Race-winner Alf Najar is said to have graffitied the words 'Murray's Corner' onto the fence later that evening, and the name stuck.

Not only has the racing circuit undergone plenty of improvements and enhancements, but the surrounding infrastructure and facilities at Mount Panorama have as well, all in line with improving safety and the experience for the thousands of fans who annually attend.

Things at Mount Panorama really started to change in the late 1970s as the Bathurst 1000's status grew and the venue evolved to keep pace.

A new pedestrian bridge on Pit Straight was installed in 1977 and a concrete wall separating the race track and pit lane was erected in time for the 1978 race.

Until then the only thing protecting crews working in the pits from the cars flashing by on the track was a painted white line on the road – hardly a barrier to stop a car or errant parts from finding a way into the pits!

The Mountain looked very, very different in the early years. Trackside barriers were few and far between and consisted of simple wire fences. It took until the major works undertaken in 1987 – to bring the track into line with international requirements to hold a round of the World Touring Car Championship – for concrete barriers to be installed all the way down Conrod Straight.

The old pit counter was bulldozed as part of these works and replaced with a new pit lane building. This in turn was flattened in late 2003 and replaced by a brand-new, state-of-the-art pit building – opened in 2004 – with bigger garages and improved corporate hospitality suites and facilities.

The area behind the pits was also flattened and the various freestanding garages and access roads replaced by a large, flat area of bitumen that now allows B-double race transporters to park right behind their team's pit bay for easy loading and unloading of cars and equipment.

These works were all part of a $24 million redevelopment jointly funded by the State and Federal governments and the Bathurst Regional Council.

Only a few years later the circuit had its own hotel, a new 133-room facility constructed at the exit of the Chase. It took a few years upon completion to finally be opened; the hotel hosted its first Bathurst 1000 guests at the 2009 Great Race.

Slowing cars down in the pit lane became a pressing issue in the 1980s as the race became more competitive and drivers looked for as many opportunities as possible to make up crucial seconds on their rivals.

Speed humps were installed in the pit lane in various places in time for the 1982 race, in order to try and curb speeds, though they were later removed as part of the upgrades for the World Touring Car race five years later.

It took until 1996 for a pit lane speed limit – 60km/h – to be adopted and enforced for the first time for the Bathurst 1000. This was dropped down to 40km/h in the V8 Supercars Championship – and therefore also the Bathurst 1000 – in subsequent years and remains in place to this day.

How the cars enter pit lane has also been tweaked in the interests of safety.

A new pit lane entry was introduced in 1984, which remains today. Rather than the cars coming around the last bend at Murrays Corner and peeling left immediately to enter the pits, the new peel-off road – just after the bridge on Conrod Straight – brought the cars off the track and through a chicane before their arrival in the pit lane itself. This prevented cars from slowing immediately coming out of the last corner – and possibly catching closely following competitors unawares.

Now over 80 years old, Mount Panorama's world-famous circuit is the perfect example of how things can evolve to move with the times but also retain the DNA that continues to make them special.

At its core it's still the same amazing racetrack that was dreamt up back in the 1930s: a challenging ribbon of bitumen that mesmerises and inspires.

It's been tweaked, tuned, improved, re-surfaced and re-developed and undergone a series of facelifts over its history.

But the bones of Bathurst's magic Mountain are such that the foundations upon which all of this change occurs will stand it in good stead for plenty of years to come.

## It Doesn't Matter Where You Start

The 2015 Bathurst 1000 stands out as the last time that the three cars that finished on the podium in the race all started outside the top 10 on the grid.

Race winners Craig Lowndes and Steve Richards started 15th, runners-up Mark Winterbottom and Steve Owen started 14th and third-placed Garth Tander and Warren Luff started 22nd.

The only other time in the race's history that this happened (since qualifying times first determined the grid in 1967) was 1987.

That day the winners – Peter Brock, David Parsons and Peter McLeod – started 19th on the grid and inherited victory after crossing the line third when the top two finishing Sierras were excluded post-race.

The fourth and fifth-placed Nissan Skylines were elevated to second and third in the official results, however their driving crews – Glenn Seton/John Bowe (who started 14th) and George Fury/Terry Shiel (who started 13th) respectively – didn't actually get to physically stand on the podium on the day. That was because the winning Fords were officially excluded some weeks after the completion of the race!

That 1987 race remains unique in Great Race history as 15 of the first 16 finishers started outside the top 10 on the grid.

The only top 10 starter to finish in the top 10 was the BMW M3 of Johnny Cecotto and Gianfranco Brancatelli. It started fifth and finished seventh.

## Try, Try and Try Again

Glenn Seton and Bruce Stewart hold the record for the greatest number of Bathurst Great Race starts without winning the race – 26.

Seton finished second three times (1987, 2003, 2004) between his debut in 1983 and his last start in 2010.

Stewart's best finish of fifth came in 1988 in a Caltex Ford Sierra RS500 alongside John Giddings.

However, he did win his class on three occasions in the Great Race. In 1969 he won Class C with George Garth in a Datsun 1600 and he came first in Class B driving solo, again in a Datsun 1600, in 1972. Stewart paired with Bill Evans to take out Class A in a Datsun 1200 in 1976.

Stewart's last Bathurst 1000 start came in 1995 at the wheel of a Perkins Engineering-built Commodore VP with Sydney privateer Bob Pearson.

# 11

# Holden's Hero

For good reason, Peter Brock is usually written up as Holden's greatest ever competitor in the history of the Great Race at Bathurst, but six-time winner Larry Perkins has just as much claim to the mantle.

Not only did the self-taught engineer win behind the wheel of Commodores at Mount Panorama – three as Brock's co-driver in Holden Dealer Team wins, in 1982, 1983 and 1984 – but he led three wins for his own Castrol-backed team, in 1993, 1995 and 1997.

In addition to running his own team and achieving success on the track, his Perkins Engineering organisation built cars and engines to allow other competitors – primarily non-professional racing customers – to tackle the Mountain for many years.

The 1997 race that Perkins and Russell Ingall won at Bathurst provides an ideal illustration of the point.

Including their race-winning car, a quarter of the field – 10 of the 40 cars on the starting grid – had originally been built by Perkins' team, who were based in a hangar at Moorabbin Airport in the southeast suburbs of Melbourne.

Perkins took his first tilt at Bathurst in 1977 at the wheel of a Torana and finished third, with colourful character and highly underrated driver, Peter Janson.

'LP' made all bar one of his 26 Great Race starts at the wheel of Holden products.

He reached the pinnacle of world motorsport in the 1970s by making it to Formula 1, including driving for the famous Brabham team – by then owned by Bernie Ecclestone. Unable to fund himself into another seat on the Grand Prix grid, Perkins returned home and later became an integral part of Holden's factory motorsport program in the early 1980s. In 1982 he joined the highly regarded Holden Dealer Team as workshop manager: the role of co-driver to team owner/driver Peter Brock was secondary in his mind.

'It was around that '81–'82 period, when I was back from Europe and not sure what I wanted to do, that Brocky rang me up to ask would I drive with him at Bathurst in '82,' Perkins recalled to me on the V8 Sleuth Podcast in 2020.

"Oh," I said, "Peter, look, I'm not that fussed about driving" … that's where I placed the touring car category of Australia on the world stage. It was just not my focus; it was as simple as that.

'I went down to the workshop and had a look around – I said, "Jesus, Brocky, it's a real shitfight, your workshop." It was dirty and scruffy and shocking. I said, "Look, if you want me to run the workshop – and, alright, if you want me to co-drive at Bathurst and Sandown – I'll do that." But it was not a big desire of mine.

'Peter just left me alone to do my preparation; he let me hire and fire. I didn't have any influence or whatever on the commercial side of his road car business or getting his sponsors or anything.'

After three wins with Brock and the HDT at Bathurst, Perkins elected to leave the team midway through 1985 to establish his own Perkins Engineering squad for 1986.

Initially a privateer squad, Perkins' team was soon after contracted, in 1988, to run the official factory Holden race program on behalf of the newly formed Holden Special Vehicles road car business led by Scotsman Tom Walkinshaw.

With Walkinshaw's team not running a factory program in the Australian Touring Car Championship the following year, Perkins was again contracted to supply services to 'the General', this time running a pair of Commodores in the endurance races under the Holden Racing Team banner.

From 1990 he returned to running his own privately run program and further underlined his reputation for expertly crafted annual Bathurst assaults.

While other teams placed plenty of resources into winning races during the Australian Touring Car Championship season of shorter races, Perkins was unwavering in his conviction that the races during the regular season were all just a warm-up for the Bathurst 1000, the race that really mattered.

His win in 1993 alongside Gregg Hansford proved to be a special one in the history books and it went over a treat with fans.

In the year of the return of V8 Commodore and Falcon competition at Bathurst, the victory really struck a chord with long-time Holden supporters, due to what sat under the bonnet of the winning #11 Commodore.

Not only did the duo defeat the mighty Gibson

Motorsport team and its Commodore of Mark Skaife and Jim Richards to win the race (and thus stop the former Nissan duo from winning three Bathursts in a row), but the Perkins team did it using a Holden V8 engine. Other Commodore teams had opted for the more expensive Chevrolet-based unit permitted under the new rules of the period.

Perkins' logic was simple. He had significant stocks of the Holden engine blocks for himself and his band of customers and couldn't see the point of going to the expense of developing a new engine.

He convinced his contacts at Holden to help fix some of the shortcomings of the Holden V8 engine and they produced a limited run of 50 blocks and 100 cylinder heads specifically for his use.

For that special run of blocks, extra metal was added in the key areas that Perkins had identified as weaknesses and the inlet ports (the part of an engine opened and closed by the intake valves) were raised by 30 millimetres.

It was yet another example of Perkins' logical, no-frills approach to racing. In his often-quoted view, Bathurst was won in the workshop in the months prior to the race – more so than on the track itself on race day.

The 1993 win was the very last time that a Holden V8 engine powered a Commodore to victory in the Bathurst 1000.

Perkins won again in 1995 but it was an unlikely victory. Though going in he had another technical development up his sleeve to help win Bathurst – in the way of a specially designed brake system – within seconds of the start, Perkins and new co-driver Russell Ingall (Hansford had been killed in a race crash earlier in the year at Phillip Island) appeared out of contention to win the race.

When slow-starting pole-sitter Craig Lowndes jinked to the right off the line, the 21-year-old clipped the Castrol Commodore and punctured its left-front tyre.

Perkins limped back to the pits and, although the car escaped steering damage, he re-joined as the last of those running on the track.

That prompted Perkins and Ingall to push their car to its limits for the rest of the day in a bid to get back onto the lead lap and stay in contention. It took 60 laps to do that. Then when a failure and subsequent crash of a car – ironically, one built by Perkins' team, the Commodore driven by former truck racer David Parsons – brought out a Safety Car with just over 30 laps to go, that brought Perkins onto the tail of the newly bunched leading pack.

Unlike his rivals, Perkins had taken himself through to the last stint of the race without needing to change his brake pads. During the year his team had developed its own brake caliper, designed in such a way that it could fit an extra-thick brake pad that would not need to be changed over the 1000-kilometre race distance at Bathurst.

'AP in England, the largest brake company in the world, didn't reckon we could have a brake pad that thick,' recalls Perkins.

'But (Japanese brand) Endless agreed to make them and we did the calliper in-house. We drove flat-out all day, and it was a big surprise to the opposition when we never pitted for a brake pad change.'

Soon the race boiled down to a battle between Perkins and leader Glenn Seton, driving a Falcon. With just nine laps remaining, Seton pulled away.

'At the end I couldn't catch Glenn,' says Perkins.

'But Glenn had picked up the pace – he hadn't been running full bore all day – and the moment he ran it up to full revs, it broke something in the valve train.

'Someone's misery is someone else's smile. [Seton's demise] was certainly a bit of fortune, but a win's a win.'

Perkins and Ingall finished sixth in the Bathurst 1000 the following year. The former had taken a characteristically logical approach to the 1996 event.

The VR Commodore had been introduced in 1995 and was the model used by the duo to win at Mount Panorama that year. But a technical change – sections of the front undertray on the front spoiler were trimmed in order to reduce front downforce and, therefore, grip that generated speed in the corners – designed to even up the Holdens with the Ford Falcons in the lead-up to Bathurst in '96 was met with grumbles by Commodore drivers and teams.

Rather than make the change to his car for Bathurst, Perkins implemented some of his trademark 'out of the box' thinking. The new rule affected the VR model Commodore, but nowhere in the rules did it say it had to be applied to the previous VP model Commodore. He took one of his existing race cars and converted it back to the older style VP bodywork in order to ensure his Bathurst challenger didn't get its front spoiler section clipped!

Perkins' theory didn't result in a race win that year, but it was fascinating to observe the way he went racing.

Perkins continued to race full-time in V8 Supercars and at Bathurst until the end of 2002 and returned to Bathurst in 2003 as co-driver for Steve Richards in one of his team's Commodores.

But a crash during Saturday practice – caused by Perkins losing concentration and spearing off the road into the outside wall at the Cutting – instantly told the six-time Bathurst winner that his time was up as a Great Race challenger.

He all but announced his retirement from race driving when he met with media in the trackside media centre to discuss the crash.

In the aftermath, there was no press release, farewell tour or testimonial dinner. That was far from Perkins' style. Typical of the man, he had made a no-emotion decision then proceeded to carrying it out with no fuss.

He continued to run his team in the subsequent years and son Jack followed in his wheel tracks when he made his Bathurst debut driving one of the team's cars in 2006.

Perkins Snr sold down his interests in his team at the end of 2008 to racing brothers Todd and Rick Kelly and their family, then stepped back from the sport.

But the family name continues at Bathurst via Jack, whose burning ambition is to win the race that his father conquered six times.

Overcoming his diagnosis of type 1 diabetes, which threatened his racing career in its early stages, Perkins Jnr has made 17 Bathurst 1000 starts, with a best result of third – alongside James Courtney in 2019.

'Bathurst, to me, is everything. I just want to win one,' he says.

'When I look at Dad's story, he's a legend. He left Australia with $180 in his pocket, made it to Formula 1 and won six Bathursts from nothing. It's pretty cool.'

## The General's Streak

With seven wins in a row between 1999 and 2005, Holden can rightfully claim the longest streak of Bathurst 1000 wins by a manufacturer in the history of the race.

Holdens also took home the winner's trophy four times in succession, from 2009 to 2012, and then again from 2015 to 2018.

The biggest ever streak of Bathurst wins by Fords sits at two runs of three straight wins. Ford Cortinas won from 1963 to 1965 and Craig Lowndes and Jamie Whincup drove Falcons to victory in 2006, 2007 and 2008.

# 12

# **Gentleman Jim**

**N**ew Zealand-born but Australian-based since the mid-1970s, Jim Richards is the unassuming humble hero of the Bathurst 1000.

Devoid of the rock-star levels of public adulation of a Peter Brock, the soft-spoken Richards built his reputation on quietly delivering sublime performances behind the wheel. It was his calling card for over three decades at Bathurst and has resulted in a body of work the envy of the industry.

Dubbed 'Gentleman Jim', a nickname many competitors have scoffed at – 'He apologised after he hit you!' they exclaim – Richards won the Great Race seven times in 35 starts spread across 33 years; he competed in both the Super Touring and V8 Supercars Bathurst races in 1997 and 1998.

Ironically, for a driver whose career has come to be so defined by his success at Mount Panorama, the Great Race was largely a blip on his radar when he first arrived to compete in the race alongside fellow Kiwi Rod Coppins in a Torana in 1974.

'You didn't hear a lot about Bathurst because there was only really one motorsport magazine that came out and it reported New Zealand events, not a lot of Aussie ones,' Richards says.

But by the end of the 1974 Hardie-Ferodo 1000 at Bathurst, far more people in Australia knew who Jim Richards was than before that year's race had kicked off. The race was struck by torrential rain and Richards and his small team found themselves in a bind. They only had a handful of wet weather and intermediate tyres, so spent the rest of the race mixing and matching sets to make it through the tricky conditions.

Badly worn front brakes meant the red V8-powered Torana was doing all its stopping by the rear drum brakes, however Richards adapted to the conditions and he and Coppins came home a brilliant third place on debut.

'Personally, I didn't even think of coming back again,' he says.

'It was brilliant; we wanted to finish, basically. The car was prepared excellently, but we'd never raced it before.

'It was so fantastic that we'd come over and come third, but we probably went a bit unnoticed; in those days the winning car and drivers were transported around the track on the back of a truck, and second and third didn't really get any recognition.'

The dangers of the Mountain were made clear to Richards late in the race too. After battling for several laps with Rod McRae's similar Torana, Richards had a front row seat as McRae endured one of the biggest accidents in the event's history.

'He passed me down Conrod and pulled in front of me down the dip, but as he did that, he must have caught one of the puddles on the inside,' Richards says.

'The car just swapped ends and went off towards the inside of the track, then back across in front of me, and knocked an old tree down. The tree hit it dead set on the floor and the car bent around it … And all he had was a cut ear.'

Richards and Coppins came back to Bathurst in 1975 and the annual endurance race became a regular date on the former's racing calendar every year afterwards.

They finished eighth in the same Torana, despite overheating, and teamed up again in a Falcon in 1977 only to fall out of the race when the engine in the big Ford blew up.

Richards' big chance to win his first Bathurst 1000 came in 1978, when he was signed by the Holden Dealer Team to share its lead Torana A9X with Peter Brock. The Kiwi had made Melbourne home and become a regular, fighting for wins in Sports Sedans at the wheel of his Sidchrome-backed Mustang and, later, a Ford Falcon hardtop.

He was the perfect choice to be paired with Brock as Holden looked to reassert its ascendancy over Mount Panorama in the wake of Allan Moffat wiping the floor with the field at Bathurst the year prior.

Richards and Brock won their first Bathurst together and made it a habit in the years that followed, scoring wins across 1978, 1979 and 1980.

'I only did six laps in practice and I don't think Brocky did much more over the practice and qualifying period,' Richards recalls of the 1978 win.

'Whenever I looked at the car, there were two or three mechanics around it polishing all the aluminium under the bonnet, polishing the rims, polishing the car ... I thought, "Geez, this is an easy job!"

'All I needed to do was qualify to drive in the race. Everything had been tested to perfection beforehand, so the plan for Bathurst was that they didn't want to wear the car out: race day was the day for getting the loot.'

Brock and Richards were a lap up on the nearest challenger by the time the chequered flag waved in the 1978 race. It was the third Bathurst victory for the former and the first for Richards. It secured him a place in history as the first New Zealand-born driver to win Australia's Great Race.

Every bit as importantly, the victory shone a light on Richards' ability behind the wheel. Those he'd raced against and those who paid attention knew exactly how talented the quiet New Zealander was; now his class was there for all to see, benchmarked against a known quantity in Brock.

'It was satisfying, but it wasn't like winning Bathurst later on, when I was the lead driver,' Richards says.

'But I do think that win changed the perception of what I was capable of: If he's going round that track as quick as Brocky in the same car, he must be a bloody good driver!'

The duo's 1979 Bathurst win was even bigger and better. Their #05 Torana led all 163 laps and Richards again performed his role to perfection, setting fast lap times without hurting the car. The end result was a crushing six-lap win.

'In that era, I believe he was the best driver,' Richards says of Brock.

'Others were close, but Brocky had the best organised team, the best funding, and I would say his team was the most professional. They were one of the first to have a really nice trailer and truck set-up, and all the team uniforms and everything like that was on the mark.'

Brock took over the running of the team for 1980, the same year that the Commodore made its Bathurst 1000 debut. It may have been a new car and a different ownership set-up, but it was again a case of situation normal for Richards. The only other deviation from the script of the two previous years was that Richards, not Brock, drove the final stint to the chequered flag. Brock had had an early charge back into contention (after an unscheduled pit stop following a collision on-track with a Gemini), which meant that, if he got in for the final stint, he'd exceed the maximum time behind the wheel that any one driver could do in the race.

'That was a nice feeling,' Richards says of driving across the line in 1980.

'To know that he trusted me and that he had no problems with me doing the finishing touches on that race win.'

Richards and Brock made one more Bathurst 1000 start together, in 1981, however their Commodore failed in the early laps and a fourth successful win evaporated when Brock was forced to pit with driveline problems.

A full-time drive with the JPS BMW squad beckoned for Richards for 1982 and he spent the majority of the '80s with the Frank Gardner-run team. Despite plenty of success, including Australian Touring Car Championship wins in 1985 and 1987, Richards and the BMW team just didn't have the speed – or luck – to finish on the podium at Bathurst in that time.

A single season back with Brock in Mobil-backed BMWs in 1988 failed to bear fruit as the little German cars were outpaced by the turbo Sierras and V8 Commodores. But then a move to Nissan for 1989 helped put Richards back on the road to conquering the Mountain.

He and a young Mark Skaife finished third at Bathurst that year in a GTS-R Skyline and the arrival of the four-wheel-drive GT-R – dubbed 'Godzilla' – in 1990 gave the Nissan team a major technical advantage, once the bugbears of the new, high-performance turbo car were ironed out.

The teething issues were all gone by the time 1991 rolled around as Richards and Skaife dominated the Bathurst 1000 to score the first Great Race win for a Japanese manufacturer. Richards drove a whopping 102 of the 161 laps, including the start and finish.

'That's my favourite Bathurst win,' Richards reveals.

'The Bathurst and championship wins that year were the most satisfying, in a way, because I was the lead driver. We knew the potential of the car in 1990; 1991 was the culmination of everything going just right.'

Richards' teammate Mark Skaife was his biggest challenger by this point and stepped up to knock him off and win the Australian Touring Car Championship in 1992. They paired up again to win at Bathurst but it was clear that the dynamics within the Gibson Motorsport Nissan team had shifted during this period.

'I figured that I was the number one driver because I was winning and Skaifey would become the number one driver when he was winning,' says Richards.

'I didn't have a problem with that; that was natural progression. I was the better driver when we started off together as teammates in 1989. Then, as time went on, he learnt everything that I knew – because if he wanted to know something, I'd always tell him – and then he ended up beating me. He just got better and better until, in 1992, he was every bit as good as I was and maybe a fraction better in some areas.

We still had some good races and I beat him on occasion but, after 1991, Skaifey became the team leader.'

The duo's win at Bathurst in 1992 remains one of the most controversial in Great Race history. Richards had been stuck on a wet track on slick tyres and crashed their race-leading Nissan GT-R. It angered the fans at the podium presentation when the Winfield-backed car was declared the winner despite sitting as a crumpled heap by the side of the track.

But by far the worst aspect of that day at the Mountain was the death of Denny Hulme, the 1967 Formula 1 World Champion who had suffered a heart attack and died.

'I was told in the pits after I'd gotten out of the car from doing my first stint,' Richards said.

'I sound a little bit callous but hearing that Denny had died had no effect on me at all during the race. It hit me after the race was over. I had a beer and shed a few tears. I've always been able to cop things like that reasonably well; I guess the younger you are, the less it affects you. If you were going to pass away, at least Denny died doing what he loved doing.'

The Gibson team swapped to Holdens for 1993 when the rules for Australian touring car racing changed, and Richards and Skaife made three more Bathurst starts together in this period.

They finished runners-up in 1993, Skaife crashed in the wet in 1994 and tailshaft failure took them out of the 1995 race while at the front of the field after Richards had seized the lead in the early laps.

The opportunity to share a car with his son Steven in the Bathurst 1000 proved the motivation for Richards to move on from the Gibson team and instead sign to drive for Garry Rogers Motorsport's smaller, single car team.

Father and son drove together at Bathurst in 1996, though Steve was caught out in slippery conditions and crashed into the wall on the exit of the Chase before Jim had a drive in the race.

There were two Bathurst races in 1997 and again in 1998, one for two-litre Super Tourers and the other for V8 Supercars. Jim and Steve drove in each of these races across these two years and wrote some special history along the way.

They teamed up to finish second together in the 1997 V8 race, then spent the entire day fighting against one another in the 1998 Super Touring race, Jim in a factory-backed Volvo and Steve in a privateer-run Nissan.

Father beat son narrowly that day: Jim and Swede Rickard Rydell sped home to beat Steve and Brit Matt Neal's Nissan by just 1.9975-seconds.

'The two of us were in first and second place, whether they were leading or we were,' Richards recalls.

'We were pretty much never more than about 4.5 seconds apart the whole day and we were driving flat-out the whole time; we weren't conserving anything. Steve and Matt, they wanted to win too, so they weren't pissing about. They were driving as hard as they could, so we had to drive as hard as we could.

'It was like four or five sprint races; when the next driver got in, they pressed on as hard as they could. And we didn't worry about saving the brakes or anything; we knew the car would go the distance.'

Despite not being a race featuring the V8 Supercar stars and the traditional Holden versus Ford Bathurst battle,

Richards rates his 1998 Volvo Bathurst victory as highly as any of his other Great Race wins.

'The two-litre racing was harder and closer, and it was flat-out the whole way, like you were doing a qualifying run on every lap. You could never have driven a V8 Supercar of the time the same way,' he says.

'The whole scenario was good: our Australian team joined (Tom) Walkinshaw's (Volvo) team for the race under the Volvo/TWR umbrella, which was nice, and we were matching ourselves against the best from Europe.

'That said, I would've been just as happy if Steve had won, to be honest. I mean, I would rather that I win, but if Steve's car was ahead and we couldn't pass him, I'd have been just as rapt.'

Richards' seventh Bathurst 1000 win – in 2002 – came when he re-united with his old friend Mark Skaife. After a few years driving Fords at Bathurst in the annual V8 Supercar 1000-kilometre classic with John Bowe and the CAT Racing team and then Glenn Seton's Ford Tickford Racing team, Richards was paired with his former Nissan partner Skaife in a Holden Racing Team Commodore.

Aged 55 by that stage and still running at the front in his Porsche of the Nations Cup class at the time, Richards was responsible at Bathurst for not only his and Skaife's Bathurst 1000-winning chances but of Skaife's V8 Supercars Championship-winning chance as well, as the Great Race by then was a points-scoring round of the championship.

That was front of Richards' mind when rain started to

hit the Mount Panorama circuit during his final stint at the wheel in the 2002 race, and his caution allowed the Castrol Commodores of Russell Ingall (shared with Jim's son Steve) and Paul Dumbrell (sharing with Larry Perkins) to skip away.

'I was hesitant; I didn't drive hard enough,' Richards declares.

'I was always thinking of the consequences of Skaifey losing both Bathurst and the championship because of a mistake that I made. I didn't want that to happen, so I drove very conservatively. You're not actively thinking about it as you're driving across Skyline, but it was always in the back of my mind: "I've got to make sure we get home."

'I would've liked to have been faster because I liked those conditions, but I wasn't game to take the extra risk and spear off the track. Yes, the car wasn't damaged and yes, the car was running well when I handed over to Mark, so I'd done my job in that sense. But those laps could have lost us the race if it had run uninterrupted to the end.'

It turned out for the best and the gap Richards lost on-track was instantly reduced when a Safety Car appeared on lap 138 of 161 due to a crash on-track. The lead pack was bunched up and a tiny mistake by Richards' son Steve on the restart from another Safety Car period soon after allowed Skaife to get by and charge away to win.

Ten years on from their infamous appearance on the Bathurst podium in 1992, Richards had mulled prior to the event over a few options of what he might say to the crowd should he win.

Expecting the inevitable comparisons to his infamous 'pack of arseholes' address, he settled on, 'You're a pack of lovely, lovely people.'

Richards didn't slow down after his seventh Bathurst 1000 win; in fact he went even faster! Aged 56 he qualified third for the 2003 race in a Holden Racing Team Commodore, setting his fastest ever lap of Mount Panorama and out-qualifying teammate Skaife in the Top 10 Shootout, although his performance was overshadowed by countryman Greg Murphy's 'Lap of the Gods' pole-winning effort.

Richards and Tony Longhurst finished a fighting fifth in that year's race. Jim and son Steve duked it out for fourth place in the closing laps and the position was eventually decided in favour of the latter.

Father and son reunited in 2004 for their last Bathurst 1000 start together in one of Larry Perkins' Castrol Commodores. Steve took pole position and their Holden appeared to be one of the fastest cars in the field.

But its chances of winning the race were dashed by two incidents. The throttle stuck partly open and sent Jim into the tyre wall at Griffins Bend in his first stint, though the patched-up car was hauled back up to third place by Steve by lap 100.

But the second incident knocked it out of race-winning contention: Jim couldn't avoid a kangaroo that bounced out onto the track in his path on the climb up to the Cutting and the car was heavily damaged.

'There was nothing I could do,' says Richards.

'It just jumped out ... BANG! I jammed the brakes on as hard as I could but the impact tore the front of the car up, then Russell (Ingall) ran me up the bum and bent the back of the car!'

Richards returned to drive for the Holden Racing Team at Bathurst and spent two years working with young Australian international drivers in James Courtney and Ryan Briscoe. Courtney crashed their Commodore out early in the

2005 race and it was Richards at the helm in 2006 when the #22 Holden hit the wall, with race-ending damage the result.

After that crash, Richards decided to call time on his days tackling the Great Race. 'Gentleman Jim' quietly stepped away from his Bathurst 1000 career after a record 35 starts.

'I wasn't going to announce a retirement or anything; I just told Skaifey a few weeks after that I wasn't going to go again,' Richards says.

*Jim Richards delivers his famous podium speech after the 1992 Tooheys 1000.*

'I still loved driving, and I prided myself on not overextending myself or worrying about spearing off. I never worried about that. So, when I crashed in the 2006 race, I just thought, "No, that's it. I've had enough."'

Richards wasn't lost to the Mountain though. He continued to race at Bathurst long after he bowed out of competing in its banner-head Bathurst 1000 race.

The Touring Car Masters class was buoyed by his arrival in 2007, when he took to Mount Panorama in a Camaro in the TCM support races for his first year of non-Bathurst 1000 driving. Then he went about building up his own Falcon Sprint and AMC Javelin to race in subsequent years in the popular muscle car class.

Jim made his last race appearance at Bathurst in 2018 in his Falcon Sprint. That same year his son Steve teamed up with Craig Lowndes in an Autobarn-backed Triple Eight-run Commodore to win the Bathurst 1000. It was Steve's fifth win in the race.

Revered on both sides of the Tasman, 'Gentleman Jim' these days tunes in to the Bathurst 1000 every year from the comfort of his armchair in Melbourne.

Once a racer, always a racer ...

## Fast Off the Mark

Six-time Bathurst 1000 winner and five-time pole-sitter Mark Skaife also has the distinction as the only driver in Bathurst Great Race history to turn in the fastest lap of the race four years in a row.

Skaife set the fastest race lap every year from 1990 to 1993. The first three years he drove a Nissan GT-R (in 1991 he did it at the wheel of the team's second car under the cross-entering rules of the period) and in the final year of the streak, in 1993, he drove a Holden Commodore VP.

The closest any other driver has come to this mark is three fastest laps in a row: David Reynolds managed this feat in Erebus Motorsport Commodores in 2016, 2017 and 2018.

## Keeping It Slow

While acknowledging the growing need for safety, Bathurst aficionados sometimes get nostalgic about the Great Race days that preceded the introduction of the Safety Car. Some say that the compulsory slow-down – and freeze on overtaking – of a Safety Car period changes the race completely.

The greatest number of Safety Car periods ever seen in a Bathurst 1000 was 13 in the rain-affected race of 2000.

The most laps of a Bathurst 1000 race affected by the Safety Car was 45 laps in 2006. That was just over a quarter of the entire 1000-kilometre race!

13

# Matters of
# Presentation

Flying around Mount Panorama at breakneck speed for nearly seven hours in the pursuit of victory in the Bathurst 1000 may seem dangerous enough, but on occasion the most volatile part of the race hasn't been on-track – it's been the podium for the post-race presentation.

Of all of the podium ceremonies to follow a Bathurst Great Race, the 1992 presentation will live on forever. That's because of the speech (or, more accurately, character reference – and it wasn't a favourable one) race winner Jim Richards delivered to the assembled fans.

The expat Kiwi's words have become part of Great Race folklore and often raise a smile and giggle these days. On the day, however, the scene was most certainly more thunder and dark clouds than sunshine and sparkles.

Richards and partner Mark Skaife had just won their second Bathurst in succession. But to the spectators, the result made no sense because Richards had crashed their Nissan GT-R in the wet conditions.

Yet it was all as laid out in the rulebook. Because the race had been stopped the results were declared as of a lap prior to the red flag.

The Nissan team's dominance had struck an unpleasant chord with certain elements of the sport's fanbase. Partisan fans were not thrilled to see another Nissan win, particularly one that had crashed out of the race! And, with Australian touring car rules set to switch to Holden versus Ford V8 action for 1993, they were keen to give Nissan's Richards and Skaife an early, raucous send-off.

The unhappy crowd saved its worst for when Richards and Skaife were called onstage. The booing and jeering intensified. Beer cans were hurled at the balcony. Richards had been smiling as he walked out, but by the time he arrived at the microphone his face had turned to stone.

Channel 7 host Garry Wilkinson invited Richards to the microphone. His words were the last thing anyone expected from the seemingly meek and mild racer.

'I'm just really stunned for words,' he started.

'I can't believe the reception. I thought Australian race fans had a lot more to go than this. This is bloody disgraceful. I'll keep racing but, I tell you what, this is gonna remain with me for a long time. You're a pack of arseholes.'

'Skaifey and I were waiting to go out onto the podium, still laughing and giggling because we'd thought we'd lost the race,' Richards explains.

'Then they called for the third placegetters to head out onto the podium, Crompo (Neil Crompton) and Anders (Olofsson), and there was all this booing and carrying on, and the crowd were throwing cans at the podium.

'There was a bar in the area we were waiting in, and Skaifey suddenly starts picking up beer cans and putting them in his Tooheys Top Gun leather jacket that they gave to the race winners. I stopped him: "No, forget it; we'll just go out, say hi, thank the sponsors and disappear, and in about one minute we'll be back here having a beer."'

The second placegetters, Johnson and Bowe, were met with raucous cheers, the former further stirring up the crowd when he voiced his disbelief that they could 'be beaten by a crashed car'.

'It was a spur-of-the-moment thing,' Richards says of his own outburst.

'If you listen to the way that I said it, I got one or two words around the wrong way because I hadn't thought about it at all, it just sort of happened. For that moment, I think it was the right thing to say. I was upset because I knew how much work Nissan and all the guys had put into that car and that race, and a percentage of the spectators were rubbishing it.

'I don't think what I said overall was that bad. I wasn't tearing strips off everybody; it was reasonably quick and I didn't say anything too bad – except I called them a pack of arseholes!'

In the aftermath Richards was hauled onto Sydney and Melbourne talkback radio shows to discuss the infamous speech, while Gibson and Skaife made an appearance on *A Current Affair* to talk over the incident.

CAMS accused Richards of bringing the sport into disrepute and asked him to apologise.

'I told them I wasn't going to apologise to the mongrels that were throwing cans and everything, but to anyone else that I may have upset, yes I did want to say I was sorry that happened,' Richards says.

If the sport's rulers were displeased, the same could not be said about Richards' sponsors.

'The week after I got home from Bathurst, I got a call from Leon Daphne, the managing director of Nissan in Australia,' Richards says.

'He and his wife Kerry, who absolutely loved motorsport, had been down among the crowd. When they started booing and carrying on, she started whacking them with her umbrella!

'Leon rang to tell me that Nissan had received only one complaint about the speech: "It was from an old lady who said the driver was disgraceful and she'd never buy another Nissan, but I told her not to worry – we'll never sell her one!"'

Richards and Skaife won the previous year's race at Bathurst – in 1991 – also aboard one of the Nissan GT-Rs that left the fan favourite Fords and Holdens in their wake.

Channel 7's Garry Wilkinson also handled that year's podium presentation; however a controversial bearded figure unexpectedly grabbed the spotlight.

'Management at Channel 7 decided that year it would be a great cross-promotional idea to have Derryn Hinch involved in the telecast,' recalls Wilkinson.

'Mike Raymond said, "Well, what the hell are we going to do with him?" They got him to record some stuff during practice to get him out of the way but someone from management said, "You've got to use him more." So, they involved him in the podium presentation!

'The punters were throwing half-full beer cans. One hit me in the shoulder, but I think it was as much as Hinch they were pissed at than Jim or Mark!'

The previous year, in 1990, the doyen of Australian sports broadcasting, Bruce McAvaney, was part of the Channel 7 broadcast team and entrusted with podium hosting duties. In a 2015 interview for the Shannons Legends of Motorsport TV series, he told me about his trepidation at facing the Mountain mob.

'It was the biggest challenge for me, I think, in my whole broadcasting career to host the presentation at Bathurst,' he said.

'It is the scariest moment, you are standing up there, it is a frightening experience. Talk about a challenge. That, for me was just about the ultimate!'

Modern-day Supercars class clown David Reynolds is always good for some comedic relief. When he finished runner-up to Jamie Whincup in 2012 at Bathurst after a tightly fought race to the chequered flag, he ventured out onto the podium determined to enjoy himself with co-driver Dean Canto.

Caught up in the emotion and the joy of his first Bathurst 1000 podium finish, Reynolds plucked one of the Channel 7 microphones from the stand on the rostrum and enthusiastically flung it out to the waiting fans below.

Quite where the microphone ended up is unknown, though Reynolds certainly found out about the cost of the high-tech audio equipment after the incident.

'I got an invoice from Channel 7 for $3000 in the mail!' he told me in a chat on my podcast in 2020.

'My bonus for finishing second in my contract was $2000 and the microphone cost $3000, so I lost $1000 for that round! I call it the "Minus Bathurst 1000!".'

Reynolds' next Bathurst 1000 podium visit – when he won the race in 2017 – didn't cost him any cash, but it did put co-driver Luke Youlden in an unexpected physical situation.

The brilliant result had given both drivers their first Bathurst 1000 win, something that Youlden had been aspiring to since 2000.

*Giving your Bathurst winning co-driver a piggy back onto the podium hadn't been done - until 2017 that is, when Luke Youlden and David Reynolds won the race for Erebus Motorsport!*

To mark the occasion he figured he should do something noteworthy. Reynolds had some colourful exploits to his name, including throwing microphones and pot plants from podiums at previous Supercars races, not to mention his love of a 'shoey' – drinking champagne from his smelly race boot.

Next thing, Youlden outdid himself by becoming the first ever Bathurst 1000 winner to piggyback his winning partner out onto the podium, a decision he quickly regretted.

'I knew I had to do something stupid, and it was stupid because not a lot of people know that I tore my ACL on the Wednesday of that Bathurst race week doing a charity basketball match!' Youlden told me on an episode of my V8 Sleuth Podcast in 2020.

'I had damaged it playing basketball in 2011 and drove at Bathurst in 2012 and 2013 with a totally ruptured right ACL. I got it fixed in 2014 and ruptured it again at Bathurst in 2017.

'When I was piggybacking him on the podium, I thought, "Geez, this is probably a bad idea!" I had to rely on that knee strength to get Dave up there on my back!

'It didn't hinder my performance in the race though. It all worked out OK.'

## A Winning Year

Kiwi Shane van Gisbergen is the latest member of the exclusive club of drivers to win the Australian Touring Car/Supercars Championship and Bathurst 1000 in the same year.

Van Gisbergen's double win in 2022 aboard his Red Bull Ampol Commodore ZB made him the third Kiwi (after Scott McLaughlin in 2019 and Jim Richards in 1991) to achieve the impressive double.

Bob Jane was the first Great Race competitor to notch up this achievement – in 1963 – though Mark Skaife has taken out both titles more often than anyone: three (in 1992, 2001 and 2002).

Peter Brock (1973, 1978), Allan Moffat (1973, 1977), Dick Johnson (1981, 1989), Jamie Whincup (2008, 2012) and Craig Lowndes (1996) are the only other members of this impressive club.

## 14

# From Across the Ditch

The Bathurst 1000 is commonly known as Australia's Great Race but it's also become the Great Race that New Zealanders aspire to win just as much as their neighbours across the Tasman Sea.

Open-wheeler racing was huge in both nations in the 1960s and '70s, but touring car racing had its place too. In New Zealand the Benson & Hedges Six Hour race at Pukekohe Park for locally assembled standard production cars became the nation's number one tin-top race.

In fact, the race – then called the Wills Six Hour – was first held at Pukekohe in 1963, the same year the Great Race moved to Mount Panorama.

Open-wheeler racer Jim Palmer was one of the first Kiwis to tackle the Great Race – as part of the Holden Dealer Racing Team Monaro squad in 1968 – and the first year of the 1000-kilometre race length in 1973 saw more Kiwis arrive in the form of Leo Leonard, Gary Sprague and Ray Thackwell.

However, no Kiwi in Bathurst 1000 history has polarised fans quite like four-time winner Greg Murphy.

Loved by hordes of adoring Holden fans and Kiwis and despised by plenty of Ford fans and Aussies, Murphy was a massive star of V8 Supercars and Bathurst in the late 1990s and throughout the early and mid-2000s. His battles both on and off the track with Mark Skaife, Marcos Ambrose and Russell Ingall are some of the best ever seen in the category's history.

With Murphy everything was black or white, never shades of grey.

'I was just in a hurry, and I didn't accept mediocrity from myself, and I didn't accept it from anyone else,' Murphy reflected in 2020 on the V8 Sleuth Podcast.

'I had strong beliefs in what was right or wrong.'

His profile grew when V8 Supercars started taking its championship to New Zealand from 2001 onwards, and was further enhanced when he won four of the first five rounds held there. However, it was his win at Bathurst in 1996 with Craig Lowndes (and then wins in a two-weekend series back home at Pukekohe and Wellington a month later) that took him mainstream 'across the Ditch' and put his name on the map in Australia.

An open-wheeler driver in his younger years, Murphy's first real memories of Bathurst are of Peter Brock's 'Big Banger' Commodore winning the race in 1984. Murphy made his Bathurst 1000 debut a decade later in a two-litre Toyota with Englishman James Kaye in 1994, and a year later he was signed by the Holden Racing Team to share one of its Commodores with Craig Lowndes – as teammates to none other than Brock.

However, the emerging Kiwi didn't get to drive the car in the race as its engine failed in the first stint with Lowndes at the wheel.

Murphy's first Bathurst 1000 laps in an HRT Commodore eventually came in 1996 and he and Lowndes went on to dominate the rain-affected race. Their #1 Mobil Commodore led 129 of the 161 laps and the duo became the youngest to win the race in its history, capping an amazing season that had seen the pair also win the Sandown 500 endurance race in Melbourne and Lowndes win the Australian Touring Car Championship.

But they were not too bright-eyed and bushy-tailed for their post-Bathurst-win media work on the Monday morning after a major night of celebrations. The photos of them keeled over asleep in their race suits in pit lane, stealing a few extra minutes of sleep in between interviews and photo shoots, remain legendary in the industry.

'The old Bathurst RSL was the go-to venue, and it didn't close at whatever time it closes now!' he laughs.

'It stayed open until the last person managed to slither themselves out the door. Those days were special.'

Hangovers and partying aside, winning Bathurst changed Murphy's life.

'It was massive. I vividly recall the phone lighting up afterwards and people wanting to talk to you and give you that time in the papers and on the television,' says Murphy.

'It does change pretty much everything because it gives you recognition that maybe you didn't have before. All of a sudden, every media outlet in New Zealand wants to talk to you and give you time and tell your story.

'Everybody over here (in New Zealand) knows what

Bathurst is. It's a big deal. That prize title is something that so many people aspire to; not many get to hold that trophy.'

Further wins in 1999 (in a Wynn's-sponsored, Gibson Motor Sport Commodore with Steve Richards) and 2003 and 2004 (both times in a Kmart-backed Commodore with Rick Kelly) cemented Murphy's place in Bathurst history.

But he's also featured in some of the Mountain's most controversial modern moments, vision of which regularly gets replayed when the annual Great Race at the Mountain comes around again.

In 2002 he was forced to sit in pit lane and serve a five-minute penalty after his Kmart team allowed his car to leave its pit bay with the fuel hose still attached. It had sent his pit crew scattering and fuel spilling all over the road, creating a potentially dangerous situation: thankfully it didn't ignite.

Murphy was incensed by the massive penalty – which effectively removed him and co-driver Todd Kelly from race-winning contention. He flew into pit lane and parked up his Commodore as officials started their stopwatches.

Then he flung open the door to clamber out, remonstrated with team manager Rob Crawford and, with time on his hands, stormed off to a port-a-loo within the team's garage.

But the Murphy footage that is more commonly replayed is his face-to-face stoush with Marcos Ambrose after the two collided in the closing stages of the 2005 race. The pair had a history of verbal stoushes (most notably in a combative post-race press conference on the Gold Coast the previous year) and they had carried it on at Mount Panorama.

The pair crashed on the approach to the Cutting while battling over fourth place on a late-race restart. This triggered a fiery confrontation – the culmination of a rivalry that had been simmering in the background of the regular Holden versus Ford battle.

'It was just one of those pig-headed moments where he wasn't going to give in and I didn't give in,' Murphy reflects.

'He had his nose ahead but there was no pass completed. I've always been quite open about the fact that I believe we both contributed to it and I always was happy to take 50 percent of the blame for it because it was a goddamned mess.

'If I had my time again and I could bloody go and repeat it, knowing what has happened, you probably would bail out of it.

'It's not like it was a great moment of my life and career, and not for him either. It just added fuel to the fire that was already burning between us.

'The other thing is there were a lot of other people caught up that didn't deserve to be caught up in our shit that blocked the track, and damage was done to other cars – all that kind of thing.

'I didn't want that to happen, and it was almost a little embarrassing.'

Murphy continued to challenge the Mountain in the years following and came close to a fifth win on numerous occasions. He finished fourth in 2007, with countryman Jason Richards for Tasman Motorsport, and second – again with Richards – in 2008, before finishing fourth with Mark Skaife for Tasman in 2009.

A podium finish in 2011 in a Pepsi Commodore for Kelly Racing, alongside Dane Allan Simonsen, marked Murphy's eighth trip to the podium at Mount Panorama.

His last start as a full-time driver came in 2012 and he spent two more years co-driving for the Holden Racing Team in a Commodore with James Courtney before electing to take up an opportunity to work as a pit lane reporter on Supercars' television coverage in 2015.

Long-time sponsor Peter Adderton lured Murphy back to Bathurst in 2022, for a wildcard entry postponed 12 months by COVID and border closures. For this, his 23rd and final Great Race start, Murphy and countryman Richie Stanaway finished a very creditable 11th. It was a nice way to end to his Bathurst career.

*Murphy always wore his heart on his sleeve at Bathurst; here, he and co-driver Rick Kelly celebrate their win in the 2003 race. Great Race legend and sponsor Bob Jane (far left) and Channel 10 commentator Mark Oastler (far right) watch on.*

Following in the wheel tracks of Murphy have been a brace of fast Kiwis who have gone on to become Supercars Championship race winners.

Of those, Scott McLaughlin and Shane van Gisbergen have joined Murphy on the honour roll of Bathurst 1000 winners. They have gone a step further than him by also becoming Supercars Champions.

McLaughlin burst onto the scene when he entered Supercars full-time in 2013 with Garry Rogers Motorsport, and became a fan favourite on the back of a three-year period racing Volvos for the team between 2014 and 2016.

Accidentally dropping an 'f-bomb' in Adelaide in 2014 in a post-race TV interview after a gripping last lap duel with Jamie Whincup endeared the young Kiwi to Supercars fans and his star continued to rise.

He hit his career sweet spot when he joined DJR Team Penske in 2017 – a powerhouse created by American racing and business dynamo Roger Penske's purchase of a majority share of Dick Johnson's famous team in late 2014 – and won the championship three times in a row from 2018 to 2020 before being taken to the United States in 2021 to take on a new challenge with Penske in the high-speed world of IndyCar racing.

But his win in 2019 at Bathurst ticked the box he desperately wanted to tick in his Supercars career. Paired with Frenchman Alex Prémat, McLaughlin fought off van Gisbergen in a last lap dash to the chequered flag to break a 25-year Bathurst 1000 winning drought for the team and its famous #17 Ford.

So excited was McLaughlin at finally winning the race on his eighth attempt that after he crossed the line he took his post-race in-car celebrations just a little too far.

'I bent the steering wheel when I hit the wheel and had to have it changed for the next round on the Gold Coast!' he said on my podcast in 2020.

'That whole weekend was such an emotional roller coaster.'

The van Gisbergen and McLaughlin battle in the closing laps at Bathurst in 2019 is but one of their numerous on-track tussles over the years. Driving for two high-powered teams at a peak in their careers – the former for the Red Bull-backed, Triple Eight Holden team and the latter for the Shell-backed DJR Team Penske Ford team – the duo often found themselves going head to head for victories on race tracks around Australia, as well as their native New Zealand.

In the case of van Gisbergen, he had to wait until the following year, 2020, to finally break through and win at Bathurst in his 14th start in the race.

Of all the years to win his first, that was the Great Race that took place with a bare-bones minimal crowd due to COVID restrictions, robbing 'SVG' of his opportunity for a full 'first-time Bathurst winner' experience.

Instead of the thousands of cheering fans below the podium for the traditional spraying of champagne and presentation of the Peter Brock Trophy, he and winning partner Garth Tander were greeted by a much smaller gathering of mainly race team personnel – thanks to the limits on crowds and where they could move around the venue.

'The car just got better and better throughout the day and the last couple of stints were really cool to drive,' he said afterwards.

'I've had some bad runs at Bathurst in the past, and today was all about making no mistakes. I made sure I capitalised when it rained – I got to the front and never let go of it.'

Van Gisbergen burst onto the Supercars scene as a 17-year-old in 2007. He was signed by Ross and Jim Stone – the heads of the Stone Brothers Racing Ford team that had won three championships in the mid-2000s with Marcos Ambrose and Russell Ingall. They saw something special in van Gisbergen's ability behind the wheel, even from such a young age.

He made a controversial jump to Holden team TEKNO Autosports for 2013 after a very short-lived retirement from Supercars in late 2012, and was signed by Triple Eight Race Engineering to join the dynamic Brisbane-based, Red Bull-backed team in 2016.

By 2022 he had hit the peak of his powers and teamed with Tander to clinch victory once again at Bathurst, the 36th and last win for a Holden in the Great Race. The same year he also won his third Supercars Championship crown.

The Kiwi brothers who gave van Gisbergen his big Supercars break, Ross and Jim Stone, were inducted into the Supercars Hall of Fame in 2016.

They too sit in the special club of Kiwi conquerors of the Mountain. Electing to leave Dick Johnson Racing at the end of 1995, they made the move in 1996 to start up their own Ford-backed team in partnership with 1980 Formula 1 World Champion Alan Jones.

The brothers bought out Jones after two years and rebranded the team as Stone Brothers Racing, winning Bathurst in 1998 with Jason Bright and Steve Richards aboard one of their Ford Falcon V8s.

Despite winning three V8 Supercar Championships with Marcos Ambrose (2003, 2004) and Russell Ingall (2005), the team ultimately didn't add to its Bathurst win count before the brothers sold out to Betty Klimenko at the end of 2012 and the team morphed into Erebus Motorsport.

However, its successful Queensland-based workshop did score further Bathurst wins via its customer engine program: SBR-built and supplied Ford V8s powered Craig Lowndes and Jamie Whincup's Triple Eight Falcons to victory in each of their winning 'three-peat' years from 2006 to 2008.

The Stones' link to the Bathurst 1000 continues via Jim's son Matt, who runs a two-car team under the Matt Stone Racing banner in the Supercars Championship.

Other Kiwis have challenged the Mountain and come close to conquering it.

Two-time FIA Touring Car World Cup winner Paul Radisich was an open-wheeler ace who became a star during the halcyon days of the British Touring Car Championship's Super Touring era of the 1990s. As a factory driver for Ford and later Peugeot, he was a world-renowned gun steerer, however Mount Panorama never quite rewarded him.

He finished runner-up in a Dick Johnson Racing Sierra in 1990 alongside Brit Jeff Allam and again finished second in a DJR-run Falcon in 2000 alongside Jason Bright.

Radisich and Steve Ellery had dominated the 1999 race, also at the wheel of one of DJR's Shell Helix Falcons, its engine power giving it a major advantage up and down the long straights at Mount Panorama.

The duo led 98 of the 161 laps of the race, but a late race clash while lapping a slower car ripped the valve out of the Falcon's front-right tyre and forced the Kiwi to pit.

Then, entering pit lane, he speared off into the sand, ripping apart the AU Falcon's flimsy front spoiler. Reportedly, the damaged front bumper had split a radiator hose and the car expired a short time after, leaving Radisich to park trackside and pass the time feeding local horses on a Mountain Straight property.

But the Kiwi is adamant that, while the race was a 'Bathurst that got away', his Ford was probably doomed to failure from the start.

'I don't think we would've got to the end anyway,' says Radisich.

'Whatever happened, the engine did expire. The chances are, without the puncture, it probably would've happened with five laps to go.'

The Mountain proved even crueller to Radisich in 2006. He suffered severe injuries in a crash at the exit of the Chase. Bumped off the road by another car, his Team Kiwi Racing Holden Commodore smashed head-on into an earth-filled tyre barrier. The car rolled onto its side, leaving 'The Rat' with a broken sternum and ankle. Race officials had to cut the roof from the car so he could be extracted.

He recovered from his injuries to return to racing partway through 2007. The following year the throttle jammed on the HSV Dealer Team Commodore he was driving at Bathurst. It sent him off the track at McPhillamy Park and, once more, cannoning into a wall.

The front of the car smashed into the concrete and again the Kiwi was carted away from Bathurst in an ambulance, this time with a fractured ankle, foot and vertebrae, cracked ribs, bruised lungs and a re-opening of the fractured sternum he'd sustained in 2006. Radisich's Bathurst 1000 career ended in an instant. The injuries took a few years to get over.

'Not so much mentally but physically. I shattered all my feet and legs and it went right up to the vertebrae in my neck, so they had to rebuild me!' he says.

Of all the Kiwis to come close to conquering the Bathurst 1000, Jason Richards' is the saddest of stories.

After a period as a BMW factory driver in his homeland in the late 1990s, Richards hit the V8 Supercars scene in Australia in 2000 with the ambitious Team Kiwi Racing, at the wheel of an all-black Commodore.

He quickly earned a reputation for being fast and, as he moved teams and stepped into cars more capable of better results in the following years, the native of Nelson in New Zealand was able to shine.

But of all the places he shone, he shone brightest at Bathurst.

Richards and a young Jamie Whincup paired in 2005 in a Tasman Motorsport Commodore to push the mighty factory Holden Racing Team all the way to the line, eventually finishing a narrow second behind winners Mark Skaife and Todd Kelly.

Richards and Greg Murphy finished fourth in 2007 for Tasman and stepped onto the podium in 2008 by finishing second. After Richards left to join Albury-based Brad Jones Racing, he again finished second at Bathurst – in 2009 – alongside Cameron McConville.

Those results confirmed that Richards clicked with the Mountain and a Bathurst 1000 win felt within reach.

But a month after competing in the 2010 Bathurst 1000 came news that rocked the Australasian motorsport scene back onto its heels – Richards had cancer.

Diagnosed with a rare and aggressive form of cancer called adrenocortical carcinoma, he was forced to stand down from his regular V8 Supercar duties to focus on treatment.

Richards was still able to compete in the occasional race in other cars and categories when his health and treatment allowed, however he was ruled out of being able to re-join BJR to race in the 2011 Bathurst 1000.

Despite being extremely ill, he somehow summoned the energy to race a Monaro in the supporting Touring Car Masters races for V8 muscle cars that weekend. His spirited drive in the Sunday morning support race just prior to the 1000-kilometre classic proved to be his last race.

Richards died that December, at the age of 35.

Inducted into the Supercars Hall of Fame posthumously in 2013, he remains part of his former team's annual campaign to finally win its first Bathurst 1000.

Brad Jones Racing, owned and run by former driver Brad Jones, has adopted Richards' 'JR star' logo since his death and carries it on the B-pillar of all the team's cars that tackle the Great Race each year. Among them is Richards' old entry, the #8 car – now driven by another fast Kiwi, Andre Heimgartner.

Team owner Jones and Richards scored nine Bathurst 1000 podium finishes between them during their racing careers without the ultimate success of winning the race.

However, should the team from Albury win the greatest race in the land and visit Victory Lane at Mount Panorama one day, there'll still be a little bit of Kiwi 'JR' flavour to the breakthrough success.

## A Chequered History

While the time-honoured game of chess has little in common with modern motorsport, chess boards did inspire the chequerboard design – alternating black and white squares – used to signal the completion of a race.

In the first two years of the Bathurst Great Race – 1963 and 1964 – officials communicated to drivers that the 500-mile race was over by holding up a wooden sign painted with the chequerboard design and bearing the word 'FINISH' in the middle.

Within two years, the board was replaced by the far more user-friendly flag. Barry Seton was first to take a chequered flag at the end of Bathurst's Great Race. He drove across the line in a Cortina GT500 he had shared with Midge Bosworth to claim overall victory. Every year since, officials waved home the field with the chequered flag.

# 15

# The Refugee Racer

**B**athurst 1000 competitors come from all sorts of backgrounds, but 1988 race winner Tomas Mezera's pathway to Great Race glory is unique given it includes time in an Austrian refugee camp.

A promising junior skier from Czechoslovakia, he hitchhiked to escape his communist-ruled homeland in 1979 at the age of 20, survived a prison-like refugee camp and wound up in, of all places, Australia.

Just nine years later he drove a Ford Sierra across the line at Mount Panorama to win the Bathurst 1000.

'I remember the Albanians and the Serbians having a huge fight in the refugee camp. They smuggled a machine gun into the camp, and it was like bloody open war there at some stage,' Mezera said on the V8 Sleuth Podcast in 2020.

'It was crazy. The people were going mad under those conditions being locked up.'

Born in 1958, Mezera grew up in Czechoslovakia behind the Iron Curtain. He developed into a talented young sportsman, playing tennis in summer and honing his skiing in winter. When it came time to pick, he opted for the latter.

'I felt well supported by the regime through my junior days to be a top skier with a view to go to the Olympics,' he says.

'I never got good enough to make the Olympics, but I was OK. At one stage I was 15 or 16 and I came second in the Czech slalom championship. If you were talented, you got the support from the government and that helped me. As I grew older, the skis were not fast enough, and I wanted to race cars. Unfortunately, racing cars under the communist regimes in Czechoslovakia was one of the sports that never was supported!

'I made a plan that if I wanted to become a Formula 1 driver, I wouldn't (be able) to do it from Czechoslovakia and that was the main reason why I decided to leave.

'My first race car was a Skoda my mate and I finished building for a hill climb. I won my first race and I thought, "That's fantastic. Here I am, Formula 1. I can't wait to get there."'

Mezera only ran the car for a few months. By August 1979 he was ready to 'do a runner' and seized upon a unique opportunity to do so.

As a junior Mezera had had a taste of the West: he'd attended pre-season skiing camps in Italy and Austria to train at their Alps and glaciers until the snow arrived for winter in his homeland.

'Fortunately a bit of an opportunity came up. That was the height of the summer and the most popular destination for a holiday was to go to Bulgaria – to go to the Black Sea.

'In the summer of '79 there was an issue with Romania, because they ran out of petrol and wouldn't sell it to tourists going to Bulgaria, so all of the Czech tourists were allowed to go through Yugoslavia.

'In those days, Yugoslavia was kind of like other Western countries: the regime wouldn't normally let you go there. But they made this exemption for a month through the summertime and, that was the opportunity to do a runner. Once you got to Yugoslavia, then it was quite easy to get to Austria – to the Western world.'

So Mezera caught a train and hitchhiked through Hungary and then waited.

For six hours.

'Some Germans finally pulled up in a Mercedes and they said, "Where are you going?"' recalls Mezera.

'They dropped me off about 50 kays out of Belgrade. It was already about eight o'clock at night, but still light, and the first truck I waved stopped. And I jumped in, and he took me to Belgrade.

'He said there was a student accommodation there. I was going to university in Czechoslovakia studying physics and had my little university card with me. I went to reception and said I was a student from Czechoslovakia, and they put me up for the night. The next day I was at the Austrian Embassy to ask for a visa to go to Austria and there was a queue 200 metres long of Czech people doing the same thing, taking the opportunity to do a runner!'

Once in Austria he was homeless, hungry, alone and had no money. Mezera ended up in the place he didn't really want to end up in – a refugee camp.

'I really didn't want to go to a refugee camp because it's not like a bloody holiday park,' he says.

'Suddenly I had no choice because – well, you have to eat. If it was the warmer months, you could sleep on the park benches with all of the other deros, but when it gets cold, the refugee camp was like the Hilton!'

Mezera immediately applied to go to America. When they told him it would take up to 36 months to get there, the thought of another three years in the refugee camp didn't sound appealing. South Africa and Australia were two other options he was presented with.

The land 'Down Under' became his next destination.

'At that time – in the summer of '79 – suddenly "AJ" (Alan Jones) started winning races in Formula 1 in the Williams,' recalls Mezera.

'So, I thought it maybe wasn't a bad thing to go to Australia, where he was from, and save up some money and go to England from there. So, two days before Christmas in '79, I arrived in Sydney.

'I had nothing when I got off the plane. I didn't even have any check-in luggage. I had a travel document the Australian Embassy gave me in Vienna with a refugee visa. Luckily, I had relatives in Sydney, and I didn't have to go through the camps there.'

From there Mezera set about making money to fund his racing dream. But his dream wasn't to race a Holden or Ford around Mount Panorama. He was all about Formula 1 and getting to England.

'Early in the morning I was on a garbage run starting at 4am; by 10am, I was in a panel shop painting cars; and I was a kitchenhand in a little restaurant in Kings Cross until about 10 o'clock at night washing dishes,' Mezera says.

He managed to save enough money to buy an old Formula Ford race car for $5000 in 1982. The car wasn't flash, but his skill shone through and by 1985 he'd gained the backing to win the Australian Formula Ford Championship and score his first Bathurst 1000 drive in a Toyota Supra, co-driving with its owner Peter Williamson. However, the Supra retired with engine problems before Mezera could get behind the wheel on race day.

Bathurst was still not on his radar long-term and Mezera headed overseas to chase his F1 dream. He finished second in the 1987 British Formula Ford Championship but quickly found himself out of money and unable to keep progressing up the ladder of the junior categories in the manner necessary to make it to Formula 1.

And that's what led to his second appearance in the Bathurst 1000 in 1988, a race that wrote his name into Australian motor racing history books forever.

Back in Australia, the Sydney-based JPS BMW team of long-time team manager and former driver Frank Gardner had shut up shop at the end of 1987. Gardner accepted a deal to run former team driver Tony Longhurst's new Ford Sierra team on the Gold Coast. But there was a problem, and that's where the British-based Mezera came into the equation: he scored himself a seat in what turned out to be a Bathurst-winning car.

'Frank was the one in 1987 that put the official protest in against the (first- and second place-finishing) Texaco Sierras at Bathurst,' recalls Mezera.

'He did it on behalf of BMW because BMW's Schnitzer team couldn't do it. They knew the Texaco cars were cheating but the Texaco team also knew the Schnitzer team was cheating! They knew too much on each other. BMW used Frank to protest and told him exactly what they (Ford) were fudging with.

'Suddenly, Frank loses the BMW deal, which goes to (Peter) Brock. Tony doesn't have a drive and gets a Ford Sierra (for 1988).

'But he and Frank couldn't get any parts for it because Frank had put the protest against them! Frank rings me in England and he says, "Oh, can you help us? We need to sort some stuff."'

Mezera knew Thomas Eggenberger, son of the Swiss Texaco team boss Ruedi. Eggenberger Jnr was racing Formula Ford in England and Mezera had previously helped him at the request of Van Diemen boss Ralph Firman. In short, the favour was returned and the access to parts opened up. And that paved the way for Tomas to share the Benson & Hedges-backed Sierra with regular driver/team owner Tony Longhurst for the Sandown and Bathurst races.

'When I first drove it at Lakeside during a test day I thought, "Geez, this thing is a shitbox!"' he says.

'It had so much turbo lag; it's heavy and it's undriveable. But I managed and it all worked out alright.'

It sure did – he and Longhurst won the Great Race at Bathurst.

'We never thought the car was going to last at Bathurst,' he recalls.

'That's why the plan was that I was going to do the last stint. Because they were 99 percent sure the car wouldn't be running by then!

'The Sierras were quick, but they were fragile. In the race – I remember in my stint – I kind of got a bit more comfortable. And I passed Larry [Perkins in a Commodore] and another Sierra and kept it in the top three all the time.

'I just nursed it home because we had a good lead. I was shifting gears at low revs and luckily the car lasted. And we ended up winning it.'

The Mountain resonated with Mezera and, though he remained focused on an international career for the next few years, the one-time refugee returned every year through to his 18th and final Bathurst 1000 start in 2004.

He drove with Holden legend Larry Perkins for three years from 1989 to 1991 before picking up the deal as the lead driver for the official factory Holden Racing Team in 1992.

In that role he gained a high-profile teammate in former World Motorcycle Champion Wayne Gardner in 1993 and then superstar Peter Brock – as teammate and endurance partner – across 1994 and 1995.

Mezera was shown the door by the Holden Racing Team in late 1995 in favour of young star Craig Lowndes (though he did return to co-drive with Brock in the 1996 endurance races) and he decided to set up his own V8 Supercar team in 1998 with a brand-new Commodore race car.

His first choice of co-driver for his team's first Bathurst was bold: then-Ferrari F1 driver Eddie Irvine, who was Michael Schumacher's teammate at the time. Irvine and Mezera had history: the former had beaten the latter to the 1987 British Formula Ford Championship.

'Eddie was dead set going to do it, but Ferrari wouldn't let him!' says Mezera.

'He came to Bathurst that year to watch the race anyway. I told him, "It's a shitbox, it's not a winning car. But it would help me to attract sponsors and get it off the ground."

'Eddie couldn't do it so I rang Alain (Swiss driver Alain Menu, the 1997 British Touring Car Champion for Williams Renault) and he did it for a holiday at Hamilton Island!'

Funds for the new team were low and Mezera couldn't afford the latest and greatest triple plate clutch. The unit in the car burnt out on the grid and the car didn't complete a single race lap.

Running his own team simply got too hard, due to a lack of sponsorship funding, so then Mezera became a gun for hire. He co-drove at Bathurst with former HRT teammate Brad Jones in a Falcon in 2000 and later returned to both the HRT and Perkins' squad at the Mountain.

He made his last Bathurst 1000 start in 2004 alongside privateer Anthony Tratt in a Perkins-run V8 Commodore.

His Czech accent and straightforward 'tell it how it is' style have endeared him to Aussie racing fans for years. For a time he served as the Driving Standards Observer for the V8 Supercars Championship, including at the Bathurst 1000, and has translated his sporting skill into becoming a semi-pro golfer on the PGA Seniors Tour.

Tomas Mezera's Bathurst story is perhaps the most unlikely of all Bathurst stories. It exemplifies the resilience of the drivers who forged long careers contesting the Mountain's most formidable race.

## Gridding Them Up

The first seven times the Great Race was run at Bathurst the field lined up in a grid format that by today's standards is strange.

For the inaugural Armstrong 500 – held at Mount Panorama in 1963 – a 3-2-3 grid format was used. Three cars shared the front row of the grid, then there were two cars on the second row, three on the third and so on.

A more traditional format of two cars per row of the grid was adopted in 1970 and, except for 1988 when a rolling start was used, this practice has stayed in place. In 2007 the format was modified slightly so that each row of cars on the grid lined up directly behind the row of cars in front of it.

## In The Blink of an Eye

Steve Richards snatched pole position at Bathurst in 2004 with a dazzling performance at the wheel of one of Larry Perkins' Castrol Commodores. But it was the margin on the stopwatch that was the real standout.

For his one-lap dash around the Mount Panorama circuit he stopped the clocks at 2 minutes 07.9611 seconds, a mindbogglingly mere 0.0012-seconds faster than fellow Holden driver Jason Bright's PWR Racing Commodore.

The margin remains the closest pole-winning margin in Bathurst 1000 history, though it was of little consequence for Richards and his co-driver – father, Jim – on race day.

The latter was at the wheel of their car when it collided with an errant kangaroo in the race, prompting a long visit to the pits to patch up the damage. They eventually re-joined the race and finished 21st, 13 laps behind the leaders.

# 16

# The Kid

If Peter Brock is the King of the Mountain, 'The Kid' Craig Lowndes is most certainly the crown prince.

A now seven-time Bathurst 1000 winner, Lowndes is the people's champion of the Supercars era of the sport at Mount Panorama; he took up where Brock left off.

Lowndes' gleaming smile and fan-first approach to racing have allowed him to transcend the sport just as Brock did, in a way few before or since have been able to match.

Born 29 years apart, they both grew up in the same region on the outskirts of Melbourne, went to school at Hurstbridge High School and played Aussie Rules football for the same Diamond Creek Football Club.

Lowndes' dad Frank was a mechanic for the Harry Firth-run Holden Dealer Team and was there working on the team's Monaros when Brock debuted at Bathurst in 1969. He was still with the team when Brock won the race for the first time three years later in a Torana XU-1.

However, despite these constant comparisons, Lowndes has carved his own groove into Mount Panorama, without getting stuck in the slipstream of Brock's sparkling Bathurst career.

His first opportunity to tackle the famous track in its most famous race came in 1994 after a mid-season phone call from Holden Racing Team manager Jeff Grech, supported by Brock's then teammate Tomas Mezera.

'Lowndes was doing alright in Formula Ford and "Hog" (Grech) and I always watched Formula Ford racing,' says Mezera, who won the 1985 Australian national series in the junior open-wheeler category.

'If you can win in Formula Ford, you can win in any category once you've (got) comfortable in the car. We sat down and went to (HRT and Holden Special Vehicles boss) John Crennan and said, "How about when we go testing, we take him with us and put him in the car? He's going to be good one day." That's where it all started.'

The team took Lowndes testing and had him do run-of-the-mill work, bedding in new brakes and running in new gearboxes. But they saw enough to know he had something special and named him on standby to drive the team's second car in the Sandown and Bathurst endurances races.

Swedish driver Rickard Rydell (who won Bathurst four years later in a Volvo but in 1994 was in his debut season in the British Touring Car Championship, driving a Volvo wagon of all things) had been signed to drive at these races. But his wife was due to give birth and he opted to stay home, opening the door for Lowndes to co-drive the second HRT Commodore – with Brad Jones at Sandown.

It went so well the team elected to leave him in the car for Bathurst, where his debut in the Great Race came with Brock on the other side of the team's garage, sharing the high-profile #05 Commodore with Mezera.

Lowndes' only Bathurst racing experience had come

earlier that year at Easter, when he shared a Nissan Pulsar SSS in the 12 Hour production car race. But by the time the 1994 Tooheys 1000 at Bathurst was over, everyone knew his name.

Lowndes' last stint joust against the far more experienced John Bowe (driving Dick Johnson's Shell-FAI Falcon) is lauded as the moment that elevated him to the national sporting conscience.

But the reality is he had done nearly everything wrong leading up to that point.

He crashed the car in the slippery Sunday morning warm-up prior to the race and later survived a massive spin on top of the Mountain mid-race that flat-spotted all four tyres and forced him to the pits for an unscheduled stop for a new set of tyres.

That left Brad Jones to turn in an amazing double-stint to drag their car back onto the lead lap and into contention, though the experienced Albury racer had to hand over to Lowndes for the final stint as he was approaching the maximum allowed driving time.

No one gave Lowndes a chance against Bowe. A seasoned pro, he'd been crowned Australian Drivers' Champion in the mid-1980s, when Lowndes was still in primary school. Everyone expected Bowe to ease ahead of the rookie and waltz to the line to win the race and enjoy a $100,000 payday.

But then came a move that would be immortalised in Bathurst history.

Climbing Mountain Straight on lap 148, Lowndes' #015 Commodore was tucked firmly up behind the rear wing of the yellow #17 Falcon. Lowndes was throwing everything he could muster to stay within striking distance of the leading car.

Bowe inched towards the inside line to protect himself from being passed by the young gun's Holden, however Lowndes simply positioned himself on the outside and sailed straight around Bowe in a gob-smacking manoeuvre.

The roar of Holden fans said it all.

A new Bathurst hero had just been born.

'I asked Bowey many years later about that whole exchange,' Lowndes told me on the V8 Sleuth Podcast in 2022.

'I still reckon he braked early because he was on the inside on the dirty line and I did brake later than I ever had (that weekend); it just happened to work, because I actually turned the corner instead of being into the tyres (on the outside of the track).

'But we were running out of fuel, so once Bowey got back past me our fuel light had come on. What I didn't know was that Bowey was in the same situation with fuel. He said he was half a lap away from yielding (the lead) because of his fuel problem, not realising I had the same issue! I could have almost ended up winning the first (Bathurst) race.'

Ultimately Lowndes had to back off to conserve fuel and ensure he would make it to the chequered flag, but the runner-up position was enough to prove he was a rare talent.

It was just the start of one of the most successful Bathurst 1000 careers in history.

Lowndes returned to the Mountain in 1995 and grabbed pole position, becoming the youngest driver in the race's history to do so. However, his HRT Commodore – and indeed the sister

Brock/Mezera car – had a terminal engine issue that dropped it out of the race within just 10 laps.

By 1996 he had replaced Mezera in the full-time Holden Racing Team line-up and the season turned into a major success story. Lowndes won the Australian Touring Car Championship and then won the Sandown 500 in partnership with Kiwi Greg Murphy, creating a blueprint for other teams to follow in terms of investing in young drivers at a time when plenty of seats were filled by team owner/drivers in their 30s and 40s.

That led on to Lowndes and Murphy teaming up to clinch their first Bathurst 1000 win, leading 129 of the 161 laps to give the factory Holden team its first Great Race win in six years.

'I still classify that car as the best race car I ever had in that era,' says Lowndes of his 1996 Bathurst-winning Commodore VR.

'Everything worked for it, we had the benefits of Bridgestone tyres; different compounds, different constructions, everything we wanted we got.'

But unbelievably it took a whole decade, until 2006, for Lowndes to taste glory at the Mountain for the second time.

Bathurst delivered plenty of 'what could have been' results for him in the years that followed.

He crashed out in 1997 at the top of the Mountain at the wheel of the HRT Commodore he shared with Murphy, and in 1998 he and Mark Skaife were dominating the race until a tyre blow-out landed Skaife in the sand trap at the Chase. They finished sixth after Lowndes also had a tyre explode at McPhillamy Park.

Second place in 1999 alongside Cameron McConville clinched Lowndes his third (and ultimately last) V8 Supercar Championship crown, then he and Skaife paired up again in 2000 to come home sixth in Lowndes' last Bathurst with the Holden Racing Team. They'd been running in the lead pack until Skaife was involved in a fracas with a lapped car driven by British touring car racer Matt Neal.

Lowndes made a highly publicised move to Ford for 2001, however his winless streak at Bathurst continued.

Pushing hard mid-race in the lead, he skated off the road on a slippery track aboard the Falcon he shared with Neil Crompton and became wedged in the wall at Forrest's Elbow; they eventually finished 17th.

Debris that blocked their Falcon's air intake cooked the engine in 2002, while Lowndes was running strongly, however his switch from 00 Motorsport to Ford Performance Racing delivered him back-to-back second places in 2003 and 2004 alongside Glenn Seton.

But their FPR Falcon lacked the outright speed of its rivals to really challenge for victory, a problem that was rectified by Lowndes making the move to the Queensland-based Triple Eight Race Engineering to drive one of its Betta Electrical-backed Falcons in 2005.

He took pole position for that year's race and led the early stages before he made an early error and slapped the rear of the car on a concrete wall. The contact busted the Watt's Linkage in the rear of his car and prompted a pit stop for repairs that dropped him down to 29th place.

But that was nothing compared to what happened a little later, once the car re-joined the track, when an errant wheel and tyre – bouncing down the road from the crashed Castrol

Commodore of Paul Dumbrell – hurtled into the windscreen of the Lowndes-driven Falcon on the exit of Griffins Bend. Thankfully its pilot was uninjured, and the team cut out the damaged windscreen, leaving Lowndes and Frenchman Yvan Muller with a very airy afternoon – minus front and rear windscreens – and an eventual 15th position.

The 2006 Bathurst 1000 remains one of the most emotional in the history of the race and perhaps the most revered of all of Lowndes' Bathurst wins.

The death a month prior of his former teammate Peter Brock had rocked the sport – and indeed the nation – to its very core, so that year's race became the ultimate Brock tribute. It was must-see and must-attend stuff.

Everywhere you turned there was something Brock. Holden provided a special silver Commodore for fans to sign – essentially a condolences book on wheels – thousands of fans had signed the Brock's Skyline wall at the top of Mount Panorama and a new Peter Brock Trophy had been created in honour of the nine-time winner.

His Bathurst-winning cars were on hand and Lowndes was given permission by Ford to drive the 1972 race-winning Torana XU-1 as part of the pre-race build-up in a parade of the legendary machines.

The minute's silence that followed the parade brought the Mountain to a standstill.

'There was not a bird chirping,' recalls Lowndes, who couldn't stop the tears from flowing down his cheeks on that emotional day in 2006.

'It was eerily silent.'

The lead-up may have been eerily silent but the race was full on.

Lowndes and new teammate Jamie Whincup started sixth, though they didn't have to worry about beating home the two cars that started up front. Pole man Mark Skaife's HRT Commodore suffered clutch failure from the start and lasted a quarter of a lap before it was rammed into retirement by the unsighted Jack Perkins, while the front-row starting FPR Falcon of Jason Bright lasted just 28 laps before its engine failed.

Whincup put the duo's #888 Falcon into the lead when he made a surprise attack on Todd Kelly at Hell Corner on a lap 110 restart, and Lowndes was able to finish off the job and hold off Todd's co-driver, brother Rick, in the final stint to sweep home to an emotional victory by a heart-stopping 0.5868-seconds.

Lowndes' Bathurst winning drought was over in the most amazing and emotional of ways and his tears on the podium underlined the sheer importance of the win.

'Jamie was still semi a rookie. I remember him being on the podium; I don't think he appreciated at that point or time how big it was for me,' says Lowndes, who carried a sticker, 'Brock Always With Us', on the visor of his helmet during the race that day.

'Jamie and I grew up in the same go-kart club a suburb apart: he was in Greensborough, I was in Plenty, his uncle (Graeme) used to race, so for Jamie he was still just trying to win races and probably didn't understand the emotional side of things going on.

'In hindsight it probably was a good thing he wasn't thinking about that. He was focused on just the race car and doing fast laps.'

Lowndes' Bathurst win drought may have lasted a decade, but the floodgates then opened as he and Whincup kept rolling on and won again in 2007 and 2008.

The 2007 win had come despite a few near misses. Lowndes buckled a wheel rim with an early race clash with Steven Johnson, but managed to get away with it, and Whincup had escaped making a crucial error entering the pits for the final pit stop to hand over to Lowndes.

'I was standing in the pit lane waiting for him to come, thinking "Where in the hell are you?" and I look up at the big screen and he'd been off in the sand trap on the way into the pits!' laughs Lowndes.

A heart-stopping last stint of the race saw Lowndes see off Johnson, James Courtney and Greg Murphy as the field tippy-toed around the Mountain in wet and greasy conditions on the limit of adhesion.

'That was a great battle in the wet because we were all on slicks and sliding around everywhere all trying to find traction,' Lowndes recalls.

He and Whincup completed their trifecta of wins in 2008 by winning the Bathurst 1000 again, leading 109 of the 161 laps on their way to victory in the year that Whincup won his first V8 Supercar Championship.

They tried to make it four in a row but fell short in 2009, when they came home fifth.

Lowndes' Triple Eight team made headlines in mid-2009 when it announced it would swap from racing Ford Falcons to Holden Commodores for 2010.

The move brought Lowndes back to the Mountain, racing a Holden for the first time in a decade, and reunited him with Mark Skaife, his partner from his most recent Bathurst assault in a Commodore in 2000.

By then Skaife had retired from full-time V8 Supercar racing, though the five-time champion was still doing the endurance races in and around his television commentary commitments.

The pathway for him and Lowndes to reunite had come via a rule change in 2010 for the endurance races, including Bathurst: teams were now prevented from pairing together their regular full-time drivers – in Triple Eight's case, Lowndes and Whincup – in the same car.

The reunification of Lowndes and Skaife worked perfectly and they won the Phillip Island 500 and Bathurst 1000 endurance race double, giving Lowndes four Bathurst wins in the space of five years.

A mid-race injury to Skaife at Bathurst – where he popped a rib out during one of his driving stints – meant Lowndes had to drive a marathon triple-stint from lap 82 right through to the end of the 161-lap race, a 79-lap trek to the Peter Brock Trophy.

'It was a fantastic drive. It will go down as one of his best drives ever,' said Skaife post-race.

'It is one of those special occasions. I think that the most laps I have done in a stint at Bathurst is about 70 – when the fuel consumption was lower and the stints were longer.

'I know that when you are in the realm of driving that long, especially around a place like Bathurst, is very, very hard. It is difficult to concentrate that hard, but it is actually more of a mental exercise than it is a physical one.

'His drive was Brock-esque.'

Lowndes and Skaife returned for another crack at the Mountain in 2011 but fell just short, pipped at the post by the HRT car of Garth Tander and rookie Nick Percat.

Warren Luff became Lowndes' Bathurst co-driver in the wake of Skaife stepping back from racing V8 Supercars, and he and Lowndes finished third in 2012 and 2013.

These results meant that Lowndes had finished on the podium in nine of the 11 Bathurst 1000s held from 2003 to 2013, a simply stunning run of success.

While his teammate Jamie Whincup had taken over the mantle as Triple Eight's main strike weapon and racked up multiple V8 Supercar Championship wins, Lowndes remained a contender at Bathurst every year and carried away more wins at the Mountain than his teammate.

He and Steve Richards paired up to win the 2015 race and they repeated the dose in 2018 with another win.

The latter came a few months after Lowndes had made an emotional announcement in Townsville that he was to retire from full-time Supercars racing at the end of that year.

Power steering problems in the lead-up to the race were solved in the nick of time and The Kid was in the perfect position mid-race, shadowing leader David Reynolds, when the Erebus driver fell victim to cramps in the cockpit. Forced to slow, Reynolds could only watch as Lowndes seized the lead and never gave it back, clinching his seventh Bathurst 1000 win.

'It's almost like '06 back again,' he said later.

'I just wanted to enjoy that last lap. I really cruised and enjoyed it for what it was, watching the crowd right across the top of the Mountain.'

Since then, Lowndes has remained on Triple Eight's books as an endurance driver for the annual long-distance races, including Bathurst.

He paired with Whincup to finish fourth in 2019 and 2021 and led a Supercheap Auto-backed, Triple Eight-run wildcard entry alongside rookie co-driver Declan Fraser in 2022.

Despite not having raced a Supercar in nearly a year, Lowndes demonstrated that experience still counts for plenty. They came home a highly competitive eighth, a result that now sits as the best by a wildcard team in the Bathurst 1000.

Inducted into the Supercars Hall of Fame in December 2022, at the time of writing, Lowndes has a date with the Mountain for its 60th anniversary Great Race in October 2023.

It will mark his 30th start in the race; only fellow seven-time winner Jim Richards (35) and Peter Brock (32) have more.

Lowndes is forever part of the history of the Bathurst 1000. His seven wins in the race have come, it could be argued, in a more competitive era than those of Brock's nine.

Whatever the case, 16 wins between the lads from the Diamond Creek Football Club isn't a bad result.

## Marathon Men

Seven-time Bathurst 1000 winner Jim Richards holds the record for most Bathurst Great Race starts – 35.

He competed in both the Super Touring and V8 Supercars races held in 1997 and 1998, meaning his 35 starts came across 33 years of competition at Bathurst, since his first appearance in 1974.

Peter Brock has the next most starts (32, including both races in 1997), though Craig Lowndes is catching them both: he started his 29th race in 2022 as a wildcard.

1969 winner Colin Bond and 1966 winner Bob Holden sit next on the leader board, with 28 starts each, and Steve Richards is narrowly behind on 27; his most recent appearance was in 2019, co-driving with Mark Winterbottom.

# 17

# Against the Clock

As much as it may seem that there's just one race at the Bathurst 1000 – on the Sunday – there's a secondary one that has generated its fair share of drama and emotion over the years: the race to take pole position for the Great Race.

At the very heart of the pathway to pole position at Bathurst is the traditional Top 10 Shootout for the coveted prime starting spot. That one solo lap of the track – a mere two minutes at the wheel, give or take – offers the 10 fastest drivers from qualifying a chance for the best drivers to measure where they want to float on the scale of risk versus reward.

Push too hard and crash, and they risk catastrophic damage to their car less than 24 hours prior to race start. Don't push hard enough, and they risk other drivers taking the glory, prize money and headlines in Sunday morning's newspaper.

Glenn Seton knows all too well how important the Bathurst 1000's Top 10 Shootout is. On two occasions, both driving V8 Falcons built and developed by his own team, he earned the right to the plum position on the starting grid.

He pipped Peter Brock for pole in 1994 and knocked off Craig Lowndes for pole two years later.

Seton was so fired up and focused to set a fast time in 1996 that he overlooked a small, yet very important pre-lap preparation detail – he forgot to do up his helmet! For those watching his every move as he muscled his red, white and blue #30 Falcon to pole position, the flapping chin strap was there for all TV viewers to see on the Channel 7 RaceCam.

'To do a Top 10 Shootout – where you're the only person on the track – and nail a great lap; look at the dash and see what time you've done, knowing what your opposition had already done; and to twice achieve pole position – and see the crowd celebrate with you – the feeling you get inside is just unbelievable,' he says.

'Nothing else has given me that reward in motor racing in my life.'

The grid for the annual Mount Panorama classic was set in order of classes for its first four years until practice times determined the starting order for the first time in 1967.

But a further twist was added in 1978 with the introduction on the Friday afternoon of 'Hardie Trophy Qualifying' – what was later dubbed 'Hardies Heroes' and more commonly known as the Top 10 Shootout in the modern era.

It was a made-for-television session inspired by the format used for qualifying at the Indianapolis 500 in the United States, where each car was given four consecutive laps running solo to record a qualifying time.

The new format gave the fastest cars the opportunity to tackle the Mountain one at a time for one flying lap to determine who would sit on pole position for Sunday morning's race start.

Traditionalists weren't fans of the new format, but it has since become a locked-in part of the Bathurst 1000's event schedule; it's been that way for more than 40 years.

At the time of its introduction it came with plenty of trimmings too: national television coverage that was perfect exposure for team sponsors, a boost in prizemoney (pole position was worth $2250 in 1977 but jumped to $8000 for 1978) and bragging rights for the driver who could lap the six-plus kilometre Mountain fastest of all.

In fact, drivers didn't just get one lap against the clock. They had a safety net of a second separate run, giving them two opportunities to nail the perfect lap. This two-lap format disappeared in 1986. To this day drivers are given one single opportunity to turn the fastest lap they can deliver.

The first Shootout at Bathurst was held on the Friday in 1978 and was taken out by Peter Brock in his Holden Dealer Team Torana A9X, the V8 muscle car propelling its pilot around the Mountain in 2m20.006-seconds – eight-tenths faster than the XC Falcon of his former HDT teammate, Colin Bond.

Brock repeated the dose in 1979 and again topped the Shootout session (which had been moved to Saturday morning), however that year's 'Hardies Heroes' came with some controversy as his HDT teammate John Harvey, who was 10th fastest in regular qualifying, was booted from the line-up and not included in the battle for pole position.

At that time the fastest eight cars from qualifying were guaranteed a spot in the 10-car Shootout, with two spots to be given at the discretion of then-race organisers, the ARDC (Australian Racing Drivers' Club). The discretionary spots allowed them to give star drivers a free ride through to the Saturday morning session should they encounter unexpected problems on Friday that left them with a time too slow to qualify in the top 10.

Harvey was booted in favour of 22nd-fastest Allan Moffat, the Ford hero deemed worthy of a spot. Reigning Australian Touring Car Champion Bob Morris (who had qualified 13th) was also added to the line-up.

Race day proved that it really didn't matter. Brock won by a record six laps. As for Harvey, Moffat and Morris: not one of them finished the 1000-kilometre race.

Weather conditions have generally proven to be fine, if not sunny, for the Shootout. That's no surprise, given the Bathurst event has largely been run in October.

But on some occasions rain has been added to the mix to make some amazing moments in Great Race history.

The first wet Shootout was in 1981, however the wet track didn't dissuade 1974 Bathurst winner Kevin Bartlett from attacking the Mountain in his Channel 9 and Kerry Packer-backed Chevrolet Camaro.

The long-time open-wheeler ace splashed and slid his way around Bathurst's famous circuit and sealed pole position by a solid 2.38-seconds over Dick Johnson's Tru-Blu Falcon XD.

It's a performance that has stuck in the memory banks of Bathurst aficionados for years since.

It took until 2000 for wet weather to again affect a Top 10 Shootout at Mount Panorama. On that occasion, 1987 500cc World Motorcycle Champion Wayne Gardner splashed his way to pole driving one of Glenn Seton's Ford Tickford Racing Falcons.

Accustomed to putting his body on the line – with no roof, doors or roll bars – on a high-powered Grand Prix motorcycle before he made the full-time switch to racing touring cars, Gardner was in his element in the wet conditions.

The slippery tarmac caught out three of the 10 drivers. Todd Kelly, Russell Ingall and Garth Tander all slipped off at the Chase, however all were at least able to plough through the wet grass, scamper back onto the track and complete their lap. Tander had the last laugh though: he and co-driver Jason Bargwanna started 10th and went on to win the race the following day.

Sprinkles of rain slowed some of the early runners in the 2005 Bathurst Top 10 Shootout and heavier rain slowed some of the big guns – Tander, Mark Winterbottom and Jamie Whincup – late in the Shootout in 2011, but 2015 was the next all-wet Shootout. It delivered a maiden Bathurst 1000 pole for the clown prince of V8 Supercars on a weekend his wisecracks landed him in hot water.

David Reynolds had been in, out and back in a full-time seat in the V8 Supercars Championship but by 2015 had found a happy home at Prodrive Racing Australia, the team now known as Tickford Racing.

He was a championship challenger that season but found himself fined $25,000 at Bathurst for comments made during the Thursday post-practice press conference regarding female drivers Simona De Silvestro and Renee Gracie. The women were driving a wildcard Falcon run by his Prodrive team and backed by Harvey Norman.

Reynolds covered $5000 of the fine by navigating the wet Shootout better than the rest of the field. He ended his fast lap 1.15-seconds quicker than the Volvo of Scott McLaughlin and secured his first Bathurst 1000 pole position.

Wet weather again returned for the Shootout in 2022 but this time it was simply too much. All the standing water and the streams running across the racing surface would have made it impossible for drivers to control their 640-horsepower-plus Supercars to acceptable levels. There was no option for officials but to abandon the session.

It was the first time in Bathurst 1000 history that the Shootout had been cancelled. Following the letter of the law, officials awarded the pole position to Cam Waters, the fastest driver in Friday qualifying.

You would have thought that 1977 – the year prior to the debut of the Shootout at Bathurst – was the most recent year the Great Race grid had been determined by regular qualifying. Not so.

The 1988 edition of the race featured a Shootout, but it didn't count for the grid. That year's Tooheys 1000 was run under international rules as a round of the 1988 Asia-Pacific Touring Car Championship.

Overseas officials had originally pushed for the Shootout to be cancelled the year prior, when Bathurst doubled as a round of the World Touring Car Championship, but the local race organisers held firm on holding the traditional one-lap session.

While they lost the battle in 1988 – along with the push to retain the traditional standing start – the local organisers ensured a Shootout did occur, although it only counted for prizemoney and not for grid positions.

German Klaus Niedzwiedz was fastest in the Shootout on Saturday, driving Allan Moffat's ANZ Bank-sponsored Ford Sierra, but started from fourth on race day, leaving Dick Johnson to start from pole position in his Shell Sierra.

The final year of Group C local touring car regulations in 1984 was dubbed a farewell for a range of cars that wouldn't return to Mount Panorama under international Group A rules, which were being introduced for 1985.

One of them was Nissan's turbocharged Bluebird, which had debuted at Bathurst in 1981 and steadily been developed and progressed into an outright contender.

Australian Rally Champion George Fury had been brought across from rallying on dirt surfaces to circuit racing on tarmac by Nissan racing chief (and former Ford motorsport boss) Howard Marsden.

The Hungarian immigrant had developed into a fine touring car driver and his lap in the 1984 Bathurst 'Hardies Heroes' that landed him pole position is regarded as the banner-head achievement of his decade-long association with the Great Race.

The little Bluebird, powered by a 1.8-litre, four-cylinder turbocharged engine, blew everyone away when Fury rocketed around the Mountain in 2m13.850-seconds to secure the first Bathurst 1000 pole position for a Japanese car.

In doing so he knocked off all the heavyweights of local touring car racing, including Peter Brock, Dick Johnson and Allan Moffat.

But, as Fury's co-driver Gary Scott recalls, a little help was involved.

'Howard and the boys came up with this idea of running air-conditioning Freon gas straight onto the intercooler,' Scott told me on the V8 Sleuth Podcast in 2022, who recalled testing the effectiveness of the system at Sandown.

'We filled a fire extinguisher [pointed at the intercooler] with the stuff and I was sent out with a thermometer in the spare car. My job was to do the read-out on the straights [via radio] to Howard [in the pits] and they would record it.

'The temperature in the intercooler chamber coming into the engine was 30 degrees, 35, whatever. I hit the button and I'm reading it out to Howard; 25, 20, 15, 10, 10, minus 5, minus 15, minus 20!

'It went from plus 30 to maybe minus 30 in half the length of the back straight. You could imagine what that could do because we could run a lot more [turbo] boost!'

Scott said the combination of that innovation and cool ambient conditions at Bathurst set the scene for Fury to record the fastest ever touring car lap of the pre-Chase Mount Panorama circuit.

'[In Hardies Heroes] I think it ran 1.8 or 1.9 [bar of boost], more than we'd ever done. George only used it on the straights, but he gave it a hit and that would have given us a lot of power.'

A very similar trick was employed under the bonnet of Peter Brock's Mobil Ford Sierra in the Bathurst Shootout in 1989. Although no technical breach was proven and Brock's pole position stood, the Mobil team was later fined $5000 for a 'moral infringement of the rules'.

As Scott points out, it's likely no coincidence that key members of the Bluebird program had by that point transitioned to the Brock team.

'What do they say? You weren't cheating at all, you were just pushing boundaries,' observes Scott cheekily.

'But don't take anything away from George. He was an unbelievable driver, a ripper teammate, ripper guy … he was one hell of a driver.'

Fury's 1984 lap set a benchmark lap time that took until 1991 to be beaten in a Bathurst Shootout. Ironically that was another Nissan in the form of the GT-R model driven by Mark Skaife.

The Bluebird's Bathurst Shootout lap still figures prominently among the legendary laps produced at Mount Panorama, but Greg Murphy's pole-winning lap in 2003 at the wheel of his Kmart Holden Commodore VY has been dubbed the 'Lap of the Gods' for good reason.

The scene was set for something special on that Saturday afternoon, 11 October, at Mount Panorama.

That particular Shootout saw a return to the traditional 'Top 10' format after two years – in 2001 and 2002 – of the Shootout field being expanded to the fastest 15 cars after qualifying.

It also was the first held on Saturday afternoon. The decision had been taken to move the fight for pole position away from Saturday morning and into a TV-friendly afternoon timeslot that would see the live action at Bathurst roll straight into the Channel 10 news. This was instead of the Shootout being shown on a delayed basis, as it had been previously.

Fans trackside and indeed watching on television at home saw some remarkable action that afternoon.

Aged 56 and making one of just two V8 Supercar starts for the year, seven-time Bathurst 1000 winner Jim Richards turned in a brilliant lap to out-qualify his Holden Racing Team teammate – and reigning series champion – Mark Skaife. In doing so, he clocked a 2m08.1466-second lap, which was the fastest he would ever lap the Mountain.

Then two-time Bathurst 1000 winner John Bowe undercut Richards' mark to lap in a 2m07.9556-second time to send Ford fans into a frenzy.

The Tasmanian, sharing a Falcon with team owner/driver Brad Jones, looked to be on target to take his first Great Race pole position.

But then something unbelievable happened.

Fastest in Friday qualifying, Murphy and his #51 Kmart Holden were the last driver and car combination to take to the track. That's because the Shootout field runs in the order of slowest to fastest.

From the start line to Reid Park at the top of the Mountain, he was four-tenths faster than Bowe. Dancing the white, red and blue Commodore across the top of the Mountain he proved to be just under three-tenths faster in the next section to Forrest's Elbow and finished off the job by completing the rest of the lap from the Elbow to the finish line with another four-tenths of a second advantage over Bowe across the final third of the lap.

The lap time that flashed up on the monitors echoes into eternity. Ask hardcore Bathurst fans to quote Murphy's 'Lap of the Gods' to four decimal places and they'll respond without delay.

2 minutes, 06.8594 seconds.

The Kiwi's record lap gave him pole position by just over one second, a margin in the modern V8 Supercars era akin to three or four seconds in previous eras of the sport.

It was a massive leap forward in lap time improvement, the likes of which hadn't been seen before in the Holden versus Ford V8 Supercar era of the sport, where keeping parity between the Commodores and Falcons was at the forefront of the minds of the rule-makers of the category.

Amazingly, Murphy's staggeringly quick lap wasn't perfect. He made a mistake dropping out of the drop at the Dipper and, instead of shifting from second gear to third, momentarily accidentally dropped into first gear.

Quickly realising his error and slotting it back into the correct gear, the Kiwi finished off the lap with precision and the time proved to be a whopping 1.1-seconds faster than he managed in Friday's qualifying session, when he'd had multiple attempts to set a fast time.

In that one single lap, he became part of Bathurst history forever.

Motorsport is a deeply competitive and combative sport built on rivalries and a burning will to win, but on that day at Mount Panorama the level of Murphy's performance and its impact on the sport was plain for all to see.

Rival team members emerged from their garages and applauded the performance as Murphy drove his pole-winning Holden back down pit lane.

It was as rare as it was special.

'I can't believe the time, I'm just shaking,' said Murphy after the lap, one that – in terms of its historical significance – overshadows the fact he and Rick Kelly went on to win the race the following day.

'The car was good, and I knew I had to push hard to beat Mark [Skaife] and JB [John Bowe], especially when I heard the roar at the end of pit lane when he had done his lap.

'My lap wasn't perfect, I grabbed first gear at the Dipper instead of third, but I was able to keep some good speed into the Elbow.

'I saw the time on the dashboard and had to check with the boys that it was right, and I could tell by Erik's [Pender, engineer] voice that it was right. I've never been so dry in the mouth on one lap before, I had to concentrate so hard on that lap.

'I wasn't going out there to be safe, I was out there to win pole.'

Another fast Kiwi, Scott McLaughlin, wrote his own piece of Bathurst Shootout history 14 years later – in 2017.

With Murphy by then retired and watching on from pit lane in his role as a TV pit lane reporter, the young DJR Team Penske Ford driver channelled a bit of Murphy magic to become the first Supercars driver to lap the Mountain in the 2m03-second bracket, a 2m03.8312-second lap the result.

His pole-winning time was 0.44-seconds faster than second-fastest David Reynolds and a whopping 1.59-seconds quicker than Jamie Whincup's 2016 Bathurst pole-winning time.

The lap was an all-in effort. McLaughlin ran the wheels of his Falcon into the dirt across McPhillamy Park but held his nerve to keep attacking the lap. The result gave Dick Johnson's team its first Bathurst 1000 pole position since Dick himself had been behind the wheel of a turbocharged Ford Sierra in 1992.

The Mountain fans erupted when the lap was complete, delivering the young gun as raucous a reception as Murphy had received when he delivered his jaw-dropping Shootout performance in 2003.

Since then the Bathurst Shootout pole position lap times have continued to tumble as teams continue to develop their cars and drivers find tenths and hundredths of seconds in places they were unable to before.

McLaughlin led the charge in 2019 when he took his DJR Team Penske Mustang to pole in 2m03.3783-seconds.

Although this time was scrubbed from the record books – a month after he and co-driver Alex Prémat had started from pole position and won the race at Bathurst – due to an engine irregularity being discovered in the powerplant the #17 Mustang had used in qualifying and the Shootout at Mount Panorama.

The lap time has subsequently been beaten anyway – by Chaz Mostert in 2021, whose Walkinshaw Andretti United Commodore ZB lapped in 2m03.3736-seconds to take his second Bathurst 1000 pole position.

His first pole sits only in the Bathurst 1000 record books, however, given he physically started second on the grid alongside poleman McLaughlin in 2019 prior to the Shell driver's post-race Shootout exclusion and Mostert's elevation to pole on paper.

It's yet another example of the Shootout contributing a sizeable slice of Bathurst 1000 drama and intrigue.

The Shootout has evolved via various tweaks, modifications and movements since its debut in 1978 but remains at its core a simple formula that is easy to understand – 10 drivers and cars versus the Mountain, with the stopwatch as judge and jury.

As the Great Race celebrates its 60th anniversary race in 2023, one of its most popular components marks the 45th anniversary of its creation.

No doubt it still has plenty more surprises and magical moments to deliver in the years ahead.

## Close Finishes

The closest finishing margin in Bathurst 1000 history came about in 1977 – in the famous Ford 1-2 form-finish – as Allan Moffat led teammate Colin Bond over the line aboard his wounded and limping V8 Falcon.

The official margin of victory was one tenth of a second. Since then, in the modern era of Bathurst 1000 racing, such narrow finishes have become far more commonplace between cars going flat out trying to win the Peter Brock Trophy.

The closest competitive race-winning margin came in 2016 as TEKNO Autosport's Will Davison held off Red Bull Commodore driver Shane van Gisbergen by just 0.1434-seconds.

## First Up Front

Former motorcycle racer Warren Weldon holds the distinction in Bathurst Great Race history as the driver to lead the very first lap of the first race. He was behind the wheel of the big V8-powered Studebaker Lark that led the first lap in the 1963 Armstrong 500.

Track safety was minimal in the early years. This is the 1965 race and the Ian and Leo Geoghegan Cortina zips through the Esses. *(an1images.com/Trevor Thomas)*

1969 race winners Colin Bond and Tony Roberts (swigging from champagne bottle) celebrate victory. *(an1images.com/Terry Russell)*

The crowds at the top of the Mountain have always loved getting close to the action. This is 1977 and eventual winner Allan Moffat's Falcon sweeps around a slower VW Golf.

*(an1images.com/Dale Rodgers)*

A pair of Falcon GTHO V8s lead a Torana and Charger through Forrest's Elbow in the 1971 Great Race.
(an1images.com/Terry Russell)

1971 Bathurst winner Allan Moffat celebrates his second consecutive Great Race win.
(an1images.com/Terry Russell)

1968 Bathurst winner Bruce McPhee heads the pack into the Cutting in 1970. Note the lack of safety fence on the outside of the track!
(an1images.com/Terry Russell)

Holden's Commodore remains the most winning car in Bathurst Great Race history. Peter Brock and Jim Richards took this Holden Dealer Team Commodore VC to victory in 1980, their third consecutive win as a combination. *(Holden Motorsport)*

The famous 'Big Banger' Commodore that Peter Brock and Larry Perkins won Bathurst aboard in 1984 still stirs the soul of Holden fans around the country. *(an1images.com/Dale Rodgers)*

The 1984 Great Race marked the last with locally built Group C specification cars. The #3 Commodore was co-driven by Garry Rogers. His team won the race 16 years later. *(an1images.com/Dale Rodgers)*

The start of the 1985 James Hardie 1000 at Bathurst. Jaguar ace Tom Walkinshaw leads the pack into Hell Corner. *(an1images.com/Dale Rodgers)*

A 1986-style Bathurst traffic jam as the large field thunders into the first corner. Note the cherry picker vantage point for the eager photographers! *(an1images.com/Dale Rodgers)*

Peter Brock's ninth Bathurst Great Race win in 1987 was also his last. He swapped from his regular #05 Commodore mid-race into his team's #10 Mobil-backed Holden. The car swap worked to perfection. *(an1images.com/Graeme Neander)*

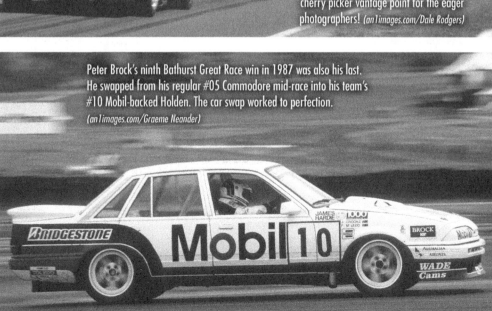

**Top:** Allan Grice sweeps to victory in 1990 for the Holden Racing Team. This was perhaps one of Holden's biggest upset wins in the Great Race. *(an1images.com/Graeme Neander)*

**Middle:** The mighty Nissan GT-R was unstoppable at Bathurst in 1991. Jim Richards and Mark Skaife won by a lap. *(an1images.com/Graeme Neander)*

**Right:** 'Larrikin' Larry Perkins acknowledges the Mountain faithful ahead of lining up on pole position for the 1993 race. He and Gregg Hansford won. *(an1images.com/Rod Eime)*

Wayne Gardner's Coke Holden heads the field shortly after the start of the 1995 race. He and co-driver Neil Crompton finished third. *(an1images.com/Graeme Neander)*

They look happy but Craig Lowndes and Greg Murphy were nursing a major hangover after they won Bathurst in 1996! *(an1images.com/Graeme Neander)*

V8 Supercars established its own Bathurst race for Holdens and Fords in 1997. The fans packed in to see the traditional rivals battle it out *(an1images.com/Graeme Neander)*

Two-litre Super Tourers didn't capture the public's attention at Mount Panorama but turned on some great racing. This is the 1998 race-winning Volvo. *(an1images.com/Dirk Klynsmith)*

The fans on top of the Mountain are the heartbeat of Australia's most famous car race. *(an1images.com/Dirk Klynsmith)*

The Bathurst 1000 is as much a challenge of beating the impressive Mount Panorama as it is of beating the other cars in the race. This is Mountain Straight in 1999.
(an1images.com/Graeme Neander)

Holden fans celebrate another win at Bathurst in 2001. The post-race podium presentation is unique in Aussie motorsport.
(an1images.com/Graeme Neander)

**Above:** Mark Skaife heads Peter Brock across the line at Bathurst in 2002. The win clinched the V8 Supercar Championship Series for the former. *(an1images.com/Graeme Neander)*

**Left:** An emotional Craig Lowndes pays tribute to Brock during the pre-race ceremony in 2006. His victory that day was his first Great Race win in 10 years. *(an1images.com/Justin Deeley)*

**Below:** Fans take in the action at Hell Corner, the first corner on the famous Mount Panorama circuit. *(an1images.com/Justin Deeley)*

The 2006 race start. Pole-sitter Mark Skaife's Commodore (right) is already crippled by clutch failure and slow to move off the starting grid. It was out of the race moments later. *(an1images.com/Justin Deeley)*

Smiles and blue Ford flags at the end of another day of racing at Bathurst. This is 2006 after Craig Lowndes and Jamie Whincup won in a Falcon, a popular win with the fans. *(an1images.com/Justin Deeley)*

2009 Great Race winner Garth Tander on his way to victory.
He and Will Davison gave the Holden Racing Team its sixth
Bathurst 1000 win. *(an1images.com/Justin Deeley)*

The 2012 Great Race kicks off with former schoolmates Paul Dumbrell (#1) and Will Davison (#6)
leading the field. Dumbrell and Jamie Whincup came out victorious. *(an1images.com/Dirk Klynsmith)*

**Left:** Steve Richards and Mark Winterbottom took to the roof of their Falcon to celebrate their 2013 Bathurst win. It ended a 10-year-win drought for Winterbottom in the Great Race. *(an1images.com/Dirk Klynsmith)*

**Below:** Chaz Mostert powerslides to the finish line to win the 2014 race. It was the only one of the race's 161 laps that he and teammate Paul Morris led all day! *(an1images.com/Dirk Klynsmith)*

The 2014 race featured a mid-race stoppage for track repairs. Teams were left parked up on the grid for nearly an hour before the race restarted. *(an1images.com/Dirk Klynsmith)*

The 2016 race kicks off. By this stage Volvo and Nissan were on the grid fighting against Ford and Holden. *(an1images.com/Dirk Klynsmith)*

Scott McLaughin greets his jubilant crew just after crossing the line to win in 2019. French co-driver Alexandre Premat is at the top of the fence. (an1images.com/Scott Wensley)

Drink up! Team co-owner Ryan Walkinshaw (left) and winning driver Chaz Mostert (right) celebrate victory in 2021 with a 'shoey'. Champagne in a smelly race boot never tasted so good! (Nathan Wong)

Fans pack all vantage points of Mount Panorama to watch the Great Race. This is 2022, the last Bathurst for Holden race cars. *(Nathan Wong)*

Bathurst Great Races of the 1970s and 1980s were decided with full laps between the podium finishers. Not so in the modern era, as this shot from 2022's closing stages shows! *(Nathan Wong)*

# 18

# Scandals, Stoushes and Stuff-Ups

For all the glorious cars, amazing drivers and momentous occasions celebrated over the course of the history of the Bathurst 1000, there have been plenty of issues, large and small, that are just as much a part of the story of the Great Race at Mount Panorama.

Featuring prominently among them are the four instances when the car that crossed the line first was later excluded or given a time penalty.

The first was in the fifth-ever Bathurst Great Race – in 1967. The chequered flag was waved at Leo Geoghegan's Falcon XR GT, which he shared with brother Ian. It was the first time the Sydney-based racers had secured a win in the race.

That caused some head-scratching for rival Ford racer Harry Firth, whose car – driven by co-driver Fred Gibson – had been leading Geoghegan. Gibson was waved home as runner-up.

A few hours later a lap scoring mistake was confirmed, and the Firth/Gibson Falcon was instated as winner, with the Geoghegan boys second.

Back in the days of manual lap scoring and no electronic timing systems, the timers had incorrectly credited a lap to the Geoghegan Falcon earlier in the race. Running short of fuel, Ian had pulled into the access road partway up Mountain Straight, driven down through the back of the paddock, got refuelled and gone back out onto the track via the pit lane – very much against the rules.

The lap scorers thus credited his #53D Falcon with an extra lap on their charts.

Once the facts were established and the result adjusted accordingly, the dust settled quickly on the matter. This was a far cry from how things played out 20 years later, the next time the car that took the chequered flag lost victory at Bathurst.

The 1987 race was run as a round of the inaugural World Touring Car Championship, bringing with it a litany of red tape, politics and additional rules. When a horde of overseas cars, teams and drivers arrived to take on the locals, the excitement was palpable.

Among the visitors was the Texaco fuel-backed Ford factory team run by Swiss boss Ruedi Eggenberger. The pair of black and red Sierras dominated the race and finished first and second.

Brit Steve Soper and Belgian Pierre Dieudonné were first and teammates, Germans Klaus Ludwig and Klaus Niedzwiedz – two laps behind – took out second place.

However, controversy had reared its head during the race. There were mutterings over the legality of the cars; specifically, it was alleged they had used illegal fuel. Ultimately, it wasn't the fuel that got the Ford Sierra team flung from the results; instead the results were overturned a month after the race had ended for the cars having illegally widened and raised wheel arches that accommodated the use of bigger tyres.

The team's appeal to the Australian Motor Sport Appeals Court (AMSAC) was rejected in December and, in March 1988, after its appeal to the highest motorsport court of FISA (now the FIA) also proved unsuccessful, third-placed Peter Brock, David Parsons, Peter McLeod and the Mobil HDT team were declared winners of the 1987 James Hardie 1000.

It took 162 days for the winners of the race to officially be confirmed in a saga that took far longer to play out than the 1000-kilometre race itself.

The exclusion of the Fords from the 1987 Bathurst race handed the inaugural World Touring Car Championship to BMW, but it was the German manufacturer that was front and centre in the headlines the next time controversy broke out over the result 10 years later at Bathurst.

The 1997 AMP Bathurst 1000 for two-litre Super Tourers again brought some of the world's best touring car drivers to Australia for the Great Race at Bathurst during the time of a dramatic divide, when V8 Supercars established its own 1000-kilometre race.

It proved to be a magic day for BMW as its pair of Diet Coke-sponsored 320i models ran home first and second – Kiwi Craig Baird (sharing with Paul Morris) leading home David Brabham (sharing with brother Geoff) to clinch victory.

But there was a problem.

Baird, who drove a marathon stint from lap 67 through to the end of the 161-lap distance, had been at the wheel of the BMW for just under four hours.

The issue was that the rules stated no driver could be at the wheel and drive continuously for any longer than three and a half hours.

Morris and Baird headed to the podium, sprayed the winner's champagne and went to the post-race press conference with the trophy. Later that night came the news they were excluded due to the driving time infringement and, additionally, BMW Motorsport was fined US$40,000.

'I was oblivious to it during the race,' reflects Baird, who made 21 Bathurst 1000 starts between 1990 and 2016 and now works with Supercars as the Driving Standards Advisor in Race Control at all Supercars Championship rounds, including Bathurst.

'I drove for three hours and 58 minutes continuously to finish the race. It should have never happened. I think the team were all a little bit concerned if we might muck up a driver change [at the last pit stop]. They should have just put Paul in the car [when Baird pitted on lap 142], and we would have won the race.

'The problem was, BMW backed us for a few hours [post-race] because the Brabham/Brabham car had supposedly passed a car under a yellow [flag, which is against the rules]. So, we were both under investigation and the worst thing that could have happened would have been both cars being disqualified.'

Even worse than that was that their great German rivals, Audi, had finished third and fourth and were poised for a 1-2 finish of their own should both BMWs get excluded.

'But when the Brabham car got let off the breach, and I understand it from a BMW marketing point of view, they didn't want bad press … Paul and I had about 3000 beers out of the trophy at a restaurant and got the phone call to say it was over,' says Baird.

'We got flung … lost it.'

Baird returned to Bathurst a fortnight later to compete in the V8 Supercars Bathurst race and shared one of Dick Johnson's Shell Helix Falcons to finish fourth with Johnson's son Steven.

Proving that the Mountain owes no driver, Baird made another 17 starts in the race and never finished higher than seventh.

The Kiwi's last Great Race start came in 2016: it was the next occasion when the first car to finish the race also had victory taken away in controversial fashion.

By that stage a four-time Bathurst 1000 winner, Jamie Whincup, took his Red Bull Commodore across the line first at the end of 161 laps.

However, race officials had handed him a post-race 15-second penalty for careless driving in an incident 11 laps earlier: he bumped Scott McLaughlin's Volvo off the track at the Chase while launching a move down the inside to pass the Kiwi.

The result was disaster as McLaughlin fired back onto the track, collected Garth Tander's Holden Racing Team Commodore (which had been bottled up behind the slower-than-usual Whincup) and put both out of contention in an instant.

Whincup sped on to cross the line first, though he and co-driver Paul Dumbrell were dropped to 11th in the final results once their time penalty (which was accessed for the initial contact with McLaughlin and not for involvement in the Tander/McLaughlin collision) was added to their race time.

That left TEKNO Commodore driver Will Davison – second across the line and narrowly holding off Whincup's teammate Shane van Gisbergen – to be awarded victory alongside co-driver/team owner Jonathon Webb.

However, it took nine days for Davison and Webb's win to be officially rubber-stamped as Whincup's Triple Eight team pushed on with fighting the penalty post-race.

The Supercars National Court of Appeal dismissed the team's appeal. All of the legal rumblings amounted to nothing when it was deemed that, under the Supercars Operations Manual – essentially the rule book of the Supercars Championship – the team's original appeal couldn't have been presented anyway, and its notice to appeal shouldn't have been accepted by the Stewards from the very beginning.

'That was brutal,' Whincup said of the Bathurst 2016 penalty – on the V8 Sleuth Podcast in 2019.

'We got done heavily there. It shouldn't have been a penalty. They [the officials] made a mistake and cost me and my team the biggest race of the year.

'They made a bad call and didn't see it correctly. Unfortunately, that's one I'll never get back.'

Scott McLaughlin, who'd been one of the minor protagonists in the Whincup 2016 Bathurst controversy, found himself at the centre of post-race controversy in 2019 after he and French co-driver Alex Prémat won the race at the wheel of their Ford Mustang.

McLaughlin had held off fellow New Zealander Shane van Gisbergen in a last lap duel to the chequered flag, giving legendary team owner Dick Johnson his team's first Bathurst 1000 win in 25 years and American racing powerhouse Roger Penske – who had become majority team owner in 2015 – his first Mountain victory.

But the close finish wasn't what got plenty of fans and rival teams up in arms; rather, it was the actions of his Kiwi teammate Fabian Coulthard. He had driven dramatically slowly when the Safety Car was called on lap 135 due to American Alexander Rossi beaching his wildcard Commodore in the Murray's Corner sand trap.

From being right behind teammate McLaughlin and Whincup partway around the lap, Coulthard's Mustang entered the pit lane 47 seconds after his teammate.

That bunched up the field as, under the rules, the following cars were not permitted to pass, and set pit lane into a frenzy.

Whincup and McLaughlin took advantage of the opportunity to pit and garner a fuel advantage. They were able to return to the track ahead of the field, denying those stuck behind Coulthard the chance to potentially leap-frog them.

Soon after, Coulthard was hit with a pit lane penalty for not maintaining a five-car length gap to McLaughlin under the Safety Car. But things really kicked off post-race when more information came to light.

Radio communications between Coulthard and his engineer were analysed, the latter's strange mispronunciation of the word 'debris' as 'debriss' three times a highlighted element. It led the Stewards to conclude that Coulthard's engineer, Mark Fenning, was speaking to a script of some kind on the pit-to-car radio.

Allegations from rival drivers and teams of race-tampering and possible race fixing flew thick and fast. Fans let their frustrations spill into vile social media posts. Horribly, Coulthard even received death threats.

The team was charged with a breach of Supercars' team orders rules but that was switched to a breach of the FIA's Obligation of Fairness rules.

The result was the largest fine in Supercars history and the biggest sanctions able to be applied by the race's Stewards.

DJR Team Penske was fined $250,000 ($100,000 of it suspended until the end of 2021), the #12 Coulthard/Tony D'Alberto car (which had finished sixth) was demoted to 21st – last place – in the results and the team was penalised 300 points in the Supercars Team's Championship.

'We find, and it has been admitted, that in giving the direction to the Driver of Car #12, DJRTP infringed the principles of fairness in competition and behaved in an unsportsmanlike manner,' read the Stewards Report.

'We do not find that there was an attempt to influence the result of the Race but it is difficult to avoid the conclusion that the result was affected to a degree, certainly for Car #12 that would otherwise have re-joined the circuit after its pit stop in a much lower position.'

Mention of McLaughlin's long-awaited Great Race win will still raise the hackles of rival fans because of the goings-on of that day before he crossed the line in front. It's a tainted win in the eyes of many non-Ford, non-McLaughlin and non-DJR Team Penske fans, a viewpoint that frustrates him.

'I drove my heart out that day in that last stint,' he recalled in an interview in 2020.

'I was oblivious to it (the Coulthard controversy) – I can't do much more than that – I had no idea what was going on. It's one of those deals where, in some ways, it's frustrating that people are always going to say things.'

But the DJR Team Penske/Bathurst 2019 controversy didn't end with the penalties issued post-race.

When the Supercars teams arrived in Melbourne the next month for the Sandown 500, there were further penalties handed down. This time they related to the engine under the bonnet of the McLaughlin/Prémat Mustang at Bathurst in the lead-up to the Great Race.

The engine in the #17 Mustang for practice, qualifying and the Top 10 Shootout – which was changed for another unit before the Sunday morning warm-up session prior to the race, an engine that was checked and passed as legal – was found to have cylinders that exceeded the maximum permitted valve lift by a very small margin, a few thousands of an inch.

The car was therefore officially disqualified from the results of qualifying and the Top 10 Shootout at Bathurst (a paperwork penalty in the record books more than anything, given the engine rule breach wasn't discovered until after the Bathurst race had been run); the team was fined $30,000; and McLaughlin and Prémat were relegated to the rear of the grid for the start of that weekend's Sandown race.

Rival team boss Roland Dane, in charge of the Red Bull team at the time, feels the goings-on at Bathurst in 2019 were 'beneath' American racing legend Roger Penske.

'I certainly will always consider what went on at Bathurst in 2019 to be beneath him, beneath Supercars and should have never happened,' he declared on the V8 Sleuth Podcast in 2022.

Controversy always finds a way of popping up at Bathurst.

Some controversies are bigger than others, but the stakes are high. Every now and again those who contest the Great Race step – sometimes unknowingly, other times knowingly – too close to, or over the line of what's permitted.

That's what happens when the end prize – in this case winning the biggest race in Australia – is up for grabs.

The Bathurst 1000 means a lot to thousands of people around the country. It's always generated more general media coverage than any other race on the touring car and, later, Supercars calendar. That's why controversial and dramatic events relating to it have always been – and always will be – big news.

It's been that way for 60 years and will be for many more.

## The Longest Name in Bathurst 1000 History

A German prince's start in the 1984 Bathurst 1000 has written him into the history books as having the longest name of any driver in the history of the race – 22 characters in total.

Prince Leopold von Bayern shared a BMW with 1967 Formula 1 World Champion Denny Hulme that year and the duo finished 15th overall and second in the Group A class.

But when you consider that his real full name is actually Leopold Rupprecht Ludwig Ferdinand Adalbert Friedrich Maria et omnes sancti Prinz von Bayern, you'd have to think he's fairly safe to hold his place in Bathurst record books for many years to come!

## Shootout Stars

Dick Johnson holds the record for the most Bathurst Shootout appearances in history – 21.

The Queensland Ford hero was in the field for the first Shootout – held in 1978 – and didn't miss the annual battle for pole position at Mount Panorama until he dipped out on a berth in 1998.

Larry Perkins sits second on the list with 18 Bathurst Shootout starts, including one in Johnson's second Ford Mustang in 1985. That was the only year that Perkins drove something other than a Holden in the Bathurst 1000.

Peter Brock and Craig Lowndes are ranked third equal, on 17 Bathurst Shootout starts, ahead of Mark Skaife (16), Glenn Seton and Garth Tander (15) and Allan Grice (13).

Kiwi Shane van Gisbergen has made 12 Bathurst Shootout starts and is best of the currently active full-time Supercars drivers in this regard. He qualified for the 2022 Shootout, however it was not held due to bad weather conditions.

# 19

# The Battle for Bathurst

Australian sport has seen its fair share of splits and brawls, however only a handful of them stand out as major turning points in the history books of individual sports.

The 'battle for Bathurst' that raged in the mid- to late 1990s filled plenty of column inches in newspapers and magazines of the era as various players fought for control of the jewel in the crown of Australian motorsport: the Bathurst 1000.

Cricket had World Series Cricket versus the establishment Australian Cricket Board in the late 1970s; rugby league had Super League versus the Australian Rugby League in the mid- to late 1990s; and Australian motorsport had its Bathurst battle rumbling around the same time the Super League/ARL fight was going on.

So how on earth did it come to pass that there were two 1000-kilometre Bathurst races in 1997?

The road that led to two separate races at Mount Panorama in 1997 and 1998 – one on Channel 7 and another on Channel 10 within a fortnight of one another – had started the previous year, 1996.

The V8 touring car teams that competed in the Australian Touring Car Championship and the Bathurst 1000 had engaged IMG, the International Management Group, to take over the group's marketing in a bid to further promote and grow the unique Holden versus Ford category.

Tony Cochrane, then the Senior International Vice President of Australasia at IMG and later the vocal chairman of the V8 group, had spent time researching the state of play of domestic V8 touring car racing.

He couldn't understand why the teams had to pay to race, rather than getting paid to race by the promoters or circuits. They were no different to a band or singer in his view; they were the star act and the stars of the show needed to be paid to perform.

In mid-1996 Cochrane met with a range of team owners, drivers and team managers in Melbourne and proceeded to illustrate why their arrangements at Bathurst were no good.

'I used [the meeting] to ram home my message that they needed better representation,' says Cochrane.

'They were good at engineering, running cars, finding the right drivers, but they weren't good at running the sport of Group A touring car racing, as it was then known. I was trying to make them see the bigger picture.

'Bathurst was the holy grail and sold to them as such, so what I said that day came to them as a big shock.

'My opening question was, "Is Bathurst financially good for you?" Someone in the room piped up, "Yes, it's fantastic. There's $300,000 total prizemoney."

'I wrote that up on a whiteboard and asked a few more questions. "So, surely you don't pay for garages – because you're the stars of the show?" They replied, "Well, no, we pay rent on those." I suggested they would get all the entry tickets they needed, and the reply was, "Ah well, no. We only get some tickets per car, and we have to buy the rest."

'Once you multiplied it all out, the nett result was that there was about $280,000 of cost in their $300,000 prizemoney total. I said, "So you're the cars and stars, and the reason why the race works, and you're earning a total of $20,000?" They all looked at one another and thought, "Holy shit, this guy's making a good point."'

Cochrane appeared at a press conference at Sandown in Melbourne in September 1996 to outline the new group's plans for V8 racing. A new television deal for the championship and a greater slice of the Bathurst financial pie for its stars were two of the immediate items of importance.

Never afraid to take a forward step, Cochrane declared that IMG wasn't an emotional company and Bathurst was not 'a sacred site', floating that an 'Australian 1000' could be run elsewhere on the same day as a rival to the Bathurst 1000. Today he says it was a calculated strategic comment and far from a reckless throw-away line.

'I come across as a raving lunatic, but I think about what I'm going to say,' says Cochrane.

'I wanted to scare the [Bathurst City] Council into doing a deal with us. I wanted them to believe this new V8 mob won't be coming to Bathurst anymore.

'That "sacred sites" comment upset a lot of people, but I really was only making it for the Councillors, Mayor and CEO of the Bathurst City Council. I wanted them to think that I was so out of control that I would stop the V8s coming to Bathurst.'

The new V8 body – including IMG and the teams – AVESCO (the Australian Vee Eight Supercar Company) soon after announced a new TV deal, in October 1996, for the 1997 Australian Touring Car Championship with Channel 10, and confirmed the category would be renamed V8 Supercars.

But Channel 7 had broadcast Bathurst since the Great Race moved there in 1963 and still held the rights to the Bathurst 1000 – the deal reportedly ran through to 2004. The TV giant was part of a three-headed entity (the Bathurst 1000 Consortium) that ran the Great Race (the event was not then part of the championship as it now is) alongside the Australian Racing Drivers' Club and the Bathurst City Council.

Ultimately it was the television rights that were the real sticking point, and the inability of the parties to reach consensus about them meant the return of V8 Supercars to the Bathurst 1000 for 1997 was dead in the water. AVESCO wouldn't go back to Bathurst without Channel 10 as broadcaster and Channel 7 refused to give up the deal to the race, which annually attracted unparalleled ratings and advertising income.

On Friday 20 December 1996, five days before Christmas, came one of the biggest bombshells in Bathurst and Australian motorsport history.

AVESCO announced it would run its own 1000-kilometre race at Bathurst, dubbed the Australian 1000, on 19 October, two weeks after the existing Bathurst 1000 which, in keeping with tradition, was scheduled for the Labour Day holiday weekend in New South Wales.

It did a deal with the Bathurst City Council, a member of the Bathurst 1000 Consortium, to make it all happen. The Council reasoned it was apolitical in the racing war despite being a member of the Consortium, and was acting in the best interests of the Mount Panorama circuit and the Bathurst rate payers to keep the V8s – and the resultant spending of visitors – in town.

The Consortium felt betrayed that the Council had broken ranks. 'They [the Council] were placed in a corner, given 24 hours to decide, and they've done it for the money,' the ARDC's Ivan Stibbard told *Motorsport News* magazine soon after.

Greg Eaton served as Channel 7's representative within the Consortium before taking on the role as its Chief Executive (the Consortium was later renamed Bathurst 1000 Event Management). Looking back, he sees the course that history took as the only one that was going to happen.

'Even if Council hadn't broken ranks, I think it was inevitable that V8 Supercars still would have taken over Bathurst,' he says today.

'It was just hastened by them [the Council] breaking ranks.

'In my mind, the writing was on the wall the day Tony Cochrane and James Erskine [also from IMG] stood up at that first meeting with the Consortium.

'It was a defining moment in time. The V8 group had clearly put a lot of thought into what they were about to do. No doubt the promoters of the tracks were making all the money and the Group A V8 touring car teams weren't.

'What happened at that time turned motorsport on its head. And it probably had to. The entrants weren't making enough money, so that laid the foundations. It really couldn't have kept going the way it was. What happened was a re-aligning of things. If they [Cochrane and IMG] hadn't done what they did, someone else would have done it.'

And Cochrane and the V8 teams had achieved the one thing they needed: the gates to Mount Panorama were now opened to them.

'The Bathurst City Council were the only part of the Consortium we needed,' says Cochrane today.

'We needed the bloody track! It's hard to do Bathurst in Sydney or Bathurst on the Gold Coast! When people say, "Oh, he got at them. The Council were weak" – it was none of those things. They had the circuit, and it was the one thing I absolutely needed on behalf of the team owners.

'I privately went and met with the Bathurst Mayor of the time, Ian Macintosh, and cut a deal to rent the circuit. I was determined to give the V8 team owners the same Bathurst history but a decent earn out of it.'

The new race, originally dubbed the Australian 1000 Classic and later renamed the Primus 1000 Classic in deference to a sponsorship deal with the telecommunications company, was to be televised on Channel 10 and promoted by IMG, with a total prize pool of $750,000 – more than double the existing Bathurst 1000 prize pool that V8 teams had raced for just over two months earlier.

The Consortium responded instantly, pressing the button on turning the AMP Bathurst 1000 Great Race into an international event for two-litre Super Touring cars, opening the door to a wide range of manufacturers and models to compete compared to the two tribes of Holden and Ford in V8 racing.

Originated in England in the early 1990s as the rules for the British Touring Car Championship, the two-litre Super Touring formula run by TOCA UK was a hit domestically. It had spread around the world by the mid-1990s, with series in North America, Asia, Europe and also Australia.

The cars were smaller than V8s, made less of a roar and weren't as fast. But with a mixture of makes and models, including Audi, BMW, Ford, Volvo, Toyota, Renault and many, many more, it turned on great races in various domestic championships.

TOCA UK was headed by expat Aussie and former Peter Brock Mobil team manager Alan Gow, who was also a partner – with Terry Morris (father of race driver Paul) and Sydney businessman Peter Adderton – in TOCA Australia, which ran the local Super Touring series.

The Consortium engaged the group to assemble a field of local and international Super Touring cars to fill the grid for the Great Race.

'I got annoyed by the fact people thought we were the bad guys in all of this,' Gow told me on the V8 Sleuth Podcast in 2019.

'We didn't start the issue. We just responded to a request from Channel 7 to put a couple of races on at Bathurst, and that's what we did.

'Looking back on it in hindsight, it was a ridiculous situation that should have never got there. It was a willy-waving competition between a broadcaster and another organisation, AVESCO. It was a shame it got to that stage and a shame it fragmented that event for a couple of years, but it wasn't our doing.'

The result of all of this was a pair of Bathurst 1000-kilometre races in October 1997, and the public was left to vote with its feet and television remote control as to which it preferred.

The 5 October race on Channel 7, the AMP Bathurst 1000, featured a small field of just 27 cars, but significantly it featured 12 different brands – BMW, Audi, Volvo, Vauxhall, Peugeot, Honda, Alfa Romeo, Renault, Hyundai, Ford, Nissan and Toyota – lining up on the grid.

Factory-backed teams from Renault (run by Formula 1 powerhouse Williams Grand Prix Engineering), Peugeot and Vauxhall (run by the Triple Eight team that later established an Australian V8 squad) were air-freighted 'Down Under' to take on the locally run, factory-backed Audi, BMW and Volvo squads.

The international flavour and star power for the race was significant. A range of British and European Super Touring stars made the trip to the Mountain. So too did legendary Formula 1 and BTCC TV commentator Murray Walker, who joined the Channel 7 commentary team.

'Channel 7 stepped in for those races and they funded those international cars,' says Eaton.

'That's the only thing that made that race happen. The amount of money Channel 7 made from Bathurst is why they invested so heavily in two litre racing. So they could continue to hold the '1000 and control the October long weekend. And, also, keep rugby league away from that date.'

Local drivers from both sides of the fence were dragged into the politics of 'their race' and 'our race' in the lead-up. Permissions for some Super Touring drivers to compete in the V8 Bathurst were withdrawn and V8 stars' attempts to negotiate pay days for appearing in the Super Touring race largely came to nought. Larry Perkins, John Bowe and Russell Ingall all were in talks to drive, but stuck fast with the V8 camp.

Not even the 'King of the Mountain', Peter Brock, was immune from commercial pressures being placed upon him. The nine-time Bathurst winner eventually locked in a deal to drive a Vauxhall Vectra with ex-F1 driver Derek Warwick in the AMP-backed race, and lined up a fortnight later in his regular #05 Holden Racing Team Commodore in the V8 Supercar race.

The Aussie racing icon had made the decision mid-year that he'd retire from full-time motorsport at the end of 1997. The brawling over his beloved Bathurst only added to his list of reasons for wanting to call it a day.

'There was a lot of drivers we had lined up for driving in cars, but they had influence exerted on them and told they couldn't do it,' recalls Gow.

'I just think that's so pathetic, and it also shows a lack of commitment on the other side of saying, "We're happy in our own skin. The V8 category is a great category. We know that Super Tourers won't take over, so who cares if some of the drivers go and race in them."

'Unfortunately, in those days, "live and let live" wasn't something that people went by. We ran those races under a lot of pressure and a real cloud, which was totally undeserved.'

On track, the Diet Coke-backed BMW team of Geoff Brabham and David Brabham claimed victory in the AMP Bathurst 1000. A reported crowd of just under 20,000 were there to see it, a markedly smaller turn-out than had seen Craig Lowndes and Greg Murphy win in a Holden Commodore 12 months earlier.

A fortnight later, on the very same tarmac, on Sunday 19 October, the new IMG-promoted Primus 1000 Classic race aired on Channel 10, featuring the cars and stars that had made up the field for the previous year's Bathurst 1000.

The V8 race was a knockout winner from a 'hearts and minds' perspective as a quoted crowd of 51,400 arrived to see a field of 41 Commodore and Falcon V8s battle over the traditional 161-lap, 1000-kilometre distance.

Loads of fans were there to see Peter Brock in his first 'last' Bathurst start, however the famous #05 Commodore suffered engine problems when co-driver Mark Skaife was at the wheel.

Larry Perkins and Russell Ingall swept home in their Castrol Commodore to take victory over the father and son combination of Steven and Jim Richards in their Valvoline Commodore run by Garry Rogers Motorsport.

The Melbourne-based GRM squad was the only team to compete in both Bathurst races because it was a regular in the Super Touring series as well and had run a Nissan Primera in the AMP Bathurst 1000 race a fortnight earlier.

'You cannot fool V8 fans. They're rusted on, they get it and they're super connected,' says Cochrane.

'I wasn't at all surprised at the success of our race. Our fans voted with their feet. We had a genuine product. The fans just didn't see two-litre cars as a truly viable proposition.'

*Some V8 Supercar fans let their feelings be known in 1997 as to which Bathurst race they were supporting.*

The double serving of 1000-kilometre races at Bathurst continued into 1998, however the V8 race switched from running in the third week of October to mid-November to work in better with the October Gold Coast IndyCar race (where V8 Supercars raced as a support category).

Again Channel 7 paid to import Super Touring cars and teams from England to add some star power to its race. A pair of factory Volvos from Tom Walkinshaw Racing, a pair of Triple Eight-run Vectras (including one driven by local Holden V8 stars Russell Ingall and Greg Murphy), a Nissan and a Honda arrived to take on the locals, headed by the Albury-based factory Audi squad of Brad Jones.

The race was a tightly contested affair at the front of the pack. After an all-day fight, Swede Rickard Rydell and Aussie-based Kiwi legend Jim Richards in their Volvo took victory over the Nissan of Jim's son Steve and leading British privateer Matt Neal.

The grid was bigger than for the previous year's race (43 cars) thanks to the addition of classes for New Zealand 'Schedule S' touring cars and local production cars. But it was still two less than the V8 race attracted the following month for what had been renamed the FAI 1000 Classic due to a sponsorship deal with the insurance company, FAI.

Having just missed out on winning at Bathurst in a Nissan in October, Steve Richards drove a Pirtek-backed Stone Brothers Racing-run Ford Falcon to victory in the V8 Bathurst race in November, alongside its regular pilot Jason Bright.

They were chased home by 1997 winners Larry Perkins and Russell Ingall and the Valvoline Commodore of Jason Bargwanna and Jim Richards, who added another Bathurst podium to his win in the Volvo just over a month earlier.

For the second year in a row the crowd for the V8 Supercar Bathurst race was again markedly larger than for the Super Touring event. Signs of the start of the end of the 'battle for Bathurst' appeared the following year.

Channel 7 stopped footing the bill to import Super Touring cars for 1999 and reverted to solely being the broadcaster (rather than an organiser) of the October event.

Basically, the Bathurst 1000 was on life support.

A new promoter (Advantage International, later renamed Octagon) replaced the ARDC and a plan was hatched to pad out the smaller field of local Super Tourers with a new V8 Falcon and Commodore class dubbed 'New Millennium Auscars'. That raised the ire of Cochrane and V8 Supercars, who deemed the category a cheap knock-off version of its own Ford versus Holden V8 product.

'This so-called new category is just a desperate, cynical attempt to get the October Bathurst race out of the mess it's in,' Cochrane told *Motorsport News* in May 1999.

'Whatever happened to the 40-car field of Super Tourers we were promised, or the 15 to 20 overseas entries? Like the last two attempts, it will fail.'

And indeed, it did.

A plan to run the new V8s and Super Tourers together was knocked back by CAMS and the 1000-kilometre race format was abandoned in favour of a festival of motorsport that included a 500-kilometre Super Touring main race (won by Paul Morris' BMW, the very same car that won the AMP race in 1997 with the Brabham brothers) and a 300-kilometre race for the new Bathurst Tourers V8 class (won by Peter Brock's stepson James in a Commodore).

But the 'Bob Jane T-Marts Bathurst '99' event was most certainly not the Bathurst 1000.

The fields were small, spectators sparse and the Sunday race day weather was horrendous: fog and rain took their own trackside seat. The event felt more like a club race event, a far cry from what it had been just three years earlier: the stop-the-nation, must-watch motorsport television broadcast attended by racing pilgrims from all over the nation.

By comparison, the success of the FAI 1000 (the word 'Classic' had been dumped from the title by this point) for V8 Supercars held in November 1999 was a clear indication that the local category was the way to go. Cochrane and his crew, powering on down their own pathway, had firmly grasped the custodianship of the Bathurst 1000.

A full field of 55 cars was on hand for the race and another big crowd turned out to see Steve Richards and Greg Murphy win in a Wynn's-backed Commodore. Craig Lowndes' second place in the race gave him enough points to seal his third championship victory. It was the first time Bathurst had counted towards the ATCC; by then it had been renamed the Shell Championship Series and is now known as the Supercars Championship.

The battle for Bathurst was over.

'If it was a war, we completely won,' claims Cochrane, unable to resist taking yet another jab.

'The only thing missing was we didn't put them on the deck of the (USS) *Missouri* to sign a peace deal.'

In June 2000, Channel 7 announced the October event would not proceed that year and confirmed its withdrawal from broadcasting at Bathurst. Subsequently, the Mount Panorama pit complex and its land were purchased from the ARDC by the Bathurst City Council. TOCA Australia shut down in 2001 when Channel 7 pulled the pin on its TV deal to cover the Super Touring Championship. And that was that.

Garth Tander and Jason Bargwanna won the 2000 FAI 1000 in November that year and V8 Supercars returned to Bathurst in the traditional month of October in 2001 to run its 1000-kilometre race. It was won by Mark Skaife and Tony Longhurst in a Holden Racing Team Commodore.

However, the race was held the weekend *after* the Labour Day weekend – and has remained so ever since (barring COVID interruptions) due to the NRL seizing the former Bathurst 1000 weekend for its Grand Final at Stadium Australia in Sydney.

IMG saw out its eight-year contract to run the V8 Bathurst event in 2004 and since 2005 the event has been run by V8 Supercars' events department, now known as Supercars Events. It has a deal with the Council for the Bathurst 1000 that runs until 2034.

'I didn't invent Bathurst. It was there a long time before me,' says Cochrane.

'It was good before we came along, but one of the things I'm most proud of is that we took it to a whole new level. It's still right up there as one of the pinnacle events in Australia, not just of motorsport but of sport full stop. I'm super proud of that.

'Bathurst is indestructible now in my opinion. It's been future-proofed for sure.'

The conflict boiled down to a story of two sides. One took the position that the traditional date, television broadcaster and race organiser was what defined the Bathurst 1000 as being 'Bathurst' to the fans and industry.

The other side was equally resolute that the star drivers and the long-running Holden and Ford V8 battle were what truly made its race 'Bathurst' in the hearts and minds of the fans.

Ultimately, who ran the race, which channel televised it and what date it ran on didn't matter to them. The V8 race smelt, looked and tasted like the Bathurst they knew, so therefore it was Bathurst.

Both races from those 1997 and 1998 years are, quite rightly, counted and celebrated today in the annals of the Great Race.

But the whole saga is proof that, despite what may be written in contracts between companies, councils or television networks, the Bathurst 1000 is really owned by the hearts and minds of Australian race fans.

## Part of a Bigger Picture

The Bathurst 1000 first became a round of the Australian Touring Car Championship (then known as the Shell Championship Series and now called the Repco Supercars Championship) in 1999.

Previously it had been either a stand-alone race or, in various years, part of the Australian Endurance Championship, which was discontinued after 1986.

The 60th anniversary race in 2023 marks the 25th year in a row that Supercars drivers have been competing for championship points as well as Bathurst glory in the Great Race.

# 20

# Women in the Great Race

**A** woman may not yet have won the Great Race at Bathurst, but there's been far more female participation in Australia's biggest race than perhaps even the most hardcore motorsport fan may realise.

A total of 29 female drivers have competed in the race dating back to the inaugural race at the Mountain in 1963, when Lorraine Hill took part. Hill shared a Morris Major Elite with Warren Blomfield and finished 35th overall.

Female participation in the race surged through the 1960s to the point where six female drivers – Sandra Bennett, Carole Corness, Diane Dickson, Christine Cole, Lynne Keefe and Ann Thomson – took part in the 1969 race, the highest number of female drivers in a single Great Race at Bathurst.

Cole (whose name changed to Christine Gibson after she and fellow racer Fred Gibson married in the 1970s) was a real pioneer for women in Australian motorsport and made her first of nine starts in the race in 1968 at the helm of a Morris Mini De Luxe alongside Midge Whiteman. Whiteman in fact still holds a special place in the history of the race alongside Jane Richardson: in 1967 they were the first all-female team to race in the Great Race at Bathurst, at the helm of a Morris 1100S.

But no other female driver has started as many Bathurst races as Gibson, and she also jointly holds the record for the best finish in the race by a woman – sixth place – achieved in the crash-shortened 1981 race in a Falcon she drove alongside car owner Joe Moore.

She shares the record with French driver Marie-Claude Beaumont, who also finished sixth and won her class in the 1975 race driving a factory-backed Alfa Romeo with Aussie open-wheeler star John Leffler before teaming with Gibson in another Alfa the following year.

'I got the opportunity for Bathurst because sponsorship had just come into the sport (it was permitted from 1968 onwards) and television coverage had just come and, consequently, people wanted something to attract both of those,' Gibson told FOX Sports in 2018.

'And if you had a bit of a gimmick, like a female (driver), I think it was welcomed. I don't think people started to consider it seriously until when the Holden Dealer Team asked me to drive for them.'

Gibson was part of a three-car HDT Torana team at Bathurst in 1970. While Colin Bond and Peter Brock (who shared his car with future Bathurst winner Bob Morris) were in the team's two headliner cars, Gibson and Sandra Bennett took their Torana XU-1 to 13th place overall (even despite a mid-race off that cost them time in the pits). They were the first of the HDT's cars to make it to the finish line in that year's race.

Unfairly though, Gibson's name is always connected to the 1981 crash that stopped the race at Bathurst.

Morris, running second in the race, tried to pass Gibson on the entry to McPhillamy Park, and the collision set off a chain reaction of cars ploughing into them that blocked the track and stopped the race.

'I was blamed because I was a female. And it wasn't right,' Gibson said in 2018 of the crash.

'I didn't want people saying it happened because of a female driver. I didn't want it to define what females were in motor racing.'

Another female Torana driver, Pat Peck, wrote herself into a chapter of Great Race history in 1972.

She remains the only woman to tackle the race single-handed, able to do so in the brief era where drivers were permitted to compete in the race without a co-driver. Disappointingly, her Holden's engine ran its bearings shortly past halfway in that year's 500-mile race.

There were other well-credentialled female racers to tackle the Bathurst 1000 during the 1970s.

Originally a rally driver, Sue Ransom made her Great Race debut with Christine Cole in 1973 in an Alfa Romeo, the first of her five starts in the Bathurst 1000.

*Christine Cole takes a stop in pit lane at Bathurst in 1970 aboard one of the Holden Dealer Team's three Toranas.*

She drove with then husband Bill Brown in an Escort in 1975 and they finished 11th. Ransom and Brown paired up again in a Ford Capri at Bathurst in 1978 – by which time they had split but they remained good friends.

The Capri ran with their names on the windscreen, however with 'Billy' upside down, a reference to his previous Bathurst roll-overs!

Knowingly, the pair ran an illegal spare engine in the race – in practice they had found that their main unit was down on power and, to ensure they could start the race, swapped to another motor that they knew wasn't legal. At the end of the race, Ransom deliberately crossed the finish line just in front of winner Peter Brock then drove into the back of the pits on Mountain Straight. This was to ensure their Capri would not be classified as a finisher: they would have finished 16th but most definitely been disqualified from the race due to the illegal V6 engine under its bonnet!

Ransom's last Bathurst 1000 start came in 1980 in a Commodore. She had a distinguished career afterwards in drag racing.

Bathurst has always attracted international drivers from all over the globe and in 1977 its bid to grow beyond Australia attracted American IndyCar racers to tackle the Great Race.

The first woman to qualify for the Indianapolis 500, Janet Guthrie, made her Bathurst 1000 debut in the same year her driving at Indy earnt her a place in the history books.

As part of the growing internationalisation of the Great Race, Guthrie paired with IndyCar legend Johnny Rutherford in a Torana. But she didn't get to turn a lap on race day: Rutherford crashed at Skyline early on.

When the world descended on Mount Panorama when the Bathurst 1000 counted for the 1987 World Touring Car Championship, two female drivers were part of the factory BMW team's roster.

Mercedes Stermitz – also Miss Austria 1983 – and Annette Meeuvissen cut their competitive teeth in Germany's Ford Fiesta Ladies Cup, before being picked up by BMW for their works-backed junior team.

Their Bathurst tilt was underwhelming. The former crashed the car heavily in practice and injured her ankle. Their BMW M3 lasted 45 laps until driveline failure put it out of the running.

Kiwi racer Heather Spurle drove a Commodore in the

1990 Bathurst 1000 alongside its owner Bob Jones. The same year she'd set the Hydroplane Woman's Water Speed Record of 271 km/h.

The next wave of international cars competing in the Bathurst race – the two-litre Super Touring era of the late 1990s – also opened the door for more female drivers to compete.

Sydney accountant Jenni Thompson drove in both years – in a Ford Mondeo and then a Peugeot 405 – and Paula Elstrek and Heidi O'Neil drove in 1998, also in a Mondeo.

One of the most high-profile female racing programs seen in Australia was the 'Castrol Cougars' race team that rolled out in 1997 in V8 Supercars.

Oil giant Castrol bankrolled a female-driven car to join the grid and racers Melinda Price and Kerryn Brewer were given the opportunity to drive a Larry Perkins team-prepared and run Commodore (the very same car he and Russell Ingall had used to win the 1995 Bathurst 1000) in select races that year on the V8 Supercar calendar.

The all-female team attracted plenty of attention from fans and finished a solid 12th overall at Bathurst in the 1997 Primus 1000 Classic after starting 41st on the grid.

'It was like every woman and daughter who was at the track wanted to come past and say hello and give a thumbs-up,' Price recalled of the Cougars program on the V8 Sleuth Podcast in 2020.

'From a fan point of view, I think everybody loved it. I remember the first year when we went down to the signing in the middle of Bathurst. I'd never had a poster with myself on it before!

'It was a bit incredible to me that people were standing there with posters of me, asking me to sign them. There wasn't a woman or a child – and some blokes as well – that walked past our garage who didn't stop to say how happy they were that there were some girls there.'

Price and Brewer went even better the following year. They crossed the line 12th but were elevated to 11th when the car that finished in front of them was excluded from the results for causing an accident.

The result remains the highest ever achieved by an all-female crew in the history of the Bathurst 1000.

Price, who made her Bathurst 1000 debut in a Toyota Corolla in 1994 – though didn't get to drive in the race – made further Bathurst 1000 starts in 1999 and 2000. She finished 17th in 1999 (from 47th on the grid) and 20th in 2000 from 56th on the grid, both times at the wheel of V8 Commodores.

With a finishing rate of 80% (four finishes from five starts), Price holds the best Bathurst 1000 finishing rate of any female driver with a significant number of starts in the race's history.

Leanne Ferrier became the next woman to tackle the Bathurst 1000 – in 2001 at the wheel of a Valvoline Holden Commodore run by Garry Rogers Motorsport.

One of the most successful female circuit racing drivers ever seen at national level, Ferrier's career deserved far more than just two Bathurst 1000 starts.

A winner in national Formula Ford competition the previous year, in a field that included future Bathurst 1000 winners Rick Kelly, Luke Youlden and Will Davison as well as future Indianapolis 500 winner Will Power, Ferrier was the real deal.

She made the jump up into V8 Supercars in 2001 in the second-tier feeder series and finished on the podium in the very first round at Wakefield Park near Goulburn. That first season had its ups and downs as Ferrier learnt the ropes, but it opened up the opportunity for her to have a seat in GRM's second Commodore for the Queensland and Bathurst V8 Supercar endurance races.

Ferrier's first Bathurst 1000 ended without her getting behind the wheel in the race after co-driver Paul Dumbrell collected Kelly at the Chase. The collision broke the steering in the former's car.

Worse news was to follow for 2002 when Ferrier's program in the V8 feeder series was abandoned by GRM and she had to patch together a late deal to race an older car in the second-tier V8 category. It took a long eight years for her to get another crack at the Great Race.

It was two-time Bathurst 1000 winner John Bowe who facilitated her return to the race in 2009, at the wheel of a Paul Cruickshank Racing-run Falcon alongside David Wall.

'He [Bowe] called and asked me if I'd be interested in running in Supercars again,' Ferrier said on the V8 Sleuth Podcast in 2021.

'John [McMellan, the then Wilson Security CEO] was keen to promote women in the sport. A lot more people were starting to understand that having a woman in the team would help lift exposure and marketing, whereas back in 2001 there wasn't as much of that awareness.

'It wasn't me searching for it. I was just fortunate that I must've been on JB's radar as a driver. I remember hanging up the phone and doing a little happy dance – this was something I never thought was going to happen again.'

Ferrier raced as Leanne Tander at Bathurst in 2009 as she and fellow racer and Bathurst winner Garth Tander had married five years earlier (they split in 2022). She placed 18th. Her then husband won the race.

That remains Ferrier's last start in the Bathurst 1000, although the well-credentialled mother of two and racer – a two-time runner-up in the Australian Drivers' Championship who later returned to racing in Formula Ford and won the national title in 2016 – does have a race win at Bathurst to her name in a Falcon.

Ferrier chalked up first place in a Touring Car Masters support race on the Sunday morning prior to the 2010 Great Race.

'It was so much fun. Driving that car across the top of the Mountain was like driving a boat across the top of the Mountain!' she says.

'That car had lots of straight-line power but not so much brakes – I was able to zoom up the Mountain, wobble across the top and zoom back down. It was a really special race, really good.'

At the time of writing, the most recent female starters in the Bathurst 1000 are Swiss-Italian racer Simona De Silvestro and Queenslander Renee Gracie.

De Silvestro made a name for herself over multiple seasons in the high-speed world of IndyCar racing in the United States, including a podium finish in Houston in 2013.

Gracie, on the other hand, had far less experience and success. Her car racing experience amounted to just two years in the Porsche Carrera Cup Australia series before a move in 2015 into the secondary Supercars category, the Dunlop Series.

The two were paired up in a one-off Bathurst 1000 wildcard entry in the 2015 race. Their Ford Falcon was run by that year's V8 Supercars Championship-winning Prodrive Racing Australia team and sponsored by Harvey Norman.

In the lead-up to the race De Silvestro and Gracie's entry received an extraordinary amount of publicity, and not all of it positive. They were dragged into a pre-race controversy when fellow Prodrive team driver David Reynolds referred to their car as the 'pussy wagon' at a post-practice press conference, a comment for which he was sanctioned by Supercars and fined $25,000.

The women's chances of a strong result in the race were hampered in the first stint courtesy of some oil at Forrest's Elbow left behind by a blown Volvo. Gracie went into a slide and was sent crashing into the wall.

The team patched up the car and the duo returned to the race to record a total of 121 laps. It was just enough for them to be classified as the 21st and final finisher in that year's race.

Deemed a hit, the 'Supergirls' concept was revisited for 2016. Harvey Norman continued to back the project and the duo drove a Nissan Altima to finish 14th, two laps behind the winning Will Davison/Jonathon Webb Commodore.

De Silvestro and Gracie took very different paths in the following years. Harvey Norman carried on its support of Supercars and backed De Silvestro as a full-time driver in a Nissan across the next three championship seasons.

Her best Bathurst 1000 finish of 13th came in 2019. That remains the last time a female driver competed in the Great Race.

Gracie carried on in the Dunlop 'Super2' Supercars development series for another few seasons before abandoning racing altogether in 2017. Within a few years she had established a flourishing career as an online adult entertainment content creator.

Though there is not currently a female driver on the grid in the Repco Supercars Championship that forms the field for the annual Bathurst 1000, female involvement in the Great Race off-track has been growing in the modern era. Women hold a range of significant positions.

There has been a far higher proliferation of women involved in roles related to mechanical, engineering and on-track performance at the Bathurst 1000 in the modern Supercars era too, as well as in management and ownership positions.

Colourful team owner Betty Klimenko made waves in 2013 when she brought her Erebus Motorsport team into V8 Supercars, with its unique Mercedes-Benz race cars.

Her colourful hair, tattoos and big personality instantly attracted a new fanbase and her team claimed the ultimate success just four years later when it won the Bathurst 1000, in 2017, with David Reynolds and Luke Youlden at the wheel.

Jessica Dane is now a significant shareholder and leader of Triple Eight Race Engineering, the team that has won the Bathurst 1000 more times in the Supercars era than any other squad.

The team also broke new ground in 2022 by making one of its engineers, Romy Mayer, the first female to be lead engineer of a Bathurst 1000 car. She called the shots for the Supercheap Auto-sponsored Commodore of Craig Lowndes and Declan Fraser that finished eighth.

Long the domain of men from an on-air perspective – especially in the early years of the Great Race – the Bathurst 1000's television coverage has also provided a platform for an expanded female perspective. Since FOX Sports took over the telecast rights in 2015, host Jess Yates has been fronting all rounds, including Bathurst, of the Supercars Championship.

Respected female pit reporters, including Briony Ingerson and Riana Crehan, have become regulars in the race's telecast over the last 15 years – over its time on Channel 7 and FOX. This is a far cry from the first few decades of the event's television coverage, when it was wall-to-wall men in hosting, commentary and pit lane reporting roles.

Women's sport has flourished in recent years in Australia with the creation of leagues and competitions, including AFLW, NRLW, the W-League in football and WBBL in cricket.

From a motorsport perspective, junior karting in Australia features plenty of girls with a passion for motorsport and a love of going fast, but it's proven to be difficult for many of them to turn their passion into a full-time career at the top level in car racing. Female participation and education sessions for girls and young women run by Motorsport Australia are helping, but there's still a long way to go.

The Bathurst 1000 has seen it all over the years, but in its first 60 years it's never witnessed a woman win its Great Race from behind the wheel.

Surely the next 60 years of Bathurst 1000 history changes that.

## Front Row Lock-Outs

Only six times in Bathurst Great Race history has one team locked out the front row of the grid for the race. It happened three times in the 500-mile era of the race – in 1967, 1970 and 1971 – and in each instance by V8 Falcons entered officially by the Ford Motor Company of Australia.

Each of the three times it happened in the 1000-kilometre era of the race, different teams were involved. The Holden Dealer Team's Toranas locked out the first row of the grid in 1974, Tom Walkinshaw Racing's Jaguars did it in 1985 and the last time it was done was 1988, when Dick Johnson Racing's Shell Sierras started in the first two positions.

There was something slightly different about 1988 though: it was the only year in the event's history that a rolling start (rather than a standing start) was used.

# 21

# You Want to Race What?

Ford and Holden loom large in the history books of the Bathurst 1000, but they haven't had Mount Panorama completely to themselves over the years.

A wide array of makes, models, sizes and shapes have lined up on the grid for the Great Race, some of them more memorable than others.

For example, only tragics would know that a Dodge once competed in the race – it was a case of 'blink and you'd have missed it'!

Retail price determined the various classes of the race in the early years. Essentially that meant organisers had to establish a price cap at the upper end so that more expensive, lavish cars didn't compete.

When this was relaxed in 1967, a class for cars retailing for anywhere over $4500 was established. It attracted, of all things, a 5.2-litre V8-powered 1963-model Dodge Phoenix TD2.

An enormous car with a three-speed auto transmission and four-wheel drum brakes, the burly Dodge was piloted by

Barry Sharp and Lindsay Derriman. It dumbfounded the pre-race critics by not only finishing, but coming home fourth in class and 19th outright, albeit 12 laps down on the winning Falcon XR GT of Harry Firth and Fred Gibson.

It beat one of the Alfa GTV 1600s that otherwise dominated its class and came home two positions in front of the other V8 automatic in the race, an XR Falcon prototype.

The Phoenix remains the only Dodge to have ever competed in the Great Race at Bathurst.

The class price rule change that allowed the Dodge to compete in 1967 also opened the way for the last Citroen to compete in the Great Race the following year.

Queensland racing star Glyn Scott (whose sons Gary and Tony would later compete in the Bathurst 1000: Gary was the pole-sitter for Nissan in 1986) and advertising executive and Formula Vee racer Bill Daly teamed up in a Citroen DS21 Pallas.

A flat bug-shaped front-wheel-drive with a 2.2-litre inline four-cylinder engine, it didn't stand a chance up against the rapid Alfa Romeo 1750 GTVs that dominated Class E. It came at a time where entrants looking to compete in the race had a wide array of cars on the market to choose from.

Unlike the Phoenix, the Scott/Daly Citroen didn't make it to the finish. Daly was at the wheel when it crashed out of the race at Forrest's Elbow and went on a wall-of-death-like ride up to the top of the clay bank on the outside of the corner. He emerged OK but the French machine was a goner.

The first year that the race was run over a 1000-kilometre distance, 1973, marked the first and last time a Subaru took part in the Bathurst classic.

In more recent years, the brand has unquestionably

become better known for its success in rally competition across the world, but a Subaru GSR did make one appearance at Mount Panorama, in the hands of Chris Heyer and Peter Mill, and finished 23rd overall and sixth in Class B that year.

That marked the first of Heyer's 11 Bathurst 1000 starts. The Sydney Volkswagen dealer stuck with racing VWs through the 1970s and into the early 1980s before making a switch to an Audi 5+5.

In 1982 this car became just the second Audi, and the first in 15 years, to tackle the Great Race. It was entered for Heyer and co-driver Peter Lander with backing from Audi's importer and assistance from Germany in the form of team manager Peter Steinmeyer.

Although the 2.2-litre, five-cylinder, front-wheel-drive 5+5 lacked the grunt of its top three-litre class rivals, the car had endurance credentials, having completed a 24-hour reliability run at Surfers Paradise in 1981.

Heyer campaigned this car in four consecutive Bathurst 1000s from 1982 and finished every year, including a best outright result of 16th (fifth in class) on its debut.

Nissan's wins in the Bathurst 1000 in 1991 and 1992 came with the mighty GT-R that was nicknamed 'Godzilla'. But plenty of fans will have forgotten the Nissan Pulsar EXA Turbo that tackled the Mountain in the 1980s.

While its Bluebirds battled for outright honours, Nissan fielded this unusual 1.5-litre turbocharged beast for Christine Gibson and Bob Muir in the under three-litre class in 1983.

The combination of front-wheel-drive with a spool differential, no power steering and a turbocharged engine delivering around 300 horsepower made this car brutal on its drivers – and on its driveshafts!

Glenn Seton joined Gibson in the car for 1984 but it failed to finish in either of its Bathurst starts.

'I drove it once and I said to Christine, "You are a hero, this is a terrible car,"' Gibson's husband, Fred, the 1967 Bathurst winner, who later took over running the Nissan team in Australia, said on the V8 Sleuth Podcast in 2021.

'It had so much power: it had a bigger turbo than it should have had, and it had different length driveshafts. One was longer than the other so it torque-steered so much.'

Two years later came the last Fiat to compete in the Bathurst 1000 and the first of the Italian brand's cars to compete in the race in a decade.

The diminutive Fiat Uno Turbo was an 800-kilogram, 200 horsepower tiny car, one of two Group A Uno Turbos brought into Australia by Fiat importer LNC Industries and sold to Perth dealer Frank Cecchele.

Both cars made the trek from Perth to Bathurst in 1986: a left-hand-drive race car and a right-hand-drive spare, which was heavily drawn on for parts during a litany of race-week reliability issues!

Western Australian drivers Gordon Mitchell and Allan McCarthy (who was a last-minute replacement for John Farrell) scraped into last place on the 59-car grid and made it through 110 race laps but were ultimately not classified.

The mid-1980s period, at the height of international Group A touring car racing, saw the introduction of even more unique cars to race all over the world.

A Maserati Biturbo competed in the 1987 race and, as far as factory-backed Bathurst entries go, they don't come much more underwhelming and unusual than the Italian brand's one-car effort that year as part of its World Touring Car Championship program.

The car appeared strong on paper, thanks to a 2.5-litre twin-turbo V6 engine, and there were two former Great Race winners among its driver line-up: German Armin Hahne and Aussie legend Kevin Bartlett. Both had shared Bathurst wins with John Goss: Hahne won in 1985 in a Jaguar XJ-S with Goss and Bartlett had shared the win with him in 1974 in a Falcon.

But the Maserati was both slow and unreliable. It qualified 34th with third driver, ex-Alfa Romeo Formula 1 driver Bruno Giacomelli, not even quick enough to make the field. The Maserati was retired from the race after just 29 laps with a broken axle and never returned to Mount Panorama.

Volvos appeared in the Bathurst Great Race in the 500-mile era in the 1960s but the entry of a near bog-standard 242 GT for David McKay and Spencer Martin in 1979 raised plenty of eyebrows.

McKay, an Aussie motoring journalist and prominent motoring identity, won the inaugural Australian Touring Car Championship in 1960 in a Jaguar, and open-wheel star Martin won the Australian Drivers Championship in a Repco Brabham for Bob Jane's team in 1966 and 1967.

But they were far from contenders to win at the Mountain in 1979 and were deemed by many to be nothing more than a mobile chicane.

They ran the whole race on a single set of standard Uniroyal steel radial tyres and completed 129 laps in the time it took the winning Torana of Peter Brock and Jim Richards to run 163!

Volvo later returned to Bathurst with success in the 1990s in the two-litre Super Touring era, the same period where a few more highly unusual cars popped up on the Great Race grid via the Super Touring rules that were in use worldwide at the time.

The appearance of a Hyundai Lantra in the two-litre class in 1994 at Bathurst added both manufacturer and model to the list of cars to tackle the Great Race.

Electrical issues took the Steve Hardman and Geoff Full-driven car out of the '94 race, and history proved that the Mountain was just a bit too much for the little Korean cars. Two started in 1997 and failed to finish and another started in 1998 and, while running at the finish, had only completed 107 laps due to various delays and wasn't classified as a race finisher. That left Hyundais with four starts and zero finishes in the Great Race.

The last Lantra appearance in 1998 came in the same year that production cars were added to the Super Touring Bathurst 1000 race to fill up the field. That cleared the way for the Honda Civic to return to the Great Race for the first time since 1976.

The car that ran in '98 (including then-Australian Formula Ford Champion Adam Macrow in the driver line-up) was far more advanced than the pint-sized Civics of the 1970s and lasted 34 laps before driveline problems eliminated it from the race.

But what made it even more unusual was the fact it had a sunroof – making it highly likely the last car to compete in the Bathurst 1000 with one!

## Fields of Dreams

The biggest Bathurst Great Race field in history sits at 63 cars – a milestone reached in 1969, 1978 and 1984. On the flip side the smallest field in the race's history is 25 cars – in 2014 and again in 2020.

Field sizes in the modern era have been capped by the number of cars permitted to compete in the Supercars Championship and how many one-off wildcards are granted by Supercars.

The lowest finishing rate came in the 1977 race won by Allan Moffat and Jacky Ickx. Only 36.6% of the cars that started (22 of 60) were classified as finishers at the end of the 1000-kilometre race.

The modern Supercars have proven to be far more reliable and finishing rates in the last decade or so at the Bathurst 1000 have been much better. The best finishing rate sits at 92% (24 of 26 starters) in the 2018 race won by Craig Lowndes and Steve Richards.

## Close but Not Quite

Three drivers – Brad Jones, Cameron McConville and Warren Luff – hold a unique place in Bathurst Great Race history as having the most podium finishes without winning the race.

Each has stood on the podium six times and come close on more than one occasion to winning the coveted prize.

These days Jones runs a four-car team in the Supercars Championship but he enjoyed a brilliant career behind the wheel and won two Australian Super Touring Championships for Audi as well as five AUSCAR and one NASCAR super speedway crowns.

He finished second in 1994 alongside Craig Lowndes in a Holden Racing Team Commodore, second in an Audi with German star Frank Biela in 1997 and was runner-up again in

2001 with Scotsman John Cleland in a Ford Falcon run by his own Brad Jones Racing team.

McConville finished second with Lowndes in 1999 for HRT and drove a BJR Commodore to second place in 2009 with the late Kiwi, Jason Richards.

Luff scored back-to-back runner-up results in 2017 and 2018 in a Walkinshaw Racing Commodore, both times alongside Scott Pye.

## 22

# They Finally Made It

**M**ount Panorama has proven to be both cruel and kind to numerous drivers over the years and it's forced plenty of Great Race winners to wait many years for their crowning moment of motorsport glory.

In the case of 2014 winner Paul Morris, his breakthrough Bathurst win came in his 22nd and, ultimately, last start in the race – in one of the most gripping finishes ever seen on the Mountain.

He still retains the record for the most starts by any driver in the history of the Bathurst 500/1000 before managing to score victory.

However, back in 1997 he was the last driver in anyone's mind to ever appear on such a list, let alone at the top of it. That's because he and Kiwi Craig Baird drove their Diet Coke BMW to victory in the 1997 AMP Bathurst 1000, the race for two-litre Super Tourers, in Morris' fifth start in the race.

But what should have been the sweetness of Great Race triumph quickly turned sour when the duo were excluded from victory: it was determined that Baird exceeded the maximum permitted driving time in his last stint in the race.

They had sprayed the champagne on the podium, held aloft the winner's trophy and experienced what it meant to be a Bathurst 1000 winner.

And then it was all taken away.

Despite this Morris returned time and time again to tackle the Great Race. He paired with Mark Skaife in a Holden Racing Team Commodore and finished third in 1999 but that remained his only Bathurst 1000 podium finish until Ford Performance Racing opted to sign him up in a co-driver role 15 years later to young gun Chaz Mostert in the team's #6 Pepsi Max-backed Ford Performance Racing Falcon FG.

Some in the industry scoffed at the selection. Not for nothing was Morris nicknamed the 'Dirty Dangerous Dude': he had a reputation for antagonistic driving and a fondness for handing out on-track payback to his rivals.

There were plenty of non-believers externally too when it came to FPR's decision to sign up Morris, but the 2014 Bathurst race delivered him his long-awaited Bathurst wish on a day where the deck was stacked against the duo for a few reasons.

Firstly, they were forced to line up on the last row of the grid – in 25th position – after Mostert was excluded from Friday qualifying for passing another car under red flags.

As well as that, Morris found himself wedged in the wall at Griffins Bend on lap 46 of 161: the track surface had broken up and he found himself skating off the road.

The delay dropped him back to 24th – last car running in the race. But it turned out that the panel damage to the front of the Falcon was mainly superficial, caused no major structural issues and ultimately didn't affect its speed.

The race was stopped for nearly an hour so officials could patch up the damaged section of track.

As to what happened next, various story lines played out. With just laps to go, Mostert found himself hunting down leader Jamie Whincup.

The Red Bull Commodore was running low on fuel and eventually coughed at Forrest's Elbow on the last lap, creating an opening for Mostert – in just his second Bathurst 1000 start – to pounce upon the slowing Holden and flee down Conrod Straight to score a popular win.

The only lap his car led all race was the lap that mattered most, lap 161.

A teary Morris flung himself out of the Pepsi Ford team's garage to greet his winning co-driver, Mostert, who was born in April 1992 – six months after Morris had made his Bathurst 1000 debut in a Toyota Corolla and won his class on his first attempt.

They were very much the odd couple but their victory – in one of the most unpredictable races – is a classic Mount Panorama moment that gets replayed repeatedly.

'I probably should've retired 10 years ago but I kept coming back because I wanted to win the thing,' said Morris post-race.

'Thanks to Chaz, now I can tick the box and can probably hang up the helmet. A lot of people thought it was a pretty weird decision when [FPR team bosses] Tim [Edwards] and Rod [Nash] gave me a gig.

'But it turned out they knew what they were doing, didn't it?'

Morris made the decision to call time on his Bathurst 1000 career and go out a winner. He's since competed in a range of motorsports, including the jumping Stadium Super Trucks. Away from the track he's helped a number of young drivers develop their careers via his Norwell Motorplex driver training complex in Queensland. Among them are current Supercars aces Anton De Pasquale, Broc Feeney and Brodie Kostecki as well as his own son, Nash, who was late taking up the sport but is making up time rapidly, having won the 2021 Super3 Supercars feeder series.

But winning Bathurst remains Morris Snr's crowning glory.

'It meant everything,' he told Greg Rust on his *Rusty's Garage* LiSTNR podcast in 2019 – speaking of how much it meant to finally win Bathurst.

'It's the only thing I ever dreamt of. It was a real life-changing experience for me. You just go from being a dickhead with a race car to a hero overnight. Guys that win multiple Bathursts, that's why they are up there. I understand why someone like Dick [Johnson] is a hero to so many people now, for sure.'

The son of former Australian Production Car Champion Kent Youlden, Luke Youlden made his Bathurst 1000 debut at the wheel of Larry Perkins' second Castrol team Commodore in 2000.

A 'nearly man', he never quite cracked it for a full-time V8 Supercar driver but he embedded himself as a trusted co-driver and was signed up by some of the top teams through the 2000s and 2010s.

He came close to winning Bathurst in 2003 at wheel of a Supercheap Auto Ford Falcon, with team owner/driver Steve Ellery, when the duo finished third. He found his services in demand for more than a decade with various teams, including Stone Brothers Racing, Ford Performance Racing and Brad Jones Racing.

Youlden forged a partnership with Kiwi Fabian Coulthard at BJR in 2013 and moved across with him to DJR Team Penske for 2016: however, his contract wasn't renewed and he found himself facing his V8 racing mortality.

'I was out of a drive at the end of 2016. It's probably the worst I've felt in Supercars,' he told me on the V8 Sleuth Podcast in 2020.

'But then I went from feeling my Supercars career was finished at the end of 2016 to winning Bathurst the year after. It was mega.'

Youlden joined Erebus Motorsport for 2017 as co-driver to David Reynolds, the team a proud self-confessed clan of misfits and rejects from other teams who had come together to create something special under team owner Betty Klimenko.

The duo overcame a day of lashing rain and tricky conditions to lead 40 laps and Reynolds brought it home to victory at the wheel of their #9 Penrite oil-backed Commodore VF. For Youlden, whose wife Stacey worked as a data engineer for Paul Morris' race team during his team's Bathurst attempts in the 2000s, it finally gave him a Bathurst 1000 win in his 18th attempt.

'We were a top two or three car all day,' he recalls of the race win.

'The Tickford cars were better in the rain but none of us had driven in the rain all week in the lead-up to the race and it started raining on the grid. I knew if we could stay top three all day, and if the track dried out, we'd be hot to trot. And that's what happened.

'Being in the right car at the right time isn't just luck. You've got to perform in other cars, and that leads you up to that point. I appreciated it more because it was so late in my career. I appreciated that win because I know how hard it is to win. I've been on to win that race a few times and it never came out. I really savoured it in 2017. It was an unbelievable feeling.'

It so easily could have been two Bathurst 1000 wins for Youlden too. He and Reynolds dominated the next year's race – in 2018 – and led 112 laps before Reynolds succumbed to muscle cramps while leading. That set off a chain reaction of problems and a pit lane penalty that dumped them back in the pack. They eventually finished 13th.

Youlden made two more Bathurst 1000 starts – in 2019 and 2021 – to take him to 21 starts in the Great Race.

But it's his 18th start he'll remember forever.

Another in the '18 starts before winning' club at Bathurst is Lee Holdsworth.

A plucky racer who grew up in Brisbane, Holdsworth cut his teeth in the one-make Commodore Cup series in the early 2000s and made moves into Supercars via the development secondary series.

He made his Bathurst 1000 debut in 2004 and was signed up by noted talent scout team boss Garry Rogers as a full-time driver in 2006.

However, barring a third place in 2009 for Rogers' team alongside Michael Caruso, Holdsworth turned up time and time again to Bathurst and came away with not much more than servings of disappointment dished up by the Mount Panorama 'gods of racing'.

One of the worst disappointments came in 2014, when he was collected by an out-of-control Russell Ingall at Griffins Bend at the top of Mountain Straight, the hit tipping Holdsworth's Mercedes-Benz up onto its side – and out of the race.

A move to former Dick Johnson Racing co-owner Charlie Schwerkolt's new Commodore team also didn't reap rewards. Holdsworth was involved in a massive crash in Darwin in mid-2016 that fractured his pelvis, a knee and multiple ribs and sent him to the sidelines for a few months.

He returned in time for Bathurst that October, but his Commodore lasted just two laps before being sidelined with engine problems. His bad Bathurst luck reappeared 12 months later: again, Holdsworth found himself out with engine trouble – on this occasion, with 76 laps completed.

Holdsworth moved to the Tickford Ford team for 2019 and placed ninth that year and seventh in 2020 before being dumped by the team post-season and left without a full-time drive in Supercars for 2021.

So he picked up a plum co-drive for Bathurst alongside Chaz Mostert in a Walkinshaw Andretti United Commodore and, like Youlden, rode the wave of a brilliant comeback to at long last seal victory at Bathurst in his 18th attempt.

Mostert took pole position in record time and their #25 Commodore was the class act of the field on race day, even overcoming a puncture during one of Mostert's stints to speed home to a popular victory after leading 106 of the 161 laps.

He and Holdsworth leapt onto the roof of their confetti-covered Commodore's in Victory Lane and lapped up the applause from the crowd. Losing his full-time driver had ultimately turned out to be a blessing in disguise for the ever-popular Holdsworth. That day, his post-race celebrations were a world away from the devastation that Mount Panorama had caused him earlier in his career.

His first five Bathurst 1000s – between 2004 and 2008 – yielded four non-finishes and a last place finish and he failed to see the chequered flag in the 2008 and 2009 Bathurst 12 Hour races run for production cars.

At the 2009 12 Hour, after his family team had packed up its damaged car, Holdsworth headed to the top of the Mountain to spectate. He cracked open a beer, dug a hole, took a sip then shared the beer with the Mountain, pleading for it to one day be good to him. After then apologising for anything he may have done in the past to upset it, he covered up the hole and gave the ground a pat.

Later that year he returned to take his first Bathurst 1000 podium finish and, nearly 13 years on, the Mountain rewarded him.

'I'm not a spiritual sort of person, but if there's anywhere where you feel the need to speak to the Mountain or the ground, it's up there,' Holdsworth told the *Parked Up Podcast* during an interview that touched on his 2021 Great Race win.

'Thirteen or so years later, he's finally forgiven me, and I guess maybe that beer has finally seeped all the way to the bottom of the Mountain now!

'You feel like there's Mountain gods and they've decided the race win before you've even got there. It's pretty special for them to choose myself and Chaz this year.'

His 2021 Bathurst win also delivered Holdsworth a return to the Supercars grid for 2022 in the form of a one-year deal with Grove Racing to drive one of its Mustangs, after its buy-out of the former Kelly Racing team.

He made the call late in 2022, not long after celebrating his 500th Supercars Championship race, to retire from full-time Supercars racing to focus on a growing real estate career and his young family.

But he'll be back as a co-driver for the 60th anniversary Great Race in 2023. After all, the Mountain has a pull that even those who have finally conquered it after many attempts just can't quite resist …

Allan Grice had been dubbed the best driver not yet to win the Bathurst classic as he headed into the 1986 race.

A one-time pastry cook in Maitland, New South Wales, Grice had a reputation as a hard charger. Unafraid to speak his mind and willing to put the nose of his car into a gap, he took pride in being the privateer Holden hero who took it up to the mighty factory Holden Dealer Team and its high-profile stars through the 1970s and into the 1980s. This approach won him plenty of fans.

He made his Great Race debut in a diminutive Fiat 124 Sport with legendary motoring journalist Bill Tuckey in 1968 and finished 18th outright and ninth in Class D, outpaced by the big V8 Monaros and Falcons in the same class.

Grice returned in a Torana four years later, in 1972, however he was a nominated reserve on the entry list and not enough cars dropped out pre-race on Sunday morning to open up a grid slot for him. Consequently he was left to watch on as the race began.

He came back to Bathurst in 1973 in a Torana XU-1 and ran every following year of the decade in a variety of V8 Toranas. But it took Grice until 1978 to see the finish line again. That year he crossed the line second in an A9X Torana alongside open-wheeler racer John Leffler.

A runner-up finish in 1982 alongside trucking business owner Alan Browne and a third place alongside Colin Bond in 1983 gave Grice two more trips to the Bathurst podium, but not the win he craved.

By 1986 he'd worked his way into a strong position for another Bathurst assault. A season racing a V8 Commodore against the best touring car drivers in the world in the European Touring Car Championship had shown he could match it with them, even if the final race results were lacking.

For Bathurst, his 15th start in the annual classic, he paired up with privateer driver – and owner of the V8 Commodore they were to drive – Graeme Bailey, a Bathurst regular in the late '70s and '80s.

Hailing from the Central Coast of New South Wales, Bailey owned Chickadee, a major poultry supplier. Although he was an amateur racer without the enormous budget of the factory-backed Holden, Nissan, BMW and Volvo teams of the era, Bailey had brought enough financial backing to Grice's European racing campaign to co-drive with him in the first three rounds of the ETCC and get the car onto the grid.

Bailey's Aussie-based Commodore – eye-catching, with its fluoro yellow-tinged paint scheme and Chickadee signage – had been built by Grice's long-time car preparation guru Les Small. The lessons learnt from a season of racing in Europe, along with Yokohama tyres and strong V8 engines, gave Grice plenty of confidence he could finally break his Bathurst drought.

He qualified second in the Saturday morning 'Hardies Heroes' Shootout for pole position and then exercised his car's superiority from the moment the green flag dropped to start the race.

Bolting into the lead, he left the field in his wake, keen to apply the same sort of instant domination that he and so many of his rivals had been on the receiving end of from Peter Brock in the late '70s and early '80s.

'Brock used to put on his "Brock Crush", where he'd go hard early at the start, then eventually look in the mirror to see if anyone was still there,' says Grice. 'I'd been quicker than Brock all year in Europe. It was time to put the "Brock Crush" on Brock.'

Brock started 11th on the grid. His Mobil Commodore had had to undergo an all-night rebuild after co-driver Allan Moffat had come to grief in it during Friday practice at the top of the Mountain.

'The King' made it up to second place by lap three but couldn't lay a glove on the Chickadee Commodore all day. Car owner Bailey did just one stint in the race and Grice drove 137 of the 163 laps (845-kilometres of the 1000-kilometre race distance) to lead home Brock's Mobil teammates John

Harvey and Neal Lowe by a minute and a half when the chequered flag flew.

Not even a small run off the road by Bailey at Hell Corner during his stint or a differential seal that was leaking oil and leaving a tell-tale dirty stain on the back of the Holden could stop Grice from breaking his Bathurst drought.

At the time Grice's 16 starts marked a record wait for a first Great Race win.

'You can win every race all year and come last at Bathurst and be a mug,' Grice grins.

'And you can be ordinary all year and win Bathurst and be a hero. It means that much to motorsport in Australia. That day we were the heroes.'

Bailey never competed in the Bathurst 1000 again. He went out a winner and still owns the '86-winning Commodore.

Of others to eventually win the race after repeated attempts, current Supercars star Shane van Gisbergen stands out. He had to wait a long while after his Bathurst debut as a teenager in a Stone Brothers Racing-run Team Kiwi Falcon in 2007.

He broke through to win the race for the first time in 2020, in his 14th start, joining Paul Dumbrell, John Harvey and John French in the '14 starts to win' club.

Dumbrell teamed with Jamie Whincup to win in 2012, after having debuted in 1999 as a teenager. He retired from full-time Supercars racing at the end of 2011 and made the move to a co-driver role alongside his long-time friend. The Bathurst result came on the way to Whincup's fourth championship win.

The legendary speedway, open-wheel and touring car driver John Harvey won in 1983 alongside Peter Brock and Larry Perkins. Famously, Harvey had driven the first stint then handed over his #25 Holden Dealer Team Commodore to the '82 winning duo after their #05 car blew its engine a few laps into the race.

Two years earlier John French co-drove the Tru-Blu Falcon XD to victory with its owner/driver Dick Johnson in the crash-shortened 1981 race.

It's ironic that French and Harvey should both take 14 starts to win the Bathurst classic given that the latter made his Great Race debut alongside the former in a Mini Cooper S in 1965. They ended up in the same place in the record books.

Regardless of how many years it took all of these drivers to finally win the race, they're all now part of the history book of the Mountain forever.

They just had to wait a little longer for their page to be included.

# The Youngest Bathurst 1000 Winners

Up-and-coming Bathurst 1000 drivers in the V8 Supercars and now Supercars Championship era of racing tend to progress to the top level of competition earlier than did those in the largely amateur 1960s and 1970s.

It's therefore no surprise to see that five of the six youngest drivers to win the Great Race have done so since the beginning of the V8 Supercars era in 1997.

Rick Kelly's win alongside Greg Murphy in 2003 wrote the Mildura-raised racer into the record books as the youngest ever winner – at 20 years and 268 days of age – eclipsing the previous mark of 22 years and 107 days set by Craig Lowndes when he won in 1996.

Chaz Mostert's 2014 win sees him third on the list (22 years, 185 days) ahead of Nick Percat (who was 23 years and 25 days old in 2011) and Percat's 2011 winning partner Garth Tander, who was 23 years and 233 days old when he won for the first time in 2000 alongside Jason Bargwanna.

Greg Murphy is the youngest New Zealander to win the race. He was aged 24 years and 44 days when he won alongside Lowndes in 1996.

## 23

# Death on the Mountain

**T**he Bathurst 1000 event has, on occasion, provided a brutal reminder that despite plenty of advancements in track and car safety, motor racing will never be an entirely safe sport.

The Mount Panorama circuit has claimed lives. It's fast, unforgiving and has delivered fatal consequences when things have gone wrong.

All up, 16 competitors have lost their lives at the Mountain in both car and motorcycle races over the years. Of those deaths, 11 had occurred before the annual 1000-kilometre Great Race's first fatality in 1986.

The death of Sydney privateer driver Mike Burgmann in that year's race provided a sombre reminder of the dangers of motorsport.

Burgmann, then 39, was a financial management consultant and board member of the organisers of the race at the time, the Australian Racing Drivers' Club. He was a married father of six – four daughters and two sons – and had started motor racing four years earlier in a twin cam Escort.

He made his Bathurst 1000 debut in 1983 in a Chevrolet Camaro with future Great Race winner Tony Longhurst and finished eighth overall in 1984 in a Mazda RX-7 with Bob Stevens, who shared a new Commodore with Burgmann the following year.

For 1986 he'd given a young driver, Mal Rose, the opportunity to co-drive at Bathurst in the very same Commodore.

Burgmann had started from 27th place on the grid and had picked up a handful of spots in the opening laps until it was spotted that his windscreen had been damaged. The call was made that he would be best to come to the pits so it could be dealt with.

But he didn't make it.

Racing down the high-speed Conrod Straight nearing the end of his sixth lap, Burgmann's Commodore was passing Garry Willmington's Jaguar XJ-S when it lost control and slammed head on into the concrete wall bordering the earth bank just before the bridge.

The crumpled wreck told the story. The impact completely crushed the front of the V8-powered Holden back to the firewall; its driver was torn out of the seat and found in the rear of the cabin when officials got to the car. The seat belt buckle had broken due to the enormous forces of the impact. He stood no chance of survival.

A plaque in his honour was unveiled at the following year's race and is affixed to the wall near the bridge at the bottom of Conrod Straight.

*Mike Burgmann (fourth from the right) poses with his team ahead of his ill-fated 1986 Bathurst race. He became the Great Race's first fatality.*

Kiwi Denny Hulme had been to the top of the pile in world motorsport long before he first tackled Mount Panorama.

The 1967 Formula 1 World Champion at the wheel of a Repco-Brabham, Hulme (who was nicknamed 'The Bear' because of his gruff manner) had raced all over the world in Formula 1, IndyCars and CanAm sportscars before he made his Great Race debut at the wheel of a JPS Team BMW in 1982 for the Frank Gardner-run team.

He became a regular in the race each year from 1984 onwards and linked up with Larry Perkins to co-drive a Commodore in 1987 and 1988. For 1989 he re-established ties with Gardner, who was managing Tony Longhurst's

Benson & Hedges team, and drove one of the team's Ford Sierras with Longhurst and 1980 Formula 1 World Champion Alan Jones to fifth place in that year's race.

He stuck with the team for the next few years and finished fourth overall and won his class in a BMW M3 in 1991 with production car and Porsche racing expert Peter Fitzgerald.

For 1992 the team paired him for Bathurst with a young gun, Paul Morris. The promising Queensland-based racer was coming off the back of his debut Australian Touring Car Championship season in a third team BMW alongside regular drivers Longhurst and Jones. He'd also given a great account of himself by finishing second in the Sandown 500 in Melbourne, the traditional warm-up race for the Bathurst 1000.

At Bathurst the team opted to put Hulme in the car for the opening stint, a logical choice given his more extensive experience and, despite two early pit stops – one to replace a flat tyre and another to swap to wet weather tyres when the rain started to fall – he had recovered to run in a solid 14th place by lap 32.

But the #20 BMW didn't complete lap 33.

It had hit the wall on the right-hand side of Conrod Straight relatively gently and come to a rest on the opposite side of the road just before the apex of the right-hand turn leading into the Caltex Chase. It appeared to be an innocuous accident at first sight, or perhaps some form of mechanical failure that had stopped the car.

But the reality was far different.

The 56-year-old had suffered a heart attack behind the wheel of the yellow and black BMW, and he was pronounced dead soon after.

Hulme became the first Formula 1 World Champion to die of natural causes and the second fatality on track in Bathurst 1000 history.

Tragedy hit the Mountain again just two years later, in 1994, but not on Bathurst 1000 race day. Rather it was during Thursday qualifying.

Victorian privateer driver Don Watson had started racing in Porsche Cup and production cars before making his Bathurst 1000 debut in a V8 Commodore in the same 1992 race in which Hulme had died.

The owner of a transport business based in Bacchus Marsh, located between Melbourne and Ballarat, Watson had bitten the bullet for 1994 and commissioned racing legend Larry Perkins to build a new VP model racing Commodore for him to use in the Australian Touring Car Championship and the two big races of the year at Sandown and Bathurst.

A hobby racer, Watson had enlisted Western Australian Ian Love to join him to co-drive in the two long distance races and they finished 14th in the Sandown 500.

But the #26 Holden didn't make it to race day.

The white and blue Commodore, the same colours and appearance of Watson's fleet of transport trucks, fired off the track at high speed at Caltex Chase on Watson's second flying lap of Thursday morning.

It didn't make the fast right-hand corner, but instead shot straight ahead down through the grass and sand, hit the concrete wall to the left at almost completely unabated speed and smashed into an earth-filled tyre barrier.

It instantly lifted and somersaulted the Commodore onto its roof, and the car came to rest on top of the wall.

The 42-year-old was pronounced dead at Bathurst Hospital a short time later.

Later inspection showed that a front brake rotor had shattered, leaving Watson without brakes and an instantly damaged left-front tyre, unable to slow down or turn at the fastest part of the track.

'The 1994 Bathurst accident was an absolute tragedy,' says Perkins.

'Don was a friend and someone I'll never forget. He had no ego; he just loved to drive. And the logical way he went about his business meant he had the total respect of all my mechanics.

'Don always took his family to race meetings – his wife Noelene and their children, who were a similar age to my kids [Jack and Nichola]. We all got on well.'

A push to improve safety at the Chase following Watson's crash in 1994 resulted in the tyre wall being moved to allow considerable expansion of the sand trap.

The V8 touring car teams paid their respects to Watson at Bathurst in March 1995 for the third round of the Australian Touring Car Championship. The front row of the grid was left vacant as a mark of respect to Watson and also to Gregg Hansford, Perkins' 1993 Bathurst-winning co-driver, who had been killed at Phillip Island a week earlier.

The Don Watson Transport business continues to thrive, its blue and white trucks a constant presence on the highways around the country and a reminder of the popular racer taken too soon.

The 2006 Bathurst 1000 became a memorial for the race's most winning driver, Peter Brock, who had been killed in a tarmac rally crash in Western Australia that September.

But, while the Australasian racing industry was still coming to terms with the death of the 'King of the Mountain', the Mount Panorama circuit again came into focus, with the death of another driver in a support race for that year's Great Race.

Kiwi Mark Porter had made his Bathurst 1000 debut in a Falcon in 2002. He became a regular in Australia racing in the second tier V8 Supercar Development Series and finished 11th in the 2005 Bathurst 1000 in a Commodore with countryman Kayne Scott.

For 2006 he'd put together his own racing team, based in his new home of Queensland, to compete in the second-tier category with a Commodore originally built by the Holden Racing Team. Additionally, he also did a deal with Brad Jones Racing to co-drive its second Team BOC Falcon in the Sandown and Bathurst V8 Supercar endurance races with Canberra-based racer Dale Brede.

That meant Porter was busy at Bathurst competing in both his own Commodore and the Jones team's Ford, given that both categories were racing in the same weekend.

But it all went tragically awry in the first Fujitsu Series race on the Friday afternoon, when Porter's Commodore spun on its own oil at the top of the Mountain and was left exposed to the following cars travelling at 200km/h coming around the preceding blind left turn.

The 32-year-old Kiwi, married with a two-year-old son, was helpless and heavily exposed to the oncoming traffic. Commodore driver Chris Alajajian flicked his car into a spin and clipped the stranded vehicle, but Falcon driver David Clark, despite his best efforts, couldn't avoid hitting it with far greater force.

The right front of his spinning Ford made heavy contact with the driver's side of Porter's car and the results were devastating.

He was critically injured and died on the Sunday, the day of the Bathurst 1000 race.

Porter's regular #111 race number was adopted by Kiwi V8 Supercar team owner Paul Cruickshank's car for the following round on the Gold Coast and his team continued to use it in Porter's honour until the team closed at the end of 2009.

## Stop Right Now!

On four occasions, the Bathurst Great Race has been halted mid-race.

The first was 1981, when a multi-car accident at McPhillamy Park stopped the race after 120 laps of the scheduled 163. It was not restarted, and results were declared, with Dick Johnson and John French the winners in their Tru-Blu Falcon XD.

The second was in 1984 after a start-line accident. Once the carnage was cleaned up the race was restarted over its full, original distance of 163 laps.

The third was in 1992 after a cluster of cars crashed in wet conditions at the exit of Forrest's Elbow. Such were the rules at the time that a restart was ruled out. Results were declared, with Jim Richards and Mark Skaife winners in their Nissan GT-R, after 143 laps of the scheduled 161.

The fourth was in 2014 after the track broke up at Griffins Bend. The race resumed after an hour delay while the circuit was patched up to be fit for racing.

# 24

# Mr 100 Percent

Forceful, dominant, tenacious and brutally uncompromising in his quest for victory, Mark Skaife is a modern master of the Bathurst 1000 who approaches everything at 100 percent throttle, flat-chat.

A six-time winner of Australia's Great Race, he evolved from a young, hungry Nissan racer into a Holden hero as leader of its mighty Holden Racing Team and, away from race driving, became a well-connected mover and shaker in the business world of Supercars racing.

With 25 starts in the Bathurst 1000, spanning 1987 to 2011, the five-time Australian Touring Car and V8 Supercars Champion has seen it all – and often been right among the action making headlines.

Skaife was around race cars as a lad. Father Russell, a racer himself – he made three Bathurst 1000 starts as a driver: in 1976, 1977 and 1982 – ran a tyre shop in Wyong on the Central Coast of New South Wales.

He had also been involved in preparing the 1968 Bathurst-winning Wyong Motors Monaro GTS 327 of Bruce McPhee and Barry Mulholland, and by the next decade had son Mark tagging along to the Mountain as a motorsport-mad kid.

'I was totally engrossed,' Skaife recalled on the V8 Sleuth Podcast in 2019.

'Dad had an XU-1 Torana at the end of 1973 and start of 1974 and I would go to Amaroo Park and sit under the Ron Hodgson tower, effectively the media room, and watch them come through the last corner and see Colin Bond and Bob Morris going at it. I was a Bondy fan, I loved his car control.

'I think it was about 1976 the first time I went to Bathurst. Dad raced there in a team with Barry Seton in a Capri. The three-litre series in those days was quite strong, with Mazda RX-3s, Triumph Dolomites, Capris, BMWs and Alfas. There was quite a good proliferation of smaller cars, and they are my earlier memories of going to Bathurst as a young bloke.'

Skaife's own Bathurst 1000 race debut was delayed 12 months. In 1986 he was due to share a Toyota Supra with its owner Peter Williamson – the same 'Willo' who had given RaceCam its debut at Bathurst seven years earlier – but the car was demolished in a nasty practice accident when Williamson crashed heavily just after the bridge at the bottom of Conrod Straight.

Such was the force of the accident the in-car mounted fire extinguisher came loose and shattered Williamson's jaw, a brutal reminder of the dangers of the sport.

*Trackside workers lift Peter Williamson from the wreckage of his Toyota Supra at Bathurst in 1986. The accident injured the popular racer and meant Mark Skaife had to wait another 12 months to compete in the Great Race.*

The following year's race presented Skaife with his first chance to actually start the Great Race, albeit in a two-litre Nissan Gazelle – not in the outright class.

Given an opportunity by Fred Gibson's Nissan team, he honed his craft, and the addition of veteran Jim Richards to the team in 1989 gave him the perfect measuring stick at the wheel of the team's screaming six-cylinder Skyline GTS-R.

They finished third in that year's Bathurst 1000, the first of 10 podium finishes in the Great Race for Skaife.

The arrival of the mighty, four-wheel-drive Nissan GT-R in 1990 gave the duo the ideal Bathurst-winning weapon and they converted it into victory in both 1991 and 1992. Skaife's rise as a racer was also evidenced by the fact he was given qualifying duties for the '91 assault and promptly claimed his first of five Bathurst 1000 pole positions the day prior to his first Great Race win.

Skaife's 1992 season was sublime. He claimed his first Australian Touring Car Championship, then won the Australian Drivers' Championship in a Formula Brabham open-wheeler, and capped off his year by sealing victory alongside Richards at Bathurst in the 1000-kilometre classic.

That day sits in the memory banks of fans for the controversial podium outburst from Richards. Consequently, it's often forgotten just how bad the conditions were as rain lashed the Mountain and turned the track into a skating rink.

The Gibson team switched to racing Holden Commodores in 1993 when Australian touring car racing's rules moved away from international Group A competition to domestic V8 racing, and Skaife and Richards remained contenders each year at Bathurst.

They were runners-up in 1993 and had a solid early lead in 1995 until tailshaft failure. Cigarette advertising was banned after that year and the team struggled to replace the money Winfield had previously been tipping in. That led to a drop in the team's competitiveness.

After various approaches in preceding years to join the Holden Racing Team, Skaife eventually agreed to move camps in mid-1997 to co-drive with Peter Brock in that year's endurance races, including the V8 Bathurst race.

While Brock largely spent his time signing autographs for his adoring fans in his farewell from full-time racing, Skaife threw his energies into making the #05 Commodore fast around the Mountain.

'I was blown away by how good the Bridgestone tyres were and how good the whole of the team was at the time,' Skaife recalls.

'We qualified pole on Sandown and Bathurst, and that year was the first time anyone had broken a 2-minute 10-second lap at Bathurst: we did a 2-minute 09.8-seconds in the warm-up before Top 10 Shootout.'

Brock led the race away from pole position and handed over to Skaife, who carried on out front until an engine issue knocked the #05 Commodore out of the race.

'It was plenty fast enough to have won,' says Skaife.

'When Lowndes crashed out behind me, we backed it off and we were cruising. Peter and I had formed a cool relationship. He was unbelievable in the first part of the race. There was no one else able to win that day unless we had a drama. And we did ...'

Skaife took Brock's seat full-time for 1998 and, matched with Craig Lowndes as a teammate, the duo's fierce but friendly intra-team rivalry pushed them individually to great heights, and spurred the team into an era where it was the benchmark for success and professionalism throughout pit lane.

Yet, as a combination, bad luck dogged them at the Mountain: Skaife and Lowndes led the 1998 race comfortably until punctures put them out of contention, while a tangle with a slower car in 2000 ended their hopes of winning and nearly derailed Skaife's championship bid.

It was once he was paired with a special Commodore – later nicknamed 'the Golden Child' – that Skaife became near-unstoppable.

He used the Golden Child to claim back-to-back Bathurst 1000 wins in 2001 with Tony Longhurst and 2002 with Jim

Richards, and clinched the V8 Supercars Championship in both years, underlining an era where Skaife and HRT couldn't lose for winning.

The closing stages of the 2002 race were particularly stressful as his Commodore's V8 engine was quickly cooking itself – plastic bags and other garbage were being scooped up and getting jammed in front of the air intake of the red, white and black Holden.

With the engine temperature soaring to dangerously high levels, Skaife continually reset the warning lights on the dash that were alerting him that failure was imminent, and pressed on. He made it to the finish line first, but was very, very lucky the race was 161 laps in distance and not 162 ...

'One more lap and we would have been in trouble, I think,' surmised Holden Racing Team Manager Jeff Grech in an interview with *Motorsport News* magazine post-race.

'Despite Mark's short-shifting, water was starting to come out of the overflow and the temperature was still going up by a degree a lap. We have a cap which breaks away at 118 degrees. On the last lap the temperature hit 117 ...'

Skaife's Bathurst-winning car looms large in the annals of the sport, given it won two Bathursts and two V8 Supercars Championships in a row.

So why was it dubbed the Golden Child?

'It was after we'd won Bathurst with it [in 2002] and we were doing a dinner at the workshop with our sponsors,' says Skaife.

'My thing has always been – and call me a bit crazy for it – that everything needed to be pristine. So, the car had won Bathurst and Craig [Kelly, 1990 Collingwood AFL premiership player and later HRT CEO] wanted to leave it as it had finished Bathurst.

'I said there was no way in the world we could have people in our workshop and not have it look absolutely mint. It was smashed with bugs; there were rubber marks all over it; it was stone-chipped – all the bad things that get done to cars over the course of 1000 kilometres of racing.

'He wanted to leave it like that, but I wanted it back to concourse condition. So, he titled it the "Golden Child" as I was so passionate about it, and it stuck!'

Skaife took over the ownership of the Holden Racing Team in early 2003 after the financial collapse of Tom Walkinshaw's racing empire, and was back in victory lane at the Mountain in 2005 alongside Todd Kelly.

The win, Skaife's fifth Bathurst 1000 success and third with HRT in the space of five years, came after a late race battle with Kiwi Jason Richards. It also gave Holden its seventh consecutive win – a record – in the Great Race at the Mountain.

Skaife and HRT were always competitive at Bathurst and the following year, 2006, proved a disaster despite the team's #2 Commodore being the fastest in the field and the hot favourite to win the first Peter Brock Trophy, created a month after the death of the nine-time race winner.

The pole position earnt by Skaife in Saturday's Top 10 Shootout was quickly forgotten when the clutch failed, and while limping along he was smashed into halfway up Mountain Straight by an unsighted rookie, Jack Perkins. The hit from the youngster was just salt in the wound as the clutch issue meant the red Commodore's day was going to be done anyway.

Skaife made two more trips to Bathurst with the factory-backed HRT outfit. His last – in 2008 – ended with a 12th place finish. He and Garth Tander were delayed by damage to their Commodore after Skaife had made a small miscue while running in the lead pack. He bounced off a tyre wall at Forrest's Elbow and, though the hit was relatively light, it required a visit to pit lane for the crew to plaster reels and reels of tape to patch up the damaged bonnet and front end.

The five-time champion made the call to retire from full-time racing at the end of the 2008 season but made three more Bathurst 1000 starts as a co-driver.

He and Greg Murphy finished a fighting fourth in 2009 in a Tasman Motorsport Commodore, though could have fought for victory, had it not been for an ill-timed Safety Car period called just as the Kiwi passed the pit entry. A pit stop at the time would have put them perfectly in position to run up the front in the final stages, but it wasn't to be.

Still, Skaife's sixth and final Bathurst 1000 victory wasn't far away, 12 months in fact, after he signed to drive alongside former teammate Craig Lowndes in one of Triple Eight's Vodafone Commodores.

The team had swapped from racing Ford Falcons to Holdens for 2010, opening the door for the reunification of the former Holden Racing Team partners, and they went on to lead a 1-2 finish for the team at Bathurst.

Lowndes was forced to do the lion's share of the driving that day, pushing home in a marathon triple stint because Skaife had popped a rib out during one of his earlier stints.

The following year they came extremely close to winning again. Lowndes stormed home to shadow race-winner Garth Tander over the line, a microscopic 0.2917-seconds behind in Skaife's 25th and last Bathurst 1000 start.

It may have been Skaife's final appearance as a driver in the race, but he's continued to play an influential part in the business of Supercars and the Bathurst 1000 ever since.

He became Chairman of the Supercars Commission when it was formed the following year and was heavily involved in the Car of the Future project, which debuted on the track in 2013.

From commentating the action on television to working on track design and sitting on the Board of Directors of Supercars, Skaife is everywhere.

He approached his race career (and winning the Bathurst 1000 on-track) at 100 percent and hasn't slowed down – even since he hung up his helmet.

Skaife's name will remain prominent in the history books of the Great Race for plenty of years to come. And while opinions about him among the motorsport fanbase may have been divided along the way, he's most certainly left his mark on the Mountain.

## Margins of Note

Victory in the Bathurst 1000 is often determined by less than a second, however it wasn't always this way. Back 'in the day' the margin of victory was more about how many laps in front a car was than how many seconds!

The record remains the six-lap win Peter Brock and Jim Richards had aboard their A9X Torana in 1979. They completed 163 laps compared to the 157 of runners-up Peter Janson and Larry Perkins.

Brock also features in the other two biggest wins in Bathurst Great Race history.

He and Brian Sampson finished two laps in front of fellow L34 Torana drivers Bob Morris and Frank Gardner in 1975 and Brock and Perkins' Commodore crossed the finish line two laps in front of teammates John Harvey and David Parsons in 1984.

# 25

# The Top Performing Teams

**M**uch of the focus on the history of the Great Race sits with the drivers and the legendary cars they've raced around the challenging Mount Panorama circuit.

Often overlooked in the record books though are the teams behind the drivers and their pilots.

Two of them from different eras – the Holden Dealer Team of the late 1960s to the mid-1980s and Triple Eight Race Engineering from the mid-2000s to the present – stand out above the pack when it comes to success in Australia's most famous race.

Leading into the 60th anniversary race in 2023, each has won the race a total of nine times – that's nearly a third of all Bathurst Great Race events held – with Triple Eight well-poised to continue on its winning ways in the race and ultimately take the record for itself in the next few years.

The HDT's winning sheet at Bathurst came via three different racing regimes, though all under the same banner.

Harry Firth originally led the team and scored wins in 1969 (with Colin Bond/Tony Roberts) and 1972 (with Peter Brock) until he finished running the operation at the end of 1977 and it was entrusted to John Sheppard. He had a 100 percent win record at Bathurst when Brock and Jim Richards won in both 1978 and 1979.

Brock took over the team for 1980 and added another four wins at the helm of Marlboro-backed Commodores. His very public bust-up with Holden in early 1987 led to the car giant withdrawing its support, though Brock continued using the HDT acronym. It was under the Mobil HDT Racing banner that he won his ninth Great Race as a driver – and HDT/HDT Racing as a team – in 1987.

On the other hand, Triple Eight's nine Bathurst wins have all come (bar the most recent one, in 2022) under the guiding hand of one man – Roland Dane. Another point of difference with the HDT is that they've come representing both Holden and Ford.

Irish-born, though now an Australian citizen and based in Brisbane for the last two decades, Dane made his fortune selling luxury cars in the UK and Asia.

He set up a team in the British Touring Car Championship in the 1990s and later founded Triple Eight Race Engineering, with business partners including ex-Formula 1 driver Derek Warwick, to run the Vauxhall (General Motors) program in the BTCC from 1997 onwards during its boom Super Touring era.

The team bought a pair of its Vectra race cars to the two Super Touring Bathurst races in '97 and '98 to give Dane his first taste of Bathurst. At the wheel of one of the cars was none other than Peter Brock, who promptly rolled it on the first lap of practice!

'My feeling and connection with Bathurst came about through watching [television] packages of the Bathurst 1000 in the 1980s that were rebroadcast on the same day into the UK. Watching things like the Jaguars driving around,' he told me on the V8 Sleuth Podcast in 2022.

'When we went there with two-litre cars, I thought, "All this pit area is a shithole and there's bugger all people here." It was underwhelming; it just didn't feel that special.

'Apart from the setting, the whole experience was underwhelming, and it wasn't until I went there the first time in [V8 Supercars] in 2003 with Triple Eight and our Australian team to Bathurst with a proper crowd, proper grid, that I really appreciated what Bathurst was all about.'

Dane sold out of Triple Eight in the UK and ended up spearheading an Australian Triple Eight team created by a buy-out of the Briggs Motorsport Ford team in 2003. After a couple of years of finding its way, the team soon became a powerhouse of V8 Supercars racing.

By 2005 it had signed up Craig Lowndes and the fan-favourite driver put the team on pole position at Bathurst that year.

The following year he and newcomer Jamie Whincup won the Great Race at the wheel of one of the team's Betta Electrical-backed, yellow and blue Falcons. Triple Eight's first Bathurst 1000 win came in one of the most emotional races ever seen at Mount Panorama. It was held just a month after the death of its most famous winner, Peter Brock.

'I was in the right place at the right time. Roland was looking around for a young bloke that was cheap, to stay out of trouble and team up with Lowndesy to win Bathurst,' recalls Whincup.

'This was a team, in my mind, that was about to take over and dominate.'

He was right.

Since then, the team has always figured in the storyline of each year's Bathurst 1000. Not once has it been an irrelevant player. Every year its cars have won, come close to winning, finished on the podium or otherwise featured prominently in the race.

'Every race since 2005, we could have won every single one of them,' says Dane.

'We've been in a position to win every single one of the Bathursts that we haven't won.'

The team won three in a row with Lowndes and Whincup between 2006 and 2008 and finished fifth in 2009, though Dane says it should have been the duo's fourth successive win.

'We should have won it. We screwed it up,' he declares.

'We were leading the race and we had a clutch bearing issue that came and went. But more particularly, at the last pit stop we wound the roll centre the wrong way. So, if we'd gone the right way on the roll centre, I think there's every chance we would have won that race. It was a massive error.'

In 2010 the team swapped to Holden and finished 1-2 at Bathurst for the first time. But that year it was Lowndes (sharing with Mark Skaife) leading home Whincup (sharing with Steve Owen), rather than them driving together.

V8 Supercars rules had been changed, prohibiting a team's full-time drivers from sharing the same car. Consequently, they were forced to drive their own regular entry with a co-driver; this rule remains in place to this very day.

'This was one of the first rule changes aimed specifically at Triple Eight,' recalls Dane.

'I say this without any rancour: I think it's the ultimate accolade. Almost all the pit lane has spent most of the last 15 years trying to stop Triple Eight through whatever means they can: politically, rules, whatever. I regard that as the ultimate backhanded compliment.

'That made what happened in 2010 quadruple satisfying, as it were – when we took two steps on the podium rather than just one.'

The team finished second in 2011, with Lowndes and Skaife, though an alternator and battery issue delayed the otherwise-dominant Whincup and Andrew Thompson Commodore ('We should have won that one very easily,' says Dane).

Whincup and Paul Dumbrell teamed up to win in 2012, with Lowndes and Warren Luff third, in the final appearance of the team at Bathurst in Vodafone colours.

Further Bathurst wins followed: in 2015 and 2018 (with Lowndes and Steve Richards) and 2020 and 2022 (with Shane van Gisbergen and Garth Tander) but for every win there were near misses.

Whincup finished just 0.47-seconds behind Mark Winterbottom in 2013 after an epic last-lap tussle, and the year after he led into the last lap until running out of fuel on the final run onto Conrod Straight.

Constant suggestions and questions from his crew over the radio in the closing stages – none of which he responded to – failed to convince Whincup to slow down and conserve fuel in the final laps. The Red Bull Commodore eventually coughed and gave up the win to Chaz Mostert's Falcon.

Triple Eight crossed the line first in 2016 but Whincup was pinged with a 15-second post-race time penalty. In 2017 it was van Gisbergen who saw a potential Bathurst win slip through his fingers.

The Kiwi led at the penultimate restart after a Safety Car period, only to slither off the wet track at Murray's Corner before he took the green flag on Pit Straight. He dropped to 14th but fought back to recover fifth place in the final 17 laps.

It's one that sticks in Dane's brain.

'That was a walkover for Shane if he hadn't made that mistake,' he says.

'Having said that, the subsequent drive in the damp conditions that Shane put in to try and recover positions was stunning. That was a biggy.'

Van Gisbergen came close to standing atop the Bathurst 1000 podium in 2019 when he shadowed Scott McLaughlin's Mustang to the line and finished second. He got the job done in 2020 to record his first win, though a delaminated tyre in the closing laps of 2021 while running second to eventual winner Mostert cost him another podium result at the very least.

That race marked Dane's last in charge of the Triple Eight team. He stepped down at the end of that season and sold his shareholding. The team's ownership is now shared between racing businessman Tony Quinn, now Managing Director Whincup and Jessica Dane, Roland's daughter.

He returned to Mount Panorama in 2022 to manage the team's wildcard entry driven by Craig Lowndes and Declan Fraser, which finished eighth. This was in the same year that van Gisbergen and Tander won again to record the team's record-equalling ninth Bathurst 1000 win.

In addition to experiencing its own Bathurst 1000 success on track, Triple Eight has built a range of customer chassis and supplied parts to other teams for their annual attacks on the Great Race.

The 2016 race was won by Will Davison and Jonathon Webb in a Triple Eight-designed and built TEKNO Autosports Commodore. It headed a lock-out of the podium by T8 chassis, with van Gisbergen's Red Bull car second and the Lucas Dumbrell Motorsport, Triple Eight-built Commodore of Nick Percat and Cameron McConville finishing third.

Nine of the 28 cars in the 2022 race – all but one-third of the field – were originally built by Triple Eight, the team that looks set – despite a change of regulations for 2023, with the arrival of Gen3 Camaros and Mustangs – to remain the organisation to beat in the Great Race for many years to come.

One of the few teams to beat Triple Eight multiple times in the Bathurst 1000 in the last 15-plus years is the squad formerly known as the Holden Racing Team, today known as Walkinshaw Andretti United.

Like the Holden Dealer Team, it too has had a few different eras and regimes over the years. But also like the HDT, Bathurst figures prominently in its logbook of success.

The team has scored eight wins in the Great Race, the first coming in 1990 with Win Percy and Allan Grice in an unfancied Commodore VL Group A SV after the HRT organisation had been set up in Melbourne earlier that year under the ownership of Tom Walkinshaw.

The Scotsman took pole position for the race in 1985 at the wheel of a howling V12-powered Jaguar XJ-S and paired up a few years later on a special vehicles road car business and racing program with Holden – this was after their split with Peter Brock.

It took another six years for the team to win Bathurst again – in 1996 with Craig Lowndes and Greg Murphy – and it added more wins in 2001 and 2002 spearheaded by Mark Skaife.

Walkinshaw's racing empire crumbled in early 2003 and his beloved HRT was part of the collateral damage of the collapse of his global Tom Walkinshaw Racing business.

Driver Skaife took over the HRT and it won Bathurst again in 2005 with him and Todd Kelly (who won on his 26th birthday) at the wheel. Then Walkinshaw returned, supplying managerial services and later as a part-owner. He regained full control again in early 2009, the year the team won Bathurst for the sixth time via Garth Tander and Will Davison.

Walkinshaw died of cancer in 2010 and his son Ryan and wife Martine continued to push the team forward, moving on to win its seventh Bathurst 1000 in 2011 with Tander and Nick Percat.

Holden made the decision to switch its official factory backing across to the rival Triple Eight/Red Bull team for 2017, forcing the former HRT to find a new banner under which to race.

In 2018 it adopted a new name, 'Walkinshaw Andretti United', after American legend Michael Andretti's Andretti Autosport team and British-based United Autosports became shareholders in the team.

While it hadn't won the V8 Supercars Championship since Skaife's 2002 title success, the team continued to prove highly competitive at Bathurst and each year from 2017 onwards it's recorded a podium finish.

Scott Pye and Warren Luff finished second in 2017 and 2018 and James Courtney and Jack Perkins were third in 2019, a result repeated by new signing Chaz Mostert and Luff in 2020.

But in 2021 the team was untouchable: the black and blue Commodore of Mostert and Lee Holdsworth was the class of the field for speed, scoring a 35th Holden win and the eighth Bathurst 1000 win for the team.

From its original British-based TWR operation the Walkinshaw name has also been connected to two further Bathurst 1000 wins. That team – separate to the Holden Racing Team and TWR Australia, which represented Walkinshaw's racing interests Down Under – ran the 1985 Bathurst-winning Jaguar driven by John Goss and Armin Hahne as well as the 1998 Super Touring race-winning Volvo S40 driven by Jim Richards and Rickard Rydell.

The future for Walkinshaw Andretti United is about to become vastly different too: it's moved to racing Fords in 2023.

While a team winning Bathurst with two different manufacturers isn't new, no family banner – such as Walkinshaw's – has ever won the Great Race connected to four different brands.

There's always new history to write when it comes to the Bathurst 1000.

The sheer weight of Holden wins versus Ford wins in Bathurst's classic race means this chapter has been dominated by teams representing the former.

Cars entered under the 'Ford Motor Company' banner won the race six times in the 1960s and 1970s, though they came under different car preparers.

Bob Jane's pair of Bathurst Great Race wins came in Cortinas in 1963 and 1964 before his old partner Harry Firth's operation prepared and ran the winning Falcon in 1967.

Firth's co-driver in that win, Fred Gibson, didn't win Bathurst again as a driver, but his Gibson Motorsport team won it three times – with Nissans in 1991 and 1992 and a Wynn's Holden Commodore in 1999.

Ford parted ways with Firth after 1968 and the rest of the 'FoMoCo' Bathurst wins with Allan Moffat – in 1970, 1971 and 1973 – were won by cars prepared and run from 'Lot 6', the secret address in Mahoney's Road in the Melbourne suburb of Thomastown where the Ford Special Vehicles unit was based and the legendary GTHO Falcon was developed.

Modern Ford hero Dick Johnson's team is a four-time winner of the Bathurst 1000. Its first three wins – in 1981, 1989 and 1994 – were under Dick's ownership and the fourth – in 2019 – was with American powerhouse Team Penske as majority shareholder.

Now known as Tickford Racing, Ford Performance Racing was set up in 2003 as the official factory-backed Ford team run by British-based Prodrive after its buy-out of Glenn Seton's existing race team.

It took the team 10 years to win at Bathurst. Its first top spot was in 2013 with Mark Winterbottom and Steve Richards and it came in the same year that local racers Rod Nash and Rusty French (both former Bathurst 1000 starters) bought the team.

The following year it won again, with backing from Pepsi Max soft drinks, this time with Mostert and Paul Morris at the wheel.

The only other team to win Bathurst for Ford in the Supercars era is Stone Brothers Racing – the team of Kiwi brothers Ross and Jim. It won in 1998 with Steve Richards and Jason Bright.

Drivers get the plaudits for a Bathurst 1000 win. However, these teams are proof that it takes a racing army to get the job done at Mount Panorama.

## Massive Minis

The Morris Cooper S dramatically redefined 'domination' at the 1966 Bathurst Great Race, then known as the Gallaher 500.

Nicknamed the 'flying bricks', the Minis locked out the first nine outright finishing positions in the 1966 race: the likes of this result have not been seen since.

The nearest any other manufacturer has come to matching this was in 1979, when Holden Torana A9Xs filled the first eight outright finishing positions.

## A Third–Generation Bathurst Racer

Young gun Aaron Seton wrote himself into Bathurst Great Race history books when he made his debut in the race in 2022, sharing a Matt Stone Racing-run Commodore with Supercars regular Jack Le Brocq.

The son of two-time pole-sitter Glenn Seton, Aaron became the first third-generation driver to ever compete in the Bathurst Great Race.

Father Glenn made 26 starts between 1983 and 2010 and finished runner-up in 1987, 2003 and 2004.

His father Barry 'Bo' Seton won the race outright in 1965 in a Cortina GT500 with Midge Bosworth.

Bo Seton made 22 starts, debuting in the very first race in 1963 in a Morris 850 and lining up for the last time in a Ford Mustang in 1984.

# 26

# Close, But Not Quite

For every tale of glory in the Great Race there are a hundred of heartbreak, brutal disappointment and yearly despair.

Mount Panorama has rightfully rewarded 63 drivers as winners of its most important race but left plenty of richly deserving racers with a big, fat zero in the Bathurst wins column on their career stats sheet.

So, just who is the greatest driver never to win the Bathurst 1000?

An important point in shaping this debate is limiting the pool to drivers who were regulars in the annual championship and the Bathurst classic, thereby excluding from the debate any one-off or very occasional international racers who, while boasting amazing racing resumes, didn't make the Bathurst 1000 a yearly priority.

Consequently, drivers the ilk of three-time Formula 1 World Champion Sir Jack Brabham and Indianapolis 500 winner and two-time IndyCar Champion Will Power have both competed in the Great Race and have won some of the most prized titles in world motorsport, but they're excluded from this analysis.

Of all of the drivers never to win Bathurst 1000 who come up in conversation, two-time Australian Touring Car Champion Glenn Seton's name comes up the most.

The son of 1965 Great Race winner and long-time racer Barry 'Bo' Seton, Glenn challenged Mount Panorama 26 times but just couldn't convince it to allow him even one single day of the ultimate glory of conquering it. He had been trackside – a five-month-old baby – when his dad won that day in a Cortina GT500.

A quiet, unassuming racer, Seton won everything else worth winning in Australian touring car racing. He bagged the championship twice – in Falcons in 1993 and 1997 – and won the Sandown 500 twice, as well as 40 races and 17 rounds of the Australian Touring Car Championship.

But, despite the best laid plans, Bathurst kept slipping through his fingers.

Seton finished on the podium multiple times – including three visits in the space of four years between 2003 and 2006 – but the top step always eluded him.

He made his Bathurst 1000 debut as a teenager – in 1983 – sharing a Ford Capri with his father and quickly found out how tricky the Mountain circuit was in opening practice.

'I'd raced karts in the wet and loved it, but I pitted and told Dad I thought the wet tyres we were running had very little grip,' recalls Seton, later nicknamed 'The Baby-Faced Assassin' by long-time Channel 7 Bathurst commentator, the late Mike Raymond, because of his boyish looks.

'He said, "Get out; give me a drive" and blasted out of the pits, before coming straight back in for a tyre change. It turned out he'd had that first set of wets lying around for years and they were well past their best!

'We were leading our class in the race by two laps when it broke a crankshaft with 30 laps to go. It was my first taste of Bathurst disappointment and a real shame because it turned out to be the only year that Dad and I drove together at Mount Panorama.'

The disappointments kept following for Glenn at Bathurst too.

He didn't see the finish line in his first three Bathurst starts until he came home in fourth place on the road in 1987 in a factory-backed Nissan.

The race had been hit by a downpour of rain and Seton had mesmerised the television audience – watching footage relayed from his RaceCam on-board camera – as he manoeuvred his slipping and sliding turbocharged Skyline on the wet bitumen. On more than one occasion it looked like an accident was on the cards, but each time Seton managed to use his immense skills – honed as a kid racing karts – to coax the out-of-control car back onto the road or back into a straight line.

Mid-race, co-driver John Bowe had found himself queuing at the exit of the pits. In keeping with the rules of the time, cars exiting pit lane were stopped there and later released to join the slow-moving queue behind the Safety Car.

In a stroke of luck – it was good timing – while Bowe was cooling his heels waiting to get the Nissan moving again, the Mobil Commodore of Peter Brock rolled by on track. It picked up third position in the race, a spot it held until the finish of the 161-lap distance despite Bowe clawing back massive chunks of time in the closing stages.

The exclusion of the first and second-placed Texaco Ford Sierras from Europe post-race meant that Brock and his Mobil teammates were elevated to victory and Seton and Bowe were lifted to second, though they never got to stand on the podium on the day or receive a trophy for their efforts.

History could have been very, very different – and Seton omitted from this chapter of this book – had the blue and white #15 Skyline not been stuck at the pit exit partway through that race. Being released back onto the track in front of the Mobil car could have changed Seton's racing life.

Seton's Bathurst luck took a dive in the years after 1987. His Skyline broke its gearbox on the first lap the following year and his first year as owner of his own Ford Sierra team in 1989 – backed by Peter Jackson cigarettes (the former Nissan team sponsor) – was fraught and ended with neither of his cars threatening the podium.

Clutch problems took him out of the 1990 race. In 1991 a misfire delayed him and Gregg Hansford and they finished ninth. For four years in a row, starting in 1992, he didn't finish the race due to various mechanical issues with his V8 Falcons.

But the last race in that four-year stretch, 1995, remains the one for which Seton is most remembered.

The background to his assault on that year's race had all the ingredients of a classic Bathurst fairy-tale result.

Race organisers had provided special incentive to win for Seton (who had used the racing number 30 since establishing his own team due to sponsor Peter Jackson's 'pack of 30' product). Should he win, he'd be given the choice of a $30,000 cash bonus or the restored 1965 Cortina GT500 his father drove to victory 30 years earlier.

Incidentally, that race was the last with cigarette sponsorship permitted: it was banned from Australian sport at the end of that year, 1995, leaving Seton without a naming rights sponsor for the following season. What's more, news had broken shortly before Bathurst that his very own teammate, Alan Jones, had done a deal with Peter Jackson's parent company Phillip Morris, and would be taking the backing with him to run his own team in 1996.

So, when Seton held the lead with just 10 laps remaining in the 1995 Tooheys 1000 at Bathurst, it's fair to say a storybook finish was on the cards.

But then came heartbreak and a failure far more bitter than any of the previous years.

Seton's Ford V8 engine started to misfire. Losing power and speed, he could do nothing to stop Holden pilot Larry Perkins from sweeping by to seize the lead.

The #30 Falcon only made it partway around the next lap when the engine failed completed and Seton gently rolled it back into a gap between the concrete barriers on the climb up towards the Cutting.

Although bewildered and in a state of disbelief, Seton still had the class to speak with Channel 7 commentators via his RaceCam in the immediate aftermath of his most soul-destroying moment at Mount Panorama.

'I ran through it with them as best I could, but it was hard to explain how I felt,' says Seton.

'At that stage I was just flat and devastated. I didn't have to stop myself from getting upset and crying in front of the camera, it was just disbelief. I was just thinking "Has this really just happened and how do I feel about it?"'

Seton made 14 more Bathurst 1000 starts but never again got as close to winning as he had been in 1995. There were plenty more years that he was fast, but time and time again a mixture of mechanical issues and bad luck kept him from winning the race.

He sold his team at the end of 2002 to British-based Prodrive but stayed on with the new owners under its new Ford Performance Racing banner.

Seton and new teammate Craig Lowndes finished second at Bathurst two years in a row – in 2003 and 2004 – allowing Seton to stand on the podium physically rather than purely on a results sheet at Mount Panorama for the first time.

He finished third in 2006 in a Stone Brothers Racing Falcon with James Courtney before drawing to an end his Bathurst 1000 career after the 2010 race.

'I don't dwell on not winning that race (Bathurst), but I certainly miss competing in it,' reveals Seton.

'I'm immensely proud of my two championships and wouldn't trade either of them for a Bathurst win. More people might remember me for Bathurst 1995 than for winning those titles, but I'm OK with that.

'I'd love to have won it, especially on the 30-year anniversary of Dad winning, but if people are still bringing it up nearly 30 years later, it's clearly made more of an impact on them than if I'd won the race.'

Marcos Ambrose's career span in V8 Supercars in Australia may have been a relatively short one, but he shares something in common with Seton: both won the championship twice at the wheel of Ford Falcon V8s, but neither was able to win the Bathurst 1000.

The Tasmanian became a Ford favourite during his five-year tenure with the Queensland-based Stone Brothers Racing team and won the V8 Supercars Championship in 2003 before backing it up in 2004.

Ambrose may have only made six starts in the Bathurst 1000, but it's a glaring omission from his list of wins in V8 Supercars. He won everything else worth winning in the category.

'I haven't had many races there: it's a percentage game,' he said of his Bathurst attempts on the V8 Sleuth Podcast in 2021.

'We've had plenty of chances to win and I screwed pretty much all of them up. They all got away.'

Ambrose had returned from racing overseas, out of financial backing, after he'd demonstrated his talents in British Formula Ford and Formula 3. Back home he decided to make a living in V8 Supercars.

The SBR team signed him up and he made his first trip with the team to Bathurst in November 2000 as an interested onlooker, soaking up as much V8 Supercar knowledge as possible. This gave him an up-close view of the rigours of racing at the Mountain and what he'd be in for in upcoming years.

After a driving stint, Kiwi Simon Wills, co-driving with countryman Craig Baird, stepped out of the team's blue and yellow Pirtek-backed Falcon – a car Ambrose would become strongly identified with in the coming five years – and promptly vomited everywhere. Ambrose jumped in to assist.

'Everyone ran for the doors. There was no one left to help the poor guy!' he laughs now.

'He was literally frothing at the mouth. And it's in his visor and it's coming down his chin and it's just a mess!'

No such clean-ups were required the following year – 2001 – when Ambrose made his Bathurst 1000 debut. He instantly made his mark on the track, becoming just the second rookie in history to take pole position for the Great Race.

The exhilaration of converting 11th fastest in qualifying into pole position in the then-Top 15 Shootout quickly dissipated on race day though. Ambrose made a crucial error entering the pits for his first pit stop and ran off the road to become buried in a sand trap.

'With the AU Falcon, we weren't the fastest car and probably wouldn't have won it, but I had no turn-off switch,' he reflects.

'I was just full-on, literally, into the pit lane and blew it into the sand. We couldn't get snatched out in time and lost a lap. And the whole thing was a bit of a disaster. That's what you do in your rookie year: you do dumb stuff like that.

'We had two years of tyre failures; we blew tyres two years in a row. In 2002 we were blowing tyres all day. And that's a lack of experience, from my perspective. We should have identified the issue going into the race. We had tyre issues at Phillip Island [earlier in the year] as well, and we ran a lot of [negative] camber.

'But that worked the tyres just too hard down the straightaway. The inside edge of the tyre gets hammered and we blew them out. We didn't learn from our mistakes, and we did it again.'

Ambrose and regular SBR teammate Russell Ingall finished sixth in 2003 and Ambrose teamed with Greg Ritter to finish fourth in 2004, his best Bathurst 1000 finish.

But the 2005 Bathurst 1000 – his final start in the race before heading off to the United States to compete in NASCAR stock car racing for a decade – was the most controversial of his Bathurst starts.

Ambrose was forced to pit by officials mid-race and put on a fireproof balaclava under his helmet, as required under the rules of the period.

The growing status of V8 Supercars as an international championship that year had spurred organisers to ramp up the requirements. Under the rules, all drivers were supposed to wear full-body fireproof underwear. But many – Ambrose included – preferred not to wear all items in the 'hot box' cockpit of their cars. Officials refused to brook any non-compliance.

The unscheduled pit stop delay dropped Ambrose back into the pack and raised his ire, which only peaked again in the closing stages when he and Kiwi rival Greg Murphy clashed as they swept up the Mountain.

On the run to the Cutting the two cars made contact, neither driver willing to concede ground. Ambrose's blue Falcon crunched into the outside concrete wall and Murphy's Commodore came to a stop with steering damage. Friction between Ambrose and Murphy had been building in the previous 12 months and blew up as they argued nose-to-nose next to their stationary cars in the aftermath of the crash.

'I'd come from leading a lot of laps to coming back through the field, and Greg made a mistake in turn two and he missed a shift,' Ambrose said in 2015 on the *Inside Supercars* television program.

'He clearly didn't give me a lot of room. It's a pretty tight corner there anyway. And I was hot and cranky from the day anyway – and he just finished me off.'

Ambrose spent nine years racing in the United States in NASCAR before a much-heralded return to Supercars in 2015 with the newly minted DJR Team Penske, after American racing powerhouse Team Penske purchased a majority slice of Dick Johnson's team.

After nearly a decade grinding away on the 30-plus weekend a year NASCAR tour, Ambrose quickly found himself unable to muster the energy required for full-time Supercars racing and stepped back after just two events in the new season. This provided the opportunity for endurance co-driver Scott Pye to become the lead driver.

Ambrose co-drove at Bathurst, though their chances ended when mechanical failure pitched Pye into the wall at Reid Park, leaving the Tasmanian without even so much as a visit to the podium in his Bathurst 1000 career.

While Ambrose only made six Bathurst 1000 starts, Brad Jones stood on the podium six times.

A native of Albury in New South Wales, he and brother Kim built a race team that won in every category it competed in on the way up the ladder.

They dominated super speedway racing at the Calder Park Thunderdome and won five AUSCAR national championships in addition to a NASCAR crown. They won in production cars and also claimed two national Super Touring crowns as the works Audi team, with Brad behind the wheel.

Brad made 24 Bathurst 1000 starts between 1985 and 2009 and finished on the podium on six occasions, but never on the top step.

He drove a mixture of top-line cars for other top teams and, later, for his own team. Jones saved his best for Bathurst. He drove for the Holden Racing Team and finished third in 1993 with Wayne Gardner and second in 1994 with Craig Lowndes. Jones was second again in a BJR-run Audi with German Frank Biela in 1997's Super Touring Bathurst race and third the following year with Cam McConville.

Another runner-up finish with Scotsman John Cleland came at the wheel of a BJR Falcon in 2001, and he and John Bowe finished third in 2004, but the Great Race always eluded Jones, even though he poured his heart and soul into the race.

'There's a moment in all of them (Bathurst starts) that are special,' says Jones.

'When JB and I finished third, I felt like we should have been second. We had a tyre delaminate. But we were one – if not *the* – team to beat up there. I felt like he and I deserved to win: every year in that period, we were the ones that were on point for Ford.'

Long-time friend, fellow Bathurst 1000 racer and now Supercars television commentator Neil Crompton knows all too well the path Jones has taken in his attempts to win the Great Race.

They drove together for the Holden Racing Team twice at Bathurst and finished fifth in 1990 and have shared each other's highs and lows.

'He put in some beautiful drives at Bathurst, and he probably would have been able to generate more recognition in his career if he'd just been able to clinch one or two wins in that race along the way,' Crompton says of Jones.

Another Jones, 1980 Formula 1 World Champion Alan Jones, also ranks as one of the best drivers to tackle the Bathurst 1000 without winning it.

He may have made his name winning Formula 1 Grand Prix races all over the world, but Jones also made 19 starts in the Great Race – most of them as a regular racer in the domestic scene – dating back to his first in a Commodore with privateer Warren Cullen in 1981.

At the time he was still the reigning World Champion as the Formula 1 season was yet to be completed. It was the first and only time a reigning Formula 1 World Champion has competed in the Bathurst 1000.

Quite literally driving for a bag of cash, Jones climbed into the car at the first driver change but was out of the race soon after with engine issues.

He quit Formula 1 at the end of that season to return home to Australia, though was lured back into F1 briefly in the mid-1980s before becoming a touring car and Bathurst 1000 regular in the latter part of that decade and into the 1990s.

'AJ' had plenty of great chances to win the race, but it never quite came off. He and Allan Grice finished second in 1995 in one of Glenn Seton's Peter Jackson Falcons and he finished third in 1988 in a Sierra with Colin Bond.

His move into team ownership in 1996 looked to be his best chance to win the race.

Sadly, it was a case of 'Oh, no; not again'. His race-leading Falcon – carrying Pack Leader signage (the generic brand wording used by Philip Morris in the wake of the ban of cigarette advertising) – caught fire and he could do nothing but watch his Bathurst challenger go, quite literally, up in smoke.

While Jones didn't get to win the Bathurst 1000, his Falcon that caught fire did. It was the very same car used by Jason Bright and Steve Richards to win two years later – after Jones had sold out of the team he had formed with Kiwi brothers Ross and Jim Stone.

Of the modern pack of Supercars racers, James Courtney's time to take himself off the list of 'best drivers never to win the Bathurst 1000' is starting to run out.

A world karting champion, British Formula Ford champ and Japanese Formula 3 champion whose Formula 1 dreams evaporated after a terrible testing crash in a Jaguar in Italy in 2002, Courtney came back to Australia to join the V8 Supercar pack full-time in 2006.

He finished third that year at Bathurst and made finding the podium a habit, finishing second in 2007 and third in 2008 – all with the same Stone Brothers Racing team that Jones had originally set up with the Stones.

But it took him until 2019 – via a third-place finish in a Walkinshaw Andretti United Commodore with Jack Perkins – for him to return to the Mount Panorama podium and he's now endured 17 Bathurst 1000s (prior to the 2023 edition) without sealing victory.

The 2010 V8 Supercars Champion during his time with Dick Johnson Racing, Courtney will be an in-demand co-driver once his full-time Supercars driving career ends. That should ultimately give him a few more Bathurst-winning opportunities.

So just who is the greatest driver never to win the Bathurst 1000?

Seton, Ambrose, the two Jones boys and Courtney are all part of the conversation, but that's the beauty of the debate.

There's plenty of other drivers who could also be nominated and, like so many other eternal Bathurst topics of discussion, there's no one single, clear, definite answer.

Everyone has their own point of view.

That's why the Great Race and its six decades of history has kept its followers and fans debating this, and so many other topics, for so many years.

## Winning Streaks

Only five drivers in history can lay claim to winning the Bathurst 1000 three years in a row.

Peter Brock and Jim Richards were first to achieve this – across 1978, 1979 and 1980. They piloted Toranas to the first two wins before taking Holden's Commodore to its debut Bathurst win to complete the treble.

Brock repeated the achievement across 1982, 1983 and 1984 with Larry Perkins, famously swapping cars in the early stages of the '83 race to carry on and claim victory.

It took until the V8 Supercar era for another duo to achieve the feat. Craig Lowndes and Jamie Whincup took three wins in a row for the Triple Eight team, driving Falcons across 2006, 2007 and 2008.

They came closest of any of the 'three peaters' to winning a fourth straight Bathurst: they finished fifth in 2009, the final year that the team raced Falcons prior to its jump to Holden Commodores for 2010.

## 27

# Supercars Stars

**M**ount Panorama and its Bathurst 1000 have been the biggest star-makers in Australian motorsport.

However, the name drivers all eventually move on, and new ones rise to take their place. Brock, Moffat, Johnson, Perkins and Richards have given way to the Supercars era's Bathurst winners for their turn in the spotlight.

2007 V8 Supercars Champion Garth Tander has become a five-time Bathurst 1000 winner and continues to add chapters to his own history book as he follows in the wheel tracks of legends.

The only Western Australian driver to ever win the Bathurst 1000, Tander was a lanky, young, raw talent when he first arrived in V8 Supercars in 1998 driving for Melbourne-based team owner Garry Rogers and his Garry Rogers Motorsport team.

He failed to finish his first two Bathurst 1000s, then scored his first win at the Mountain in 2000 in partnership with Jason Bargwanna at the wheel of one of Rogers' Valvoline-backed Commodores.

Since then, he's topped the podium in the race four more times – in 2009 and 2011 for the Holden Racing Team, and in 2020 and 2022 with Triple Eight's Red Bull team alongside Shane van Gisbergen.

Over time he's come to appreciate the significance of winning the Bathurst 1000. It isn't *just* another race.

'When I won it in 2000 at GRM with Bargs, I did not appreciate what it meant,' said Tander on the V8 Sleuth Podcast in 2019, who didn't finish on the podium again in the race until his next win – in '09 – with Will Davison.

'I remember saying to Will before we walked out onto the podium, "Mate, your life is about to change.' He said, "What do you mean?" I said, "Don't worry, you'll understand in a minute when you go out." It's pandemonium.'

A moment on-track on the way to that 2009 victory underlines just how important winning Bathurst is.

Tander pounced on former teammate Rick Kelly to take the lead in the closing stages, and aggressively moved over to push his fellow Holden driver to the grass on the run up Mountain Straight to ensure his opponent couldn't fight back.

'It was pretty ruthless,' recalls Tander.

'He made a mistake at turn one and ran a little bit wide. And I just passed him and didn't give him any opportunity to be next to me when the pass was finished!

'You don't have any friends in the last stint at Bathurst. It's the race we're all going there to win. As long as it's within the rules ... and that was deemed to be within the rules. They [officials] said it was borderline, but I'm happy with borderline.'

Tander had to fight hard again for his third win in 2011,

overcoming a late charge from Triple Eight Holden driver Craig Lowndes to seal a victory he shared with rookie co-driver Nick Percat.

The young gun also escaped a close call of his own. Mid-race he ran wide at Griffins Bend at the top of Mountain Straight and bumped the trackside concrete wall. To his relief the red and black #2 Holden had escaped major damage and he pressed on to score the Holden Racing Team's 200th all-time race win.

'Yes, Nick clipped the wall but anyone that has won Bathurst has a story like that; some little drama happens during the day and had the potential to derail you,' says Tander.

'2011 just happened to be our day.'

Tander has added two more Bathurst wins to his resume since he stopped racing Supercars full-time.

After battling against Triple Eight for so many years – during his days at the HSV Dealer Team and Holden Racing Team – he joined the team as Shane van Gisbergen's co-driver for Bathurst in 2019. They finished second that year then won in 2020 and 2022.

Tander, who works as part of the Supercars Championship television broadcast team (save for the Bathurst 1000 and endurance races, where he continues as a co-driver), has been around long enough to have tasted the highs and lows of the Mountain.

'You always know within the first three laps of the start of the week (in practice) if your car's a chance to win the race or not,' he says.

In 2014 he didn't even get to compete in the race, so badly had his Commodore been damaged in Saturday practice

– in a crash after the brakes failed on co-driver Warren Luff. The duo was in the lead pack late in the 2016 race too, until Tander was taken out in a multi-car crash involving Jamie Whincup and Scott McLaughlin and another chance of victory was snuffed out in an instant.

There are other days at Bathurst where, despite everything seemingly going wrong, a car can still finish on the podium. That happened to Tander and co-driver Cameron McConville in 2010 when they finished third.

Tander narrowly avoided hitting a kangaroo that had bounced out on the track, and later his Commodore's driver's door fell off when he and McConville were changing over during a pit stop.

'It's not an easy job to line it up on the door pins,' says Tander.

'One of the few standard things on the race cars in those days was the door hinges. And they had to be lined up on two – tiny – four-millimetre pins.'

The door was quickly re-mounted by a crew member during the pit stop. But even worse was to come: Tander was hit in the front passenger's door as he entered the pit lane for a separate pit stop.

It wasn't another race car that did the damage: it was the event Medical Car making a rapid get-away in response to a radio call. It was rushing to an accident site on track!

*Jason Bargwanna and Garth Tander savour their victory at Bathurst in 2000.*

Tander's first Bathurst 1000 win – in 2000 – forever links him in Great Race history with Sydney-raised racer Jason Bargwanna.

A pint-sized pilot, who drove with a big heart and filled his post-race interviews with red-cordial levels of enthusiasm, Bargwanna made a name for himself driving Garry Rogers' Valvoline Holden Commodores during the impressive growth period enjoyed by V8 Supercars in the late 1990s and early 2000s.

Bargwanna's first Bathurst 1000 start had come 10 years earlier – in 1990 – at the wheel of a then already elderly VL model Commodore.

Aged 18, he was wide-eyed and couldn't believe his luck. Taken to the event as largely a reserve driver by the Callaghan family's team, he proved faster than his co-drivers and ended up driving in qualifying and then the race.

'I remember the driver's briefing – sitting next to Brock and Grice and Johnson, the blokes you idolise – and I was in among them all!' exclaims Bargwanna.

'The team asked me to drive the second stint in the race, so it had gone from the team asking me to come along as a spare driver to then practice, qualifying and racing the car!'

Bargwanna's smaller frame also meant some 'out of the box' thinking was required in order to improve his seating position in the team's Commodore.

'The only way I could reach the pedals was to sit on a pillow!' he laughs.

'I'm not kidding! We pulled a pillow out of the motel, and I shoved it into the seat. The car had no power steering, so we had to manhandle it around the track.'

Bargwanna teamed up with cousin Scott to return to the Mountain in 1992 at the wheel of a Toyota Corolla, and they won their class, but five years later he really made a name for himself when he was selected as part of the Holden Racing Team-run Young Lions youth development program to race at Bathurst.

He stunned the V8 Supercar regulars by topping Friday's qualifying session, outpacing the entire pack of stars, including Mark Skaife, Glenn Seton and Greg Murphy. Bargwanna converted that pace into a fifth place in the Saturday Shootout but his grid position was vacant when the race started on Sunday morning.

His #97 Commodore was packed away by that point – a twisted, smashed piece of metal – after a simple driving mistake had put paid to the hopes and dreams of Bargwanna and co-driver Mark Noske.

It had all turned to junk on Sunday morning in the

pre-race warm-up session. Bargwanna lightly brushed a wall on the run down the Mountain and was catapulted into the concrete wall at Forrest's Elbow.

It was a hard hit with the wall. The car was heavily damaged and there was not enough time to repair it prior to the race start time.

The crash could have instantly ended Bargwanna's career, but he'd shown enough speed and skill during his appearances in the Young Lions Commodore during 1997 to land a drive with Garry Rogers' team for 1998.

He scored his first V8 Supercar win at Calder later in that first season with GRM and teamed with Tander to win at Bathurst in 2000.

'I remember being quite nervous at the start of the race. We knew we were in with a shot to win,' said Bargwanna on the V8 Sleuth Podcast in 2019 of the 2000 win.

'I don't often get quite nervous at the start of race meetings, but I felt on that day we knew we could do it. That first stint in the pouring rain, I remember driving off the start down to turn one, pulling gears and not being able to see anything outside the windscreen. And looking out the side window, passing cars I couldn't even see. That set the tone for the day.'

Bargwanna's winning partner, Tander, ended up with a very sore backside after the race too!

'We've all had burnt feet and bits and pieces driving V8 Supercars but because we had a difference in height, the seating was very different. And his butt was very low in the seat and a bit closer to the exhaust, and he ended up with blisters on his bum,' recalls Bargwanna.

'He was literally cooked on the podium!'

The modern era of Bathurst has seen a host of other Supercars stars conquer the Mountain and dictate their own special piece of Bathurst history.

Another of Tander's Bathurst partners, Will Davison, went on to win his second Great Race in 2016 as lead driver for the single car, Queensland-based TEKNO Autosports Commodore team alongside team owner/co-driver Jonathon Webb.

The grandson of four-time Australian Grand Prix winner Lex, Will has emerged as the modern star of the Davison racing clan.

Australian Formula Ford Champion in 2001, his eyes were firmly on making it in Formula 1 overseas and, after progressing through the junior open-wheeler categories in England (where one of his rivals in Formula Renault included Lewis Hamilton), he even got to the point of testing an F1 Minardi in Italy at the end of 2004, alongside countryman Will Power.

But Davison's funding ran out and he was forced to come home to Australia and change his pathway to one in V8 Supercars.

After stints with Dick Johnson Racing, the Holden Racing Team (including a Bathurst win with Tander in 2009) and Ford Performance Racing, he signed a big bucks deal to drive one of the ambitious Erebus Motorsport team's Mercedes-Benz AMG E63 race cars, however found himself on the move again after just two years to join TEKNO.

He and Webb started a lowly 17th on the grid in 2016 at Bathurst, however Davison was able to hold off an attacking

Shane van Gisbergen to claim victory by the smallest ever margin in the history of the Great Race: 0.1434-seconds separated the two competing cars.

Davison's wasn't the first car to complete 161 laps that day. Red Bull pilot Jamie Whincup crossed the line ahead of him, however had a 15-second penalty added to his race time for careless driving after colliding with Scott McLaughlin's Volvo with 11 laps to go. It dropped the four-time Bathurst winner to 11th in the results.

None of that affects Davison, who counts his 2016 drive – and holding off a flying van Gisbergen – as one of the best of his career.

It nearly all went wrong though. His #19 Commodore choked up right before winning the biggest race of the season.

'It coughed for fuel going down into the last corner!' recalls Davison.

'I'd pulled fourth gear and it had a huge fuel surge (on the run into Murray's Corner). I went to hit the throttle coming out of the corner and I thought, "Please, please go. If it surges on the exit, I'm gone!"

'It got momentum as I hit full throttle, but it was fully coughing, and I pulled left to block Shane. I knew he'd be coming up next to me. If the finish line was 100 metres further up ahead than it was, he would have driven past me!

'That elation of crossing the line wasn't a feeling of numbness by not being the first car to cross it. Jamie's car was exceptionally fast, but it was penalised. In tennis, how many people would have won Wimbledon but got a call they felt was wrong? You don't get the point back.

'He got a penalty. That was that. Simple. Whether it was received post-race or within the race, it's no different.

'I forgot Jamie was even there ahead of me crossing the line. I was so focused on Shane. Looking back, I reckon I did a great job with no fuel left in the car. I held him off and drove one of the best races I've ever driven.

'I'm a firm believer that if you bring your A-game to Bathurst year in, year out, ultimately somehow it comes back to you in a roundabout way. Some days it pays you back on a day you didn't expect it to, like 2016.

'Winning that race is an incredible privilege; it's not a right. I go there every year to execute my best personal performance. If you get outcome-focused, you get too emotional. You go there to execute your perfect day, and you don't think about things outside your control, which is what we did in 2016.'

Chaz Mostert has become one of the stars of the current Supercars Championship grid. While his career still has a long way to run, it is the perfect example of how – more than any other race – the successes and heartbreaks that are part and parcel of the Bathurst 1000 can dominate an otherwise consistent report card.

Now a two-time winner of the Great Race, his warm and goofy personality, constantly changing hair colour and relaxed nature out of the car are a far cry from his style when behind the wheel. He's all business when his race helmet is on.

Mostert replaced Davison at Ford Performance Racing in 2014 and delivered victory at Bathurst that October at just his second Great Race attempt in a spellbinding finish to announce himself to those outside the world of hardcore V8 Supercars fans.

Seizing the lead on the last lap after leader Whincup's Commodore ran low on fuel, Mostert skipped away to win a race that had taken nearly eight hours to complete after a one-hour mid-race stoppage to repair a fractured track surface.

His #6 Falcon was beaten and bruised after co-driver Paul Morris had run off the road on the damaged track prior to the race being stopped. He'd headbutted a trackside tyre barrier too – and all of this came after they'd started at the back of the grid.

This unlikely victory proved the launchpad for Mostert to become a star of the championship, but the Mountain quickly reminded him 12 months later just how quickly fortunes can change.

The young speedster was carted away from Friday qualifying in a helicopter bound for hospital in nearby Orange after pin-balling his Pepsi Max Falcon between the brutal concrete walls on the run to Forrest's Elbow, the very corner where he'd seized the lead of the race from Whincup on the last lap the previous year.

His left femur and left wrist were fractured, and he damaged ligaments in his knee in the crash, which had sent trackside officials scurrying as the out-of-control car vaulted onto the top of a concrete wall and crashed through their marshal's post.

Mostert was laid up for the rest of the 2015 season but returned at full speed in 2016 and hasn't slowed down since.

He finished fourth at Bathurst with James Moffat in 2018 but blotted his copybook by accidentally taking out Tickford teammate Cam Waters in 2019 at the Chase.

A move to Walkinshaw Andretti United for 2020 delivered a podium finish – third – at Bathurst before Mostert and Lee Holdsworth delivered one of the most dominant wins in the modern era of the race in 2021.

Mostert set a new qualifying lap record in the Top 10 Shootout and not even a flat tyre could derail his flying Commodore on race day. It had a significant pace advantage over the field, led 106 laps and sealed a popular victory.

'We were pretty confident we were the car to beat but, as this race goes, a (proverbial) dollar part can end your day,' said Mostert.

'The (failed) tyre in the third stint put us on the back foot and we changed our driving style a lot to look after the tyres and stay off the kerbs.'

So excited was he by the win, Mostert couldn't resist ignoring the protocol. Instead of driving post-race to the podium via the access road from partway up Mountain Straight, he went on a full victory lap around the Mountain.

'It's one of the most special laps I've ever done around here,' he grinned shortly afterwards.

'To see the fans who have been there all week, the cheer will stick with me forever.'

Mark Winterbottom's journey to win the Bathurst 1000 spanned the same decade it took the team he won it for – Ford Performance Racing – to also achieve its goal of conquering the Mountain.

A karting and junior category star from Western Sydney, Winterbottom's first Bathurst 1000 came in 2003 at the wheel of the Stone Brothers Racing team's second Falcon, the very same year FPR (later known as Prodrive Racing Australia and now known as Tickford Racing) also debuted at the Mountain in its first season in V8 Supercars.

There was no room for career progression at the Stones' team as they had reigning champion Marcos Ambrose and Russell Ingall on their books, so Winterbottom found a home with Mark Larkham's Orrcon Ford team and spent the next two seasons learning the ropes of the main V8 Supercars category.

His big break came in 2006 when he signed to join Jason Bright at FPR, the official Ford-backed team, which was just starting to hit its straps.

But despite being with one of the best funded teams in pit lane, Bathurst victory continued to elude Winterbottom and his crew. They were fast each year, so quick in fact that Winterbottom took pole position in both 2007 and 2010.

But the unsuccessful attempts were starting to pile up.

Engine failure early in 2006 sidelined him and Bright. Then he and Steve Richards had led more laps than anyone in 2007 when Winterbottom was caught out by rain at the Chase while in front, which sent him spearing off the track.

Fourth place in 2008 was agonisingly close to the podium and his race in 2009 ended when a replacement battery in the boot of his Falcon came loose and sparked a fire. Co-driver Luke Youlden had a tyre delaminate that sent him into the wall in 2010 and bent their steering, and fourth and 11th-placed finishes with Richards in 2011 and 2012 left Winterbottom without a single Bathurst podium finish from 10 attempts.

That all changed in 2013.

It wasn't just the fact Winterbottom (paired again with Richards) won Bathurst that was special – it was how he did it.

He and Jamie Whincup had battled one another through karting into junior car racing and then into V8 Supercars.

The latter had already won four Bathurst 1000s and was on his way to winning his fifth V8 Supercars Championship, his successes very much overshadowing Winterbottom's to that point.

But in the final stages of the 2013 Bathurst 1000, Winterbottom was the man of the moment. The duo ran nose-to-tail for the last 16 laps and the Ford ace withstood every attack Whincup could throw at him.

He staved off one final desperate attempt from Whincup, who attacked down the outside at Griffins Bend on the last lap but to no avail. That allowed 'Frosty' to skip away and at long last conquer the Mountain.

'I felt under pressure,' said Winterbottom post-race.

'There have been points throughout your career. Whether it be go-karts, getting a scholarship to get into Ford – there's been some big moments, but nothing as big as this. To cross that line, to do it with this team, and with Richo as well. To hear the FPR chant on the podium – I've never heard that before.'

The team's fans kept cheering for Winterbottom in the years that followed. He won the V8 Supercars Championship in 2015, assuring his name would appear in the history books forevermore – as winner of the two things that matter most in the sport: Bathurst and the Championship.

A Ford favourite through to the end of his tenure with the team in 2018, Winterbottom made the move to driving a Commodore – and later a Camaro – for Team 18.

However, so powerfully are opinions shaped by the goings-on at Mount Panorama that Ford fans will forever have a soft spot for Winterbottom. To them, he'll always be one of 'theirs' for the result he delivered in 2013 at Bathurst.

## A Very Select Club

Remarkably few drivers who start the Great Race at Bathurst ever get to experience the feeling of winning it.

In fact, only 63 drivers from a total of 1333 to have started the race have been able to conquer the Mountain – that's 4.7%.

The club gets more exclusive when you consider that just 22 of those 63 winning drivers – 1.65% of all drivers – have won the race on more than one occasion.

# 28

# The Weirdest Bathurst 1000

T he Bathurst 1000 has had its fair share of weird things pop up over the years.

From kangaroos and even an echidna wandering out onto the racetrack to wild and wacky weather, the Great Race has had it all.

But in 2020 a completely new curveball emerged threatening Australia's most famous race – a global pandemic.

Given it was first held in 1963 – 18 years after the end of World War II – the Bathurst classic had never had its streak of annual events threatened by serious goings on in the wider world.

Other classic motorsport events around the world older than Australia's Great Race, including the Indianapolis 500 in the United States and the Le Mans 24 Hour sportscar race in France, had already experienced paused periods in their history due to war.

The '500 began in 1911 but was put on hiatus twice (for two years in the 1910s, during World War I, and for four years in the 1940s, during World War II), and the 24 Hour – which started in 1923, was not run in 1936 (it was cancelled due to general strikes in France) or from 1940 to 1948 due to the outbreak of World War II and the required reconstruction of circuit facilities post-war.

Bathurst's annual race had no such gaps in its history, however the COVID-19 pandemic that stopped the world in its tracks in early 2020 did indeed threaten it.

The race that year was far from the Bathurst 1000 that fans knew and loved. It was a weird one, the likes of which had never been seen before.

Border closures and restricted numbers meant thousands of regular Bathurst 1000 attendees were forced to stay home to watch the race.

It all made for a very strange sight when they turned on their televisions to see bare spectator areas, no trackside tents and plenty of grassed areas not seen during a race weekend given they're normally covered by throngs of fans.

Camping was not permitted, and restrictions meant a maximum of 4000 spectators per day were allowed to attend the event. All were in temporary reserved plastic seating, spread out for social distancing reasons at the bottom of the Mountain on Pit Straight, Murray's Corner and Hell Corner.

The top of the Mountain was closed to the public; viewing at the Chase was banned; the paddock and the area behind the garages were not accessible to spectators.

Thanks to the annual crowds being largely absent, local business missed out on its biggest week of the year.

'The biggest issue at the time was how much of an ability would we have to be able to have a crowd for the race,' says Phil Shaw, Events Manager of Supercars.

'If we'd have been unable to have any public there, the next step would have been for it to have been a TV-only production.

'In the end, under the agreement we had with the New South Wales Government, we had to install all those chairs along the slope of Pit Straight. The biggest challenge for us wasn't so much if the race was to be run, it was whether it could be run with any form of crowd there to see it trackside.'

If there was a moment in time in 2020 where the Bathurst 1000 was seriously under threat though, it was some months prior: on Monday July 6, to be exact.

That was when skyrocketing COVID cases in Melbourne triggered the first border closure in 101 years between Victoria and New South Wales.

To keep the Supercars season rolling, the five Supercars teams based in Victoria, which made up 12 of the 24 cars on the Supercars Championship grid – Tickford Racing, Walkinshaw Andretti United, Erebus Motorsport, Kelly Racing and Team 18 – scrambled. Hurriedly, they packed their transporters, assembled their crews and made sure they were across the border before the 11.59pm cut-off that night.

Crew members left partners and children at home, not knowing how long they would be gone for. As it turned out, the Bathurst 1000 formed the last race of the championship and was pushed back a few weeks later than normal, to Sunday 18 October, making for a marathon three-month stint away from home for the Melbourne-based teams.

That marathon eventually ended after the Great Race, a race that culminated in victory for Shane van Gisbergen and Garth Tander as fifth-placed Scott McLaughlin sealed his third consecutive Supercars Championship in his last Supercars start before heading to the United States to race an IndyCar.

The race on track ran for just over six hours, time for hardcore and casual Bathurst 1000 fans to briefly forget about the pandemic and its associated struggles and difficulties and take in another chapter of Great Race history.

A total of 19 of the 25 starters finished the 2020 race, with 14 of them finishing on the lead lap after 161 laps of racing.

But none of those stats stick in the minds of the countless long-time Bathurst 1000 spectators who were forced to miss attending that year's race.

Plenty still bristle about being excluded from seeing the 2020 race in person. For many, what hurt was that the enforced break ended their streak of multiple years attending the Great Race. In some cases, people had passed through the gates to Mount Panorama up to 40 or 50-plus years in a row.

It's the fans that make the atmosphere during Bathurst 1000 race week so very special.

The 2020 Bathurst race was a lot of things but, above all else, it was proof that the Great Race is not as great when the venue isn't packed with spectators.

# The Frequent Finishers

Alex Davison and the duo of Jamie Whincup and Craig Lowndes share a special place in Bathurst 1000 history, sitting tied for the record of most race finishes in a row – 17.

Whincup and Lowndes' streak started in 2003 and came to an end in 2020 when the former crashed the duo's Commodore at the Cutting in the race's early stages.

Davison's chance to break the record in 2022 also ended in much the same way when younger brother Will crashed the duo's Shell/Dick Johnson Racing Mustang in the late stages at Griffin's Bend.

The only difference between Davison's streak of 17 straight finishes and that of Lowndes and Whincup was that he missed a race – 2016 – when he didn't have a drive in that particular year.

Next on the list of consecutive finishes sits Canberra's Ray Gulson, who finished in 16 straight starts between 1964 and 1985. Like Davison, he also missed some years: twice in that timeframe he didn't qualify, and he didn't compete in four of the races.

Shane van Gisbergen has the third highest number of back-to-back finishes. His 2022 victory was his 14th straight finish in a streak that began in 2009.

# Lucky Numbers

Peter Brock's famous number 05 (inspired by a 1970s drink-driving campaign highlighting the 0.05% permissible blood alcohol level in Victoria) and Dick Johnson's iconic 17 are two of the most recognised numbers in Bathurst 1000 history.

But they're not the most successful numbers carried to victory in the Great Race.

The number 1 has featured in seven wins, beginning with Allan Moffat/Jacky Ickx in the extraordinary Ford 1-2 form finish of 1977 and most recently by Jamie Whincup and Paul Dumbrell in 2012.

One reason the number is linked to so much success is that it's generally reserved for use by the Australian Touring Car/Supercars Champion in the season after their championship win. The odds favour the top teams and drivers at Bathurst.

Mark Skaife and Jim Richards carried number 1 to victory on their Nissan GT-Rs in 1991 and 1992 and Craig Lowndes and Greg Murphy took their first Bathurst 1000 win driving the #1 Holden Racing Team Commodore in 1996.

Skaife also had back-to-back wins with number 1 in 2001 and 2002 (with Tony Longhurst and Richards respectively) for the Holden Racing Team.

With the rise and success of the Triple Eight Race Engineering team and star signing Craig Lowndes, the 888 race number has become the second most frequent winning number in Bathurst 1000 history thanks to his triumphs in 2006, 2007 and 2008 with Jamie Whincup, 2010 with Mark Skaife and 2015 and 2018 with Steve Richards.

In perhaps something of a surprise to some, Brock's famous 05 took him to only five of his nine Bathurst wins (1978, 1979, 1980, 1982 and 1984). His other winning numbers were 28 (1972), 5 (1975), 25 (1983, after swapping cars mid-race) and 10 (1987, after again swapping cars mid-race).

The number 2 has made the winner's list four times, however it doesn't ring a bell with most fans like Johnson's famous 17. It has been the race's winning number four times (three with Johnson at the wheel and once in 2019 when his team's Mustang was driven by Scott McLaughlin and Alex Prémat).

Number 11 is synonymous with another Bathurst legend, Larry Perkins. He first won the race in 1995 as 11 – 30 years after it was on the side of Barry Seton and Midge Bosworth's race-winning Cortina.

Perkins carried the 11 to victory three times in the 1990s, each time in odd years – 1993, 1995 and in 1997's V8 Supercar race.

29

# The Retired Racers

**T**he deeds of Bathurst-winning race cars live long in the history books, and, in most instances, the race cars outlive the actual pilots that took them to glory at Mount Panorama.

The fate of Bathurst-winning cars has been varied over the years. Some, particularly many of the winning cars of the 1960s, have been lost to the ravages of time and are victims of a lack of period record-keeping. They may exist somewhere out there, but proving the provenance of a dusty old Cortina, Mini, Falcon or Monaro as a genuine Bathurst winner is nigh on impossible.

There's plenty of debate about many of the winning cars of the early 1970s too. For instance, three different parties all claim to have the GT-HO Phase II Falcon that Allan Moffat drove to his first of four Bathurst wins in 1970!

No one in the 1960s and 1970s could have forecast the explosion of interest in the race and how it's become a part of the nation's sporting conscience over its 60 years, let alone the resultant collectability – and value – of these winning cars.

In more recent years the value of Bathurst-winning race cars has soared, as collectors wheel and deal to get these famous Mountain machines onto their asset sheet. Competition for getting to the front of the queue for these cars has been particularly frantic in the wake of Ford and Holden discontinuing production in Australia and the latter exiting the local market.

Deals have been done in the last few years of the Supercars era for cars to be acquired by collectors while the teams are still actively racing them – often the offer is made before they've even competed in the Bathurst 1000 in October.

The funds paid for them mid-season become important race team income and the value of the car has the potential to increase should it then go on and win the Bathurst 1000 and/or the Supercars Championship prior to delivery to its new owner.

Take for example Sydney-based PremiAir Hire business owner Peter Xiberras, who joined the Supercars and Bathurst 1000 grid in 2022 with his own Gold Coast-based team.

A champion Top Fuel drag racing driver/team owner, he inked a deal with the mighty Red Bull-backed Triple Eight Race Engineering team during the 2020 Supercars season to purchase the team's pair of ZB model Commodore race cars, driven by Kiwi Shane van Gisbergen and four-time Bathurst 1000 winner Jamie Whincup.

The value of van Gisbergen's car instantly jumped when the Kiwi scored his maiden Bathurst 1000 win in it in 2020 alongside Garth Tander. The value has continued to climb ever since: van Gisbergen and the car racked up so many race wins over the course of 2021 and 2022 that it's became the most winning individual chassis in the history of the Supercars Championship.

But just to add another cherry to the already sugar-coated cake, van Gisbergen and Tander won Bathurst again in it in 2022 and scored Holden's 36th and last Great Race victory.

The van Gisbergen/Tander two-time Bathurst winning car sits in rare company as one of only three cars to score two Great Race victories. The first to achieve the feat was Peter Brock's Holden Dealer Team VH Commodore that won in 1982 and again in 1983.

The other two-time winning car, Mark Skaife's 2001 and 2002 Holden Racing Team Commodore was retained by Skaife for many years before he elected to sell it to a passionate Sydney collector. It sits tucked away in the owner's collection.

The National Motor Racing Museum, located just outside the bottom of Conrod Straight at the Mount Panorama circuit, houses all sorts of Bathurst racing memorabilia from over the years.

It's very much the 'retirement home' for Bathurst winners and other notable Great Race cars and has five winning cars on permanent display.

Among the Museum's collection is the 1965 Armstrong 500-winning Cortina GT500 driven by Barry 'Bo' Seton and Midge Bosworth.

Also on permanent display is the 1977 Falcon that Allan Moffat and Belgian Jacky Ickx drove to victory in the famous 1-2 form finish.

The 1976 race-winning Torana L34 driven to victory by Bob Morris and Englishman John Fitzpatrick is another permanent resident, as is the 1988 winning Benson & Hedges Ford Sierra RS500 Cosworth of Tony Longhurst and Tomas Mezera.

One of the most iconic cars in Bathurst history – the 1984 winning Holden Dealer Team Commodore VK driven by Peter Brock and Larry Perkins – is the fifth, and perhaps most famous, of the museum's cars.

The Museum's Coordinator, Brad Owen, has a job all rev heads will be jealous of. But it's one he doesn't take lightly.

'People say, "It's just a car" and you should just treat it like a mechanical object, but no, they are pieces of art,' he says.

'They've moved on from being a mechanical object and a tool and now they're of the same significance as a fine art piece and need to be treated that way. Even when we operate these cars, we treat them like that. We try to minimise their movement. Some of them have issues caused by their age or their history. For example, the Brock 1984 VK Commodore has a cracked windscreen, so we're very careful not to accelerate any decay or deterioration.

'These cars jog memories and evoke emotions. All motorsport fans spent Bathurst race day every year on the couch in front of the television and these cars unlock those memories. Whether it's the same type of car as your parents drove, or the same type of car you watched on TV, or the car you were physically there to see race, everyone with an interest in the sport and the race has their own special connection with these cars.'

The five cars are all part of the Bathurst Regional Council's collection. In fact, the Brock Commodore and Moffat Falcon predate the museum, which wasn't opened until 1988. Other than when used for special displays and public relations activities, they spent the rest of the time in the council's workshop. That changed when the Bathurst Light Car Club put its weight behind the establishment of a permanent museum.

'All of our cars have slightly different stories,' says Owen.

'The Brock Commodore only ever raced at Bathurst once and only did four races in its racing life (Sandown, Bathurst, Surfers Paradise and Calder in 1984), whereas the Moffat Falcon did two more Bathursts – in different colours – after its win, and the running gear was used for his next XD Falcon in 1980.

'The body shell was all that was left behind. And that, along with a set of wheels, was what was donated to the Council, which set about rebuilding the car and had to source the parts to turn it back into a running vehicle.

'The Sierra spent time with Colin Bond's Caltex team and was raced and used as a test car, but it stayed in its Group A touring car specification and was acquired by its original sponsor, WD & HO Wills/Amatil, who then donated it to the council in the last year it sponsored cars at Bathurst in 1994. That was the year prior to cigarette advertising being banned in Australian sport.

'The 1976 Bob Morris Torana became a Sports Sedan in the 1970s and was modified somewhat but it had a lot of the original parts still with it. It was later returned to its correct race-winning configuration. Terry Morgan, who was the long-time workshop manager for the council, had a contact who found out where the car was, and a deal was done for the council to acquire it.'

So how much are they worth? Owen smiles but refuses to be drawn on offering up a particular figure.

'From an insurance point of view, it's a decent number when you add them up,' he says.

'I think they're priceless. They've all got a dollar value for insurance and evaluation purposes, but if you lost these items then whatever you buy to replace them just doesn't have the same history. There's only one car every year that wins the Bathurst 1000 and that makes them very special.

'We've had a few offers over the years to sell them, but they're not for sale. No amount of money could buy them.'

Five Bathurst-winning cars have met their demise in the years since the race's distance was extended from 500 miles to 1000 kilometres in 1973.

That year's winning car, the Falcon XA GT 'Superbird' of Allan Moffat and Ian 'Pete' Geoghegan, didn't even last out that season and was destroyed within just two months of its Bathurst win.

The blue and white coupe was written off when a flat-spotted tyre blew – with Moffat at the wheel through a high-speed sweeper at Phillip Island. The Ford hero veered off the track and into a small earth bank, and the car was flung into a series of end-for-end rolls. It came to rest perilously close to a storage dam.

Moffat was taken away on a stretcher with a cracked sternum and the wreck was given to privateer Ford driver

Murray Carter to salvage what mechanical components were still useable. Then the stripped body shell was scrapped.

Phillip Island also ended the racing life of the 1994 Bathurst-winning Falcon that Dick Johnson and John Bowe drove to victory in their second win as a duo. An EB model Falcon when it won at Mount Panorama, it was upgraded to the newer EF model bodywork for the following season and won the 1995 Australian Touring Car Championship in Bowe's hands.

The Tasmanian drove it for the early rounds of the 1996 championship as he attempted to defend his crown, however he and Craig Lowndes both ran off the road in close proximity to one another on the opening lap of an ATCC race at the high-speed circuit.

The yellow, blue and red Ford powered into one of the trackside banks then was shot high into the air. Disappointingly, the impact was missed by the Channel 7 television cameras covering the event. The car eventually landed on its side after a series of rolls.

The damage was so bad that the team decided to strip the usable parts and scrap the Falcon body shell at the tip.

A hard racing life, rather than a specific accident, brought forward the end of the line for another Ford, the Falcon XA GT coupe that John Goss and Kevin Bartlett used to win the rain-affected 1974 race. It later became a road car and, riddled with fractures and stress cracks, was considered beyond repair. As with the Moffat and Bowe crashed cars, it was stripped of its parts then dumped at the tip.

Two of Peter Brock's Bathurst 1000-winning Holdens also belong to the list of casualties. His 1975 Torana L34, the privateer car he drove to victory with Brian Sampson, raced on in the years following its Bathurst win in the hands of various drivers.

Eventually it was sold, minus engine, to a young Tasmanian, Michael Rowell, who removed its racing roll cage and rebuilt it as a road car. But he wrote it off in a road crash on a New Year's Eve in the late 1970s.

The story of the Brock 1975 Bathurst Torana didn't quite end there. After the accident the body shell was cut in half. The front half – from the B-pillars forward – went to a local racer, who grafted it onto a damaged speedway car, and the back half went to the local tip!

The other Brock Bathurst winner to meet its demise was his 1980 VC model Holden Dealer Team Commodore. The first Holden Commodore to win Bathurst, it was the car that Brock and Jim Richards used to claim their third successive win, which wrote them into the record books as the first duo to win the race three years in a row. After further time with Brock's team and privateer driver Jim Keogh, it was converted to race at the Calder Park Thunderdome superspeedway. It was crashed and destroyed in an accident in 1995.

Holden and Ford have collectively dominated the Bathurst classic over the years, winning all bar six of the 62 Great Races run at Mount Panorama since the first in 1963.

However, of all the Bathurst-winning cars from over the years, there's only one that continues to race competitively and it's neither a Ford nor Holden.

The howling V12-engined Jaguar XJ-S that won in 1985 (one of three brought out to Australia by Scotsman Tom

Walkinshaw, who later owned and ran the Holden Racing Team) is the only Bathurst winner that continues to actively race competitively on a regular basis.

Melbourne-based Jaguar enthusiast Mike Roddy is a regular in historic racing at the helm of the 'big cat', the car John Goss and German Armin Hahne used to break the Holden and Ford winning streak that dated back to 1967.

'I don't think they're meant to be in museums,' he said in 2015.

'You have to let them run wild. I'm pretty careful with it though. I drive it pretty hard, but I don't like to get side-by-side with other guys, particularly if I don't know them too well.'

The last non-Holden or Ford to win Bathurst prior to the Jaguar was the tiny Morris Cooper S (more commonly known as a Mini) that Bob Holden and Finn Rauno Aaltonen used to win the 1966 race. It was on-sold after its victory and entered in the following year's race by new owner John Millyard.

Millyard was a musician who played at a Sydney CBD nightspot and one night the Mini was reportedly stolen from outside the venue, never to be seen again!

The petite Cooper S Bathurst winner was a four-cylinder, front-wheel-drive car that went around Mount Panorama with a best lap time in the race of 3 minutes 11 seconds, almost exactly one minute per lap slower than the six-cylinder, four-wheel-drive, turbocharged Nissan GT-R achieved when it won 25 years later – in 1991.

Mark Skaife and Jim Richards gave the Japanese manufacturer its first Bathurst 1000 win, repeating the dose a year later in another GT-R, this time sponsored by Winfield cigarettes.

Both Bathurst-winning Nissans now belong to a Queensland-based collector, who owns a number of retired Nissan touring cars.

The 1991 car spent time racing in Asia before returning to Australia to be restored to its Bathurst-winning factory red, white and blue colours and specification.

The 1992 winning car required repairs to damage sustained when it crashed in the dreadful wet conditions that brought that Bathurst race to an early end. It has since raced in Historic competition.

The other non-Holden and non-Ford winning cars came in the two years – 1997 and 1998 – that there were two Bathurst 1000-kilometre races, one of which was held for international two-litre Super Touring cars.

The Diet Coke BMW 320i that Geoff and David Brabham (sons of three-time Formula 1 World Champion, Sir Jack) drove to victory in '97 was used by Paul Morris to win the 1999 and 2000/01 Australian Super Touring Championships and is now in the ownership of a private collector in New Zealand.

Appropriately, the Volvo S40 that won the following year's race is now to be found in Sweden – with Rickard Rydell, the Swedish racing star who drove it to victory at the Mountain alongside Jim Richards.

The Bathurst 1000 is a world-famous race, and that's been further underlined by the increase of overseas collectors snapping up its historic winning cars in recent years.

A one-time Peter Brock Mobil team gopher, American-based Aussie Kenny Habul has made his fortune in solar energy. His passion for Bathurst and Brock is so deep he paid big bucks to own Brock's last Bathurst 1000-winning Commodore, the VL model V8 that won the 1987 Great Race – at which Habul was a teenaged member of the Brock team.

In addition to his McLaren Racing CEO duties in Formula 1, Zak Brown is a partner in the Walkinshaw Andretti United Supercars team these days. But prior to that buy-in the American snapped up a deal to purchase the 2011 HRT Bathurst-winning Commodore VE II driven to victory by Garth Tander and Nick Percat.

A racer long before he was a motorsport marketing guru or team principal, Brown is as passionate as they come and has jumped behind the wheel of his Bathurst winner in recent years at tracks across Europe and the United States.

It so happens that the States is also the destination of the 2019 race-winning Shell V-Power Racing Team Mustang driven by Scott McLaughlin and Frenchman Alex Prémat. Repaired after a devastating crash in McLaughlin's hands on the Gold Coast a few weeks after its glorious day on the Mountain, the car is to be sent to America to join the extensive race car collection of American racing giant Roger Penske.

Penske bought in to Dick Johnson's team for the 2015 season and, after selling out at the end of 2020, retained some of the team's cars from his time as majority owner.

Johnson doesn't own any of his Bathurst 1000-winning cars. Financial difficulties in the mid-2000s forced him to sell his collection in order to keep his race team afloat. Among those cars were the 1981 winning Tru-Blu Falcon XD and 1989 winning Shell Ford Sierra.

Sunshine Coast collector David Bowden and his family are the custodians of these pieces of Johnson Ford Bathurst history, part of a major collection that also includes Peter Brock's famous 1978 and 1979 Holden Dealer Team Torana A9Xs.

Further south in Melbourne, race team owners Ben and Rachael Eggleston have acquired their own pieces of Holden Bathurst history. The husband-and-wife partnership run a team in the Supercars support category, Super2, and several Bathurst winners have pride of place in their ever-growing collection.

It includes the 1990 VL Commodore that claimed the Holden Racing Team's first Bathurst win with Allan Grice and Win Percy. Then there's Mark Skaife and Todd Kelly's 2005 HRT winner, fully restored to its factory red colours and technical specification.

They also have the historically significant 1996 Craig Lowndes/Greg Murphy HRT VR Commodore under restoration and have earmarked the 2010 race-winning Lowndes/Skaife TeamVodafone VE II Commodore as a future project to restore.

Only a handful of Bathurst winners have retained their successful cars or indeed been able to buy them back.

1986 winner Graeme Bailey's Chickadee Chicken Commodore has remained in his hands ever since Allan Grice drove it across the line, while Garry Rogers Motorsport has kept the VT Commodore in which Garth Tander and Jason Bargwanna won back in November 2000. In fact, the GRM Valvoline car never raced again!

Larry Perkins bought back his 1993 Castrol Commodore a few years ago and he and son Jack have spent thousands of hours restoring it over a stretch of years. Given it's the last Holden to win the Great Race with a Holden V8 engine (rather than the Chevrolet V8 engine used by every Commodore that's won the race since), it's an incomparable piece of Bathurst history.

Seven-time Supercars Champion Jamie Whincup won Bathurst in 2012 in a Commodore he'd nicknamed 'Kate' and, when it was retired from racing at the end of that season, he did a deal with team boss Roland Dane to acquire it. These days Kate is usually on display at The Bend Motorsport Park's visitor centre museum in South Australia. An occasional blast in the hands of its owner keeps the fuel flowing through.

The 2012-winning Commodore is a complete running car, in stark contrast to the bare, stripped chassis of the 2017 race-winner driven by David Reynolds and Luke Youlden for Erebus Motorsport.

It was heavily crashed at Bathurst in 2019 when the throttle jammed on driver Anton De Pasquale. One day the team intends to return it to its former glory – the way it looked the day it conquered the Mountain.

# Starting Them Young

Mildura-raised racer Cam Waters is a two-time runner-up in the Bathurst 1000 and a modern star for the Tickford Racing team aboard its Ford Mustangs, but he holds a very special place in the history books as the youngest ever driver in the race's history.

Born in August 1994, he was just 17 years and 67 days old (not old enough to hold a road car licence in his home state of Victoria) and in Year 11 at high school when he lined up on the grid for the 2011 race in a Commodore as co-driver to TV personality and experienced racer Grant Denyer.

Waters, an emerging Formula Ford junior open-wheeler driver at the time, had just won the *Shannons Supercar Showdown*, a reality-TV series hosted by Denyer that offered a Bathurst 1000 co-drive to its winner. None of the competitors had been your 'off the street' reality show contestants; far from it. They were a diverse group of young racers looking for a big break in their careers.

Waters was forced to keep his win and Bathurst co-drive prize a secret until the program aired – a few months after it was filmed.

'I crashed in the race at Bathurst, but the team fixed the car and got us going again. That event set me up for the next five years,' he said on the V8 Sleuth Podcast in 2022.

'It got my name out there more and made getting sponsorship easier to get.'

His name got out there a heck of a lot more during practice at Bathurst when the teenager survived a high-speed spin approaching Skyline. It's a miracle Waters didn't collide with the awaiting concrete wall after flicking the car into a wild 360-degree loop. Afterwards, he simply drove it back to the pits to have the flat-spotted tyres replaced.

'I wasn't fazed at the time, but it could have been the biggest crash of my life!' he says.

On the Tuesday after the race at Bathurst, the young gun did his licence driving test and collected his P-plates!

## 30

# **Biker Boys**

**M**ount Panorama hasn't always purely been about car racing.

Motorcycle racing has been part of the history of Bathurst's famous track since it first opened in 1938, and the two-wheeled events at Easter in the 1970s and 1980s sit firmly in the history books, both for the on-track racing and off-track riots and spectator wildness that typified the era at the top of the Mountain.

Motorcycles haven't raced at the Mountain since an ill-fated attempt to revive the Easter motorcycle meeting in 2000, however a range of two-wheeled heroes have made successful transitions to car racing, particularly in the Bathurst 1000.

Heading the list is 1993 Bathurst 1000 winner Gregg Hansford, who is in a class of his own, given he won top-tier events at Mount Panorama on both two and four wheels.

His first triumphs at the Mountain came at the traditional Easter bike meetings before he set his sights on the world championship, where he claimed 10 Grand Prix wins for Kawasaki in the 250cc and 350cc classes between

1978 and 1979. Then injuries brought down the curtain on his two-wheel career.

Hansford soon switched full-time to four wheels, recruited by Allan Moffat to share his Mazda RX-7s and Ford Sierras. They won the 1988 Sandown 500 and nearly captured that year's Bathurst 1000 before they dropped out while leading when their turbo Ford's engine overheated.

He finally etched his name in Bathurst's four-wheel record books in 1993, co-driving a Commodore with Larry Perkins. The duo tasted victory in that year's Tooheys 1000. Hansford then backed it up with a win in the James Hardie 12 Hour production car enduro in a Mazda RX-7 with Neil Crompton just a few months later.

In fact, Perkins had opted to sign up Hansford off the back of chasing him around the Mountain in the previous year's 12 Hour race. The Holden hero was racing a Lotus Esprit in a one-off and found himself chasing the beach-blond Gold Coaster's Mazda.

'I remember following him closely for many, many laps,' Perkins says.

'I was aware it was a 12-hour race, and you didn't have to pass the guy and win in the first corner. His pace was very, very good so I thought I'd just follow him and see how it goes.

'Over those many, many laps, he never ever made a mistake, his line on the first lap was the same as his last lap, etcetera.

'When I finished my stint or that meeting finished, I contacted Gregg and asked him what he was doing for Bathurst because I've got a seat for him whenever he wants it.

'That's how I met dear old Gregg and the rest of it is history.'

The pair teamed up again to finish third in the 1994 Bathurst 1000, but their partnership sadly ended in early 1995 when Hansford was killed driving a Ford Mondeo in the opening round of that year's Australian Super Touring Championship at Phillip Island.

'Give him something to drive and he'd go and drive it,' his great friend, and veteran of 20 Bathurst 1000 starts, Charlie O'Brien, told the V8 Sleuth Podcast in 2022.

'A true champion of Bathurst is someone who wins on two and four wheels, and he didn't just win once at Bathurst on two wheels.

'He was quite a remarkable driver and smooth to go with that. He certainly deserved everything he achieved.'

A contemporary of Hansford's on two-wheels, Venezuelan Johnny Cecotto claimed the 350cc world title in 1975 at age 19, setting a record for the youngest motorcycle world champion that stood for 15 years.

He also triumphed in the prestigious Daytona 200 in 1976 and won three 500cc Grand Prix across the 1977 and 1978 seasons but retired from motorcycle racing at just 24 years of age in order to pursue a career in car racing.

Cecotto made it all the way to Formula 1, where he was teammate to Ayrton Senna at Toleman in 1984. But then a horror shunt in qualifying for the British Grand Prix at Brands Hatch left him with leg injuries that curtailed his open-wheel career.

Instead he turned his attention to touring cars, securing a role as a factory BMW driver. That brought him to Mount

Panorama on three occasions. On his first visit he expressed his surprise that anyone would even consider racing a motorbike around the circuit!

Cecotto finished second alongside Roberto Ravaglia on debut in 1985, put his BMW M3 into the Top 10 Shootout at the 1987 World Touring Car Championship round on his way to seventh with Gianfranco Brancatelli, and finished fourth with Tony Longhurst in 1992, despite crashing their M3 in the Sunday morning warm-up.

Cecotto's last Bathurst 1000 in 1992 was Wayne Gardner's first and the 1987 500cc World Motorcycle Champion was arguably the highest profile Australian racer to go from two wheels to four.

Gardner rode motorcycle racing into the mainstream in the 1980s; his World Championship led to Australia getting its own world title round in 1989 at Phillip Island – which he won in typically dogged, emotional fashion.

Although further world titles eluded him, Gardner remained a regular winner until his retirement from the 500cc series at the end of the 1992 season. In a matter of months he was saddling up in a privateer Commodore to make his Great Race debut.

He joined the official Holden Racing Team for 1993 and finished third at Bathurst with Brad Jones before making the step to set up and run his own Sydney-based Commodore touring car team with Coca-Cola sponsorship and Neil Crompton as teammate. They finished third at Bathurst in 1995 and were leading in 1997 when the engine blew apart.

Gardner became a gun for hire after he closed his own team. He had lost none of his daring and splashed his way to pole position at the Mountain in 2000 in one of Glenn Seton's Ford Tickford Racing Falcons, though clutch failure took him and rally ace co-driver Neal Bates out of the race.

The former bike supremo raced GT cars in Japan but kept an annual date with the Bathurst 1000. He drove with Mark Larkham in 2001 and did a deal to share a Stone Brothers Racing Falcon with David Besnard for 2002 to make his 11th Bathurst 1000 start – but he didn't make it to race day.

His luck deserted him on only the fifth lap of Friday morning's final practice session before qualifying.

'When I got into the car my overalls hit the lever at the front of the seat that turned the brake bias off; it's for bleeding the brakes when they come in to change pads,' said Gardner on the V8 Sleuth Podcast in 2020.

'The leg of my suit dragged the lever across (and) turned the brake valve off, so I had no brakes. I went up Mountain Straight and had no brakes; it went straight to the floor. I pumped and pumped but I couldn't make it, downshifted, nearly made it but hit the wall and it then flicked me off across the other side of the road.'

The Caltex Falcon was destroyed, ruling the Besnard/ Gardner pairing out of the race. The crash prompted Gardner to retire from four-wheel racing and he never raced at Bathurst again.

'I got offers to come back after that, but to be honest, that scared me a bit, that crash. It scared the f*** out of me,' Gardner says.

'It knocked me out. Luckily I was OK – they're pretty strong cars – but the amount of impact really shocked me.

It was my first real crash that I'd had. I'd had little crashes, but certainly not at that high a speed. My kids were growing up and they wanted to start racing, so I figured it was time to stop.'

Gardner may not have made the grid for the 2002 Bathurst 1000, but Daryl Beattie – another former Honda 500cc World Motorcycle Championship racer – most certainly did.

Beattie was one of a host of Australian riders to make it to the 500cc world championship in the wake of Gardner's breakthrough success in 1987, and he made his 500cc debut replacing the injured Gardner at Eastern Creek in the 1992 Australian Motorcycle Grand Prix.

He took over a factory Honda seat in the world championship in 1993 after Gardner's retirement and won the German Grand Prix in his rookie full-time season. He then took two more race wins for Suzuki in 1995 while battling Mick Doohan for the world championship, but a series of injuries the following year led to him retiring at the end of the 1997 season.

Beattie carved out a successful TV and commentary career with Channel 10 after returning home, which led to a chance to have a test in one of Paul Morris' V8 Supercars in 2002.

Later that year Beattie made his V8 race debut, sharing an Imrie Motor Sport Commodore at the Queensland 500 and Bathurst 1000 enduros, but that was as far as his Supercars aspirations went.

Alongside Tyler Mecklem he started 32nd at Mount Panorama and completed 84 laps, of which Beattie did 32.

But then Mecklem crashed out at Griffins Bend at the top of Mountain Straight.

Flick through the Bathurst 1000 history books and you'll find Michael Dowson's name listed as class winner in the 1989 race.

Dowson and Gregg Hansford are the only racers who have been victorious on both two and four wheels at Mount Panorama.

A contemporary of Kevin Magee and Mick Doohan, Dowson didn't quite get the international breaks that his Marlboro Yamaha teammates had. Nevertheless, Dowson was a winner at the annual Easter bike races at Bathurst in the 1980s, won a pair of World Superbike Championship races and was successful in the domestic championships in both Australia and Japan.

He made just one appearance in the 500cc World Championship, finishing ninth in the 1989 Australian Grand Prix at Phillip Island. Remarkably, Dowson made his touring car racing debut one week later.

He was one of a handful of racers from various levels and disciplines selected to race a Toyota Team Australia Corolla by the manufacturer's 'Star Search' program.

Dowson crashed out early in Lakeside's Australian Touring Car Championship round and the class victory he claimed at Bathurst alongside future rally star Neal Bates was his first and only start in the Great Race.

Kiwi motorcycle ace Graeme Crosby was a mentor of Wayne Gardner's when the 'Wollongong Whiz' first headed to Europe in the early 1980s in pursuit of his dream of becoming world champion.

One of the most colourful racers of his era, 'Croz' rose to prominence through Superbike racing in the 1970s and was victorious in some of the most prestigious two-wheel races on the planet, including the Daytona 200, Suzuka 8 Hour and at the Isle of Man TT.

He translated that success into the world of 500cc racing; although he never quite cracked it for a Grand Prix win, Crosby claimed a slew of pole positions and podium finishes across the 1981 and 1982 seasons riding for Suzuki then Yamaha.

Despite finishing second in the championship in the latter season, Crosby abruptly quit racing at the end of the year. He'd grown tired of the politics involved in racing and retired home to New Zealand.

Crosby was soon tempted back to the racetrack, albeit in a touring car rather than on a bike.

While his four-wheel career was relatively short, it was also spectacular. His best – and only full-time – season came in 1986 at the wheel of a Holden Commodore, when he proved fast enough to make the Top 10 Shootout for the 1986 Great Race.

That particular Commodore was run by Ross Stone, one half of the Stone Brothers Racing team he ran with brother Jim that Gardner later drove for at Bathurst in 2002.

Crosby returned to race in four more Bathurst 1000s – including two as co-driver to Colin Bond in the Aussie legend's Caltex Sierra – but failed to finish on all four occasions. He and Bond would have finished sixth in 1991, however their engine died mere minutes from the finish, and they were left in the long list of non-finishers.

Multiple World Superbike Champion Troy Bayliss was another two-wheeled hero who couldn't help but have a crack at the Bathurst 1000.

His storybook rise from club racer to multiple World Superbike Champion and MotoGP race winner was incredible and his career included a couple of motorcycle races at Mount Panorama in the early 1990s as a support event to the James Hardie 12 Hour production car race.

After retiring from motorcycle racing at the end of his championship-winning 2008 WorldSBK season, Bayliss expressed a desire to make the move into V8 Supercars. He tested a Craig Lowndes Vodafone Triple Eight Falcon at Queensland Raceway in mid-2009 and sealed a deal with Western Australian Dean Fiore to share his Commodore at Bathurst later that year.

'I love V8s. I was a bit of a Dick Johnson man back in the day,' said Bayliss on the V8 Sleuth Podcast in 2019.

'I felt like I couldn't do anything wrong (in the Lowndes car) and a few months later I jumped in Dean's Commodore (on a Queensland Raceway test day). And as soon as I left the pit box, I didn't feel comfortable in that thing.

'We went to Phillip Island (for the pre-Bathurst 500-kilometre race) and that was OK but then we went to Bathurst. It was such a big task and so many people don't understand how fast these cars are. They were really hard work.'

He and Fiore started 32nd – last on the grid – and spent time in pit lane dealing with a fuel injector problem. They lasted 59 laps in the race before Bayliss got caught out in greasy conditions and crashed at the top of the Mountain.

His Bathurst 1000 career ended on just his eighth race lap in a V8 Supercar.

'To drive in the rain at Bathurst, I didn't feel really safe at all,' he recalls.

'When that car got out of shape, I felt like I was along for the ride. I overshot Skyline a little bit, ran a bit wide, and then that just links into a lot of corners and I spun and crashed into the XXXX [beer] sign.

'It didn't do a lot of damage, but it was enough to put us out. And that was sort of the end of that.'

The most recent world motorcycle star to tackle Bathurst in a V8 Supercar did it at a Bathurst 1000, but not in the big race on Sunday.

Casey Stoner earnt his place as a legend of Australian motorsport with a pair of MotoGP world championship wins in 2007 and 2011 for Ducati and Honda respectively.

But Stoner grew weary of the politics within the sport and retired at the end of the 2012 season to spend more time at home with his family.

Part of that time at home in 2013 included a season in Supercars' second-tier Dunlop Series driving a Red Bull-backed Holden run by Triple Eight. In fact, it was the very same Commodore that Craig Lowndes and Mark Skaife had used to win the 2010 Bathurst Great Race.

The spotlight was well and truly on Stoner throughout his first season of car racing. Every one of his rookie mistakes garnered far greater scrutiny and headlines than would have been given to a driver of similar experience who didn't happen to be a multiple MotoGP champion. Unsurprisingly, Stoner elected not to carry on for a second season.

His best race result was a fifth placing in the final race of the Queensland Raceway round, although he was on for a better result in the Saturday afternoon race at Bathurst until he hit the wall at Reid Park on a late restart.

'Believe it or not, I didn't actually want to race at all in 2013,' Stoner told *Rusty's Garage* podcast host Greg Rust in 2019.

'I didn't want to do anything. I wanted to have the whole year off to myself – just do the testing program, drive some cars to get used to them and then do the Development Series in 2014. But I was forced into doing it in 2013. I wasn't ready for it. I was worn out; I was burnt out.

'I made a couple of mistakes, I got driven into a few times, things just didn't go our way. I was busy as hell off the track. It was just a very, very stressful year that I wanted to get away from and I couldn't.

'Unfortunately, once you sign the contract to go into it … that was us: we were stuck.'

Stoner competing in the Bathurst 1000 would have made news all over the world, but sadly it wasn't to be.

Perhaps the most unheralded motorcyclist to compete in the Great Race is Japanese racer Kunimitsu Takahashi.

Takahashi might not be the highest profile name in Bathurst history, but the Japanese legend enjoyed a ground-breaking career in motorsport.

A motorcycle racer in his teens, he joined the factory Honda team at the turn of the 1960s and was one of their first riders at world championship level. In 1961, he won the West German 250cc Grand Prix at Hockenheim, taking Honda's second victory in a world championship race and becoming the first Japanese rider to win at that level.

Like Johnny Cecotto, he retired from two-wheel racing at age 24 and switched to cars, enjoying a career that included a Formula 1 start in the 1977 Japanese Grand Prix and a host of Le Mans 24 Hours tilts through the Group C and GT eras, as well as touring car racing.

It was the latter that brought him to Mount Panorama in the mid-1960s as a driver for the factory Datsun squad. Paired with Moto Kitano, Takahashi won Class A in the 1966 Gallaher 500 and made two further starts in the Great Race.

But this was far from his most outstanding contribution to motorsport.

Takahashi, who passed away aged 82 in March 2022, is regarded as the father of the sport of drifting.

# The Longest Waits Between Wins

When Steve Richards stood atop the podium after taking out the Bathurst 1000 in 2013 for Ford Performance Racing, much of the focus was placed on his car's lead driver, Mark Winterbottom. After holding off Jamie Whincup in a thrilling contest, Winterbottom had at long last claimed his first Great Race win. It was his 11th attempt!

But Richards' third Bathurst 1000 victory wrote him into the history books for the longest wait between Great Race wins: some 14 years since his previous win – alongside Greg Murphy in 1999.

It beat the previous mark – set by Tony Longhurst in 2001. That win alongside Mark Skaife came 13 years after Longhurst's first win – in a Ford Sierra in 1988.

Jim Richards (1980 to 1991) and John Goss (1974 and 1985) each had to wait 11 years between their first and second Bathurst 1000 wins, while Craig Lowndes broke a 10-year drought on an emotional day in 2006 to claim the first Peter Brock Trophy in the wake of Peter Brock's death a month earlier.

# 31

# The Future

**S**o, what's next for Australia's Great Race?

The 2023 Bathurst 1000, the 60th anniversary of the Great Race at Mount Panorama, marks the start of a new era and the beginning of its history without Holden.

Every year since 1963 there were Holdens on the grid for the annual Mount Panorama classic, a streak that ended in 2022.

General Motors announced in early 2020 that it would retire the brand from the marketplace that year, though Supercars teams continued using the 'Gen2' ZB Commodore race car through to the end of 2022 as plans to introduce a new era of cars, dubbed 'Gen3', were delayed to 2023.

GM has stayed in Supercars via the development of the new Chevrolet Camaro ZL1 Supercar that is pitted against the new-look Ford Mustang GT.

The appearance of Camaros on the grid at Bathurst in 2023 marks the first time the Chev halo car has competed in a Bathurst 1000 since the last Group C era race in 1984 when a pair of Z28 models lined up for the start.

The new cars feature a range of control components common across each car and, for the first time in Supercars and Bathurst 1000 history, control engine suppliers. This is a move designed to save money for teams and avoid them having to maintain expensive engine development programs.

The Gold Coast-based Herrod Performance Engines build and supply all Ford teams with a 5.4-litre engine while Brisbane-based KRE Engines build and supply each of the 5.7-litre Chevrolet engines.

But the big question remains: will Holden fans adopt the famous Chevrolet 'bow tie' as their own to replace their historic lion – and trigger a new rivalry?

Will the Bathurst 1000 lose its appeal to the hardcore, long-time fan and will the next generation embrace the race in an increasingly crammed world of sports, entertainment and content options?

American-based Aussie Leigh Diffey is well placed to provide a worldly view of what comes next for the Great Race from his base in Connecticut.

A Queenslander who started commentating Ipswich Motorcycle Club events as a 19-year-old, he's become Australia's biggest motorsport television export in the United States, his home for the best part of the last two decades.

Diffey's connection to Mount Panorama goes back to his big local break as lead commentator of the V8 Supercars Bathurst races on Channel 10 in the late 1990s and 2000s. He's since gone on to call more of the world's iconic famous races including the Indianapolis 500, Monaco Grand Prix, Le Mans

24 Hour and Daytona 24 Hour, not to mention covering the Olympic Games for NBC, his employer since 2013.

'Bathurst is the thing everyone asks me about,' says Diffey.

'I get asked about Supercars and the very next question is about Bathurst. It's like IndyCar and the Indianapolis 500 or when people talk sportscar racing and they ask about Le Mans or Daytona or Sebring. They go hand-in-hand.

'The fact people over here still ask me about it means it's very relevant on the international level. It's in the same realm they talk about the great races of the world.

'As time has gone on, the general awareness of that event has grown, enhanced by where we are with modern day TV and internet and streaming and social media. With every decade that goes by, it becomes more of an easy topic to talk about because it's so accessible now.

'Here in the US, one of the biggest things that helped the Bathurst 1000 from a promotional standpoint and awareness was in 2011 when me, [NASCAR legend] Darrell Waltrip, Mike Joy and Calvin Fish came down and we broadcast Bathurst live to the US, which had never been done before.

'That was a landmark moment for the event, it was very special to be a part of that. People still talk about it over here to this very day. Even though the race was on at a crazy time [in the United States], they didn't care, they thought it was so cool to see it live.

'As an Australian I'm saddened by the fact there's no more Ford versus Holden, it's what I grew up with, but I think Bathurst is bigger than any brand or any manufacturer,' he says.

'It's about the Mountain and the quest to try and conquer it. Manufacturers come and go, but the race and the challenge of the Mountain is still there. It's one of the most daunting places in the world.

'The challenge remains the same, that to me quells the sadness of no more Ford versus Holden. It makes me proud that event has, and always will, stand the test of time.'

Regardless of what cars compete in the Bathurst 1000 in the future, its 60 years of history, firm commercial foothold and the dominant position of Supercars in the local motorsport landscape will ensure it continues to be the biggest race on the calendar for years to come.

Repco announced in late 2022 that it had signed a new long-term contract through until the end of 2028 to continue as naming rights partner of the race and the Supercars Championship on the whole; a sign that the connection the race has to its audience is still going strong.

It's clearly a vote of confidence in the Bathurst 1000 remaining 'box office'.

The Bathurst 1000 has a history of attracting the big names from sport, politics and entertainment.

Being at the Bathurst 1000 is being seen.

Prime Ministers Malcolm Fraser and Bob Hawke knew it when they made appearances at the Great Race at Mount Panorama.

The former was on the podium with Allan Moffat in 1977 and the latter presented Peter Brock with the winner's trophy in 1983. That was only a week after Australia had won the America's Cup and Hawke had delivered his famous line that any boss who sacked a worker for watching the sailing classic and missing work the next day was 'a bum'. Brocky and Hawkey at Bathurst – could there be anything more 1980s Australia?

Scott Morrison made two Bathurst 1000 appearances – in 2018 and 2021 – while Australia's Prime Minister. Former Opposition Leader John Hewson is another politician with a love of motorsport. He took his passion into the pits and worked on the Ford Sierra and Falcon pit crews of Queensland racer Kevin Waldock in the 1990s.

Hollywood star Eric Bana is a massive Dick Johnson Racing fan and has been a Great Race visitor when schedules permit. The race has even hosted royalty: Prince Philip, the Duke of Edinburgh, visited and toured the pits mid-race in 1986.

Australian cricket legend Steve Waugh was appointed Grand Marshall of the 2004 race, 10 years after Olympic swimmer Kieren Perkins gave the pre-race command for drivers, 'Start your engines', for the 1994 Great Race. Some of Australia's biggest acts have also been at Bathurst to perform the pre-race national anthem – Jimmy Barnes, John Farnham, Delta Goodrem, Billy Thorpe, Ian Moss, James Morrison, Natalie Bassingthwaighte and Iva Davies to name but a few.

These days the Mount Panorama circuit is permitted by law to be closed and used for at most, five major motorsport events each calendar year.

Behind the Bathurst 1000 the next biggest race is undoubtedly the Bathurst 12 Hour GT race. Like the '1000, it's owned and run by Supercars.

It's become the Bathurst race that attracts international drivers and teams in lightning-fast GT3-specification Audis, Mercedes-Benzes, Porsches and Lamborghinis, reminiscent of the era when the Great Race would attract visiting teams, cars and drivers from beyond Australian shores.

The lack of international drivers taking part in the modern Bathurst 1000 does take away some potential storylines, however there are good reasons for it. Among them are the one-of-a-kind nature of the domestic Supercars, the limited time for pre-race testing and international racing calendars, and schedule and sponsor clashes. All these factors tend to favour teams generally sticking to signing local drivers familiar with the cars, track and racing.

'I think it (the lack of international drivers in the Bathurst 1000) is to the event's detriment,' says Diffey.

'It added an element of flair when you could include that international flavour. It gave it a point of difference.'

The biggest barrier is that the rules don't permit full-time Supercars drivers to share the same car at Bathurst.

'If you could massage the rules (so overseas drivers could drive a team's second or third car with less pressure) that it would allow it to happen again, it would be a fantastic selling point for the event.

'If the young drivers coming out of the Supercars Super2 series are good enough, they'll get their opportunities, but a sprinkling of internationals would be a good thing.'

Diffey points to 2019 when IndyCar stars, American Alexander Rossi and Canadian James Hinchcliffe, drove a Walkinshaw Andretti United-run wildcard Commodore entry in the Bathurst race.

'One guy [Hinchcliffe] had sat on pole position for the Indy 500 and the other [Rossi] won the 100th running of it in 2016,' he says.

'They've done so many other cool things in their career and they would put the Bathurst 1000 up there in the top five coolest and most challenging things they've done, certainly one of the most daunting too.'

There's been a limited list of international winners of the Bathurst race over the years and it would appear this will remain a select group. Not counting New Zealanders, it includes Finn Rauno Aaltonen (winner in 1966), Brit John Fitzpatrick (1976), German Armin Hahne (1985), Brit Win Percy (1990), Swede Rickard Rydell (1998) and Frenchman Alexandre Prémat (2019).

Prémat had signed to drive a Tickford Racing Ford Mustang in the 2020 Great Race and joined the team in the Supercars pre-season test at The Bend Motorsport Park in South Australia earlier that year. Unfortunately the pandemic that escalated a short time after put paid to that and a subsequent attempt to return in 2021 also came to nought.

It would seem extremely unlikely that there'll be many more international co-drivers on the grid for a Bathurst 1000, let alone a winner hailing from overseas.

The Bathurst 6 Hour production car race held at Easter and run by the Australian Racing Group has some of the hallmarks of the early Great Race. The participation of more standard race cars harks back to the road-registerable production cars that competed in the Armstrong 500 in the 1960s.

It's this Bathurst endurance race – attainable for amateur, enthusiast racers – that always features a full field packed with cars of all kinds.

ARG also debuted a new 'Bathurst International' inclusion to its schedule in 2022 with a tiny crowd on-hand. It featured visiting two-litre turbocharged, front-wheel-drive touring cars competing against cars from the local series. The ARG announced that the event would become a part of the TCR 'World Tour' from 2023 onwards.

The fifth Bathurst event is Challenge Bathurst, a four-day SuperSprint and Regularity event that gives semi-pros and amateurs the chance to hot lap the famous Mount Panorama circuit in a closed, non-racing, safe environment.

They're all Bathurst events, but they aren't 'the' Bathurst event.

Summing up what makes the Great Race truly 'great' and why it will stay that way is tricky.

At its core it's about everyone and everything being at their best.

It's Australia's top-tier racing category, with the best drivers, best teams, best competition and biggest and best support – from both public and commercial interests – at the best track in the country.

Everybody – drivers, teams, officials – at a Bathurst 1000 is aiming to be at their best for that one special day every year.

It's the way it's always been and the way it looks like staying for many years to come.

## Counting Them Up

The 60th anniversary of the Bathurst Great Race – in 2023 – will mark the 63rd running of the race. That's because two races were held in 1997 and 1998: one for Super Tourers and one for V8 Supercars. The 'extra' two races are both recognised in the history books.

# ACKNOWLEDGEMENTS

**B**athurst has consumed my professional life for as long as I can remember. I've written and spoken countless numbers of words about its famous races, cars, drivers, teams and fans, but this is the first time I've bolted such a vast amount of this material together in a book of this kind.

I'm indebted to those that have spent time with me discussing their Mount Panorama memories – both of magical days of victory that define their careers and days of bitter defeat when the Mountain gave them nothing but heartache.

Many of the quotes in this book are from interviews I've conducted for episodes of my V8 Sleuth Podcast. The podcast started in 2019 and over the course of nearly 300 episodes there's very few of them that don't mention Bathurst in some way, shape or form.

It's important for me to thank all those that have contributed, directly or indirectly, to bring this project together.

My special thanks to Stefan Bartholomaeus and Will Dale, two of Australia's best and brightest motorsport writers, who write for my V8 Sleuth team, and whose extensive interviews with Glenn Seton, Allan Grice and Jim Richards have made for great material for this book.

Thanks to my long-time friend and mentor David Hassall for his fantastic insight into the famous duo, Peter Brock and

Allan Moffat, and Allan himself for further insight into his famous 1977 Bathurst win.

My great friend, racing ace and TV talker Neil Crompton has, as always, been generous with his time and insight, as well as his former Channel 7 commentary colleague Garry Wilkinson.

Now based in America, Leigh Diffey is one of the best Australian motorsport export stories. Many moons ago he agreed to be a guest on a radio show I co-hosted as a teenager back in Ballarat and I've been bugging him about racing ever since.

Dick Johnson, Larry Perkins and Mark Skaife have always answered my many questions about their amazing careers, thanks gents.

Thank you to the National Library of Australia for access to archive interviews with Bob Jane and Harry Firth and 1966 Bathurst winner Bob Holden for our great chat at the Phillip Island Historics in 2017.

Covid kept the world apart physically for a few years, but the wonders of Zoom allowed for time and chats with Bathurst 1000 winners Greg Murphy, Scott McLaughlin, Tomas Mezera and Luke Youlden. Four great guys.

A range of interviewees opened the doors to their homes and race teams too. Thanks to Colin Bond and Craig Baird for the hospitality in Sydney and on the Gold Coast respectively, and Brad Jones for the time at the global headquarters of Brad Jones Racing in Albury.

Brad Owen, the tireless co-ordinator of the National Motor Racing Museum at Mount Panorama, has one of the best jobs in Australia too – my thanks to him for talking further about the amazing pieces of automotive history he takes care of every day.

My additional thanks to David Reynolds, Craig Lowndes, Gary Scott, Jamie Whincup, Roland Dane, Tony Cochrane, Greg Eaton, Alan Gow, Melinda Price, Leanne Ferrier, Fred Gibson, Marcos Ambrose, Garth Tander, Jason Bargwanna, Will Davison, Cam Waters, Charlie O'Brien, Wayne Gardner and Troy Bayliss for their time and Bathurst insights and memories.

Some of Australia's best motorsport photographers have their work published in this book – thank you to Graeme Neander, Dirk Klynsmith, Justin Deeley, Terry Russell, Scott Wensley, Andrew Hall, Rod Eime, Trevor Thomas and Dale Rodgers for entrusting me with your archives in recent years.

The HarperCollins' team has been so supportive of bringing this publication to life. Thank you to you all, in particular Roberta Ivers and Chris Kunz, for helping me bring motorsport and the Mountain to the masses.

My eternal thanks to my wife, Jaylee, for support that never waivers and acting as sounding board to my seemingly neverending Bathurst facts and figures. You're a gem.